Best Practices for Teaching Introduction to Psychology

Best Practices for Teaching Introduction to Psychology

Edited by

Dana S. Dunn
Moravian College

Stephen L. Chew
Samford University

LAWRENCE ERLBAUM ASSOCIATES, PUBLISHERS

2006   Mahwah, New Jersey   London

Lawrence Erlbaum Associates, Inc., Publishers
10 Industrial Avenue
Mahwah, New Jersey 07430

Cover design by Kathryn Houghtaling Lacey

Library of Congress Cataloging-in-Publication Data

Best practices for teaching introduction to psychology / edited by Dana
   S. Dunn, Stephen L. Chew
      p. cm.
Based on a conferences held Sept. 26-27, 2003 in Atlanta, GA.
Includes bibliographical references and indexes.
ISBN 0-8058-5217-4 (cloth : alk. paper)
ISBN 0-8058-5218-2 (pbk. : alk. paper)
   1. Psychology—Study and teaching.   I. Dunn, Dana.   II. Chew,
   Stephen L.

BF77.B48 2005
150'.71'1—dc22   2005041464
                                                                   CIP

Books published by Lawrence Erlbaum Associates are printed on acid-
free paper, and their bindings are chosen for strength and durability.

Printed in the United States of America
10   9   8   7   6   5   4   3   2   1

For our students—past, present, and future

Contents

Contributors

Craig E. Abrahamson, Department of Psychology, James Madison University, Harrisonburg, VA; e-mail: abrahace@jmu.edu

Drew C. Appleby, Department of Psychology, Indiana University-Purdue University Indianapolis, Indianapolis, IN; e-mail: dappleby@iupui.edu

Victor A. Benassi, Department of Psychology, University of New Hampshire, Dunham, NH: e-mail: vab@cisunix.unh.edu

William Buskist, Department of Psychology, Auburn University, Auburn, AL; e-mail: @auburn.edu

John Carton, Department of Psychology, Oglethorpe University, Atlanta, GA; e-mail: jcarton@oglethorpe.edu

Stephen L. Chew, Department of Psychology, Samford University, Birmingham, AL; e-mail: slchew@samford.edu

David Daniel, Department of Psychology, University of Maine at Farmington, Farmington, ME; e-mail: dbdaniel@maine.edu

Dana S. Dunn, Department of Psychology, Moravian College, Bethlehem, PA; e-mail: dunn@moravian.edu

Amy C. Fineburg, Spain Park High School, Birmingham, AL; e-mail: fineburg@hotmail.com

Diane L. Finley, Prince George's Community College, Crofton MD; e-mail: dfinley@pgcc.edu

Gary S. Goldstein, Department of Psychology, University of New Hampshire at Manchester, Manchester, NH; e-mail: gsg@cisunix.unh.edu

Richard A. Griggs, Department of Psychology, University of Florida, Gainesville, FL; e-mail: rgriggs@ufl.edu

Regan A. R. Gurung, Department of Human Development and Psychology, University of Wisconsin at Green Bay, Green Bay, WI; e-mail: gurungr@uwgb.edu

Amy Hackney, Department of Psychology, Georgia Southern University, Statesboro, GA; e-mail: ahackney@georgiasouthern.edu

Mitchell M. Handelsman, University of Colorado at Denver, Denver, CO; e-mail: mitchell.handelsman@cudenver.edu.

Jane S. Halonen, Office of the Dean of Arts and Science, University of West Florida, Pensacola, FL: e-mail: jhalonen@earthlink.net

Charles M. Harris, Department of Psychology, James Madison University, Harrisonburg, VA; e-mail: harriscm@jmu.edu

G. William Hill, IV, Center for Excellence in Teaching and Learning, Kennesaw State University, Kennesaw, GA; e-mail: bhill@kennesaw.edu

Charles J. Huffman, Department of Psychology, James Madison University, Harrisonburg, VA; e-mail: huffmacj@jmu.edu

Elizabeth Johnson, Department of Psychology, Oglethorpe University, Atlanta, GA; e-mail: bjohnson@oglethorpe.edu

James H. Korn, Department of Psychology, St. Louis University, St. Louis, MO; e-mail: kornjh@slu.edu

Thomas E. Ludwig, Department of Psychology, Hope College, Hope, MI; e-mail: Ludwig@hope.edu

Marcia McKinley, Department of Psychology, Mount Saint Mary's University, Emmitsburg, MD; e-mail: mckinley@msmary.edu

David G. Myers, Department of Psychology, Hope College, Hope, MI; e-mail: dmyers@hope.edu

Dena A. Pastor, Department of Psychology, James Madison University, Harrisonburg, VA; e-mail: pastorda@jmu.edu

Charles W. Perdue, Department of Psychology, West Virginia State College, Institute, WV; e-mail: perdue@wvsc.edu

Michelle E. Schmidt, Department of Psychology, Moravian College, Bethlehem, PA; e-mail: memes01@moravian.edu

Randolph A. Smith, Department of Psychology, Kennesaw State University, Kennesaw, GA; e-mail: rsmith@kennesaw.edu

Rebecca Stoddart, Department of Psychology, St. Mary's College, Notre Dame, IN: e-mail: stoddart@saintmarys.edu

Joseph E. Trimble, Center for Cross-Cultural Research, Department of Psychology, Western Washington University, Bellingham, WA; e-mail: joseph.trimble@wwu.edu

Stacey B. Zaremba, Department of Psychology, Moravian College, Bethlehem, PA; e-mail: mesbz01@moravian.edu

Foreword

G. William Hill, IV
Kennesaw State University

Introductory psychology is undoubtedly the most commonly offered course in the psychology curriculum across all levels of education. Unlike specialized, upper-level courses in psychology that are focused on a relatively narrow content area and often taken primarily by psychology majors or as a required elective for another degree program, an introductory psychology course serves multiple student audiences and purposes simultaneously, presenting unique challenges to teaching this course.

For the majority of students, the course is both their first and their last exposure to the discipline of psychology. Many students enter the course with a somewhat narrow view of psychology driven by how it is represented in the popular media. Thus, it can be our only opportunity to expose students to psychology's breadth and depth, as well as an appreciation of psychology as both a scientific and an applied discipline. Further, some students may be taking the course simply to fulfill a core curriculum requirement, which may entail demands to address specific learning outcomes associated with general education, such as critical thinking, scientific reasoning, diversity, and social issues.

For other students, the introductory psychology course may stimulate an interest in taking additional advanced coursework in psychology, either as a psychology major or minor or as related coursework to another degree (e.g., nursing, education). For these students, the course needs to function as a foundational prerequisite for more specialized courses. Thus, when teaching the course, faculty must also address learning outcomes that will prepare students for advanced courses. The course also can help the future major or minor better understand career paths and opportunities within psychology and make informed selections from among specialized course offerings.

Beyond the issues associated with differing student expectations and needs, the course's design and delivery often presents challenges to the teacher, compared to teaching specialized courses. Although faculty have struggled with many of these issues for years, the search for possible solutions to the difficulties inherent in teaching this course continues to be a major area of discussion and research among teachers of psychology. After over two decades of attending as well as organizing teaching conferences, for example, my experience is that every conference includes one or more presentations on teaching introductory psychology and these sessions are among the best attended at the conference. Although some topics and issues seem to remain the same over the years (e.g., the search for effective demonstrations or activities to enhance learning, the question of what to cover or breath versus depth, selecting a text, teaching content out of one's specialty area), new challenges have been added in recent years such as the impact of technology both in the classroom and through online delivery, the changing demographics of students, changes in the field of psychology that impact the content and focus of our texts, and the emphasis on clearly defined learning outcomes and their assessment.

After the phenomenal success of the first "Best Practice" conference in September 2002 (*Measuring Up: Best Practices in Assessment in Psychology Education*), the Society for the Teaching of Psychology (STP) realized that there was a strong interest among psychology faculty at all educational levels in a new type of conference, one that focuses on a specific issue or course in psychology. Partnering with the National Institute on the Teaching of Psychology, the Kennesaw State University Center for Excellence in Teaching & Learning, and the American Psychological Association (APA), STP co-sponsored the *Taking Off: Best Practices in Teaching Introductory Psychology* in Fall 2003. Like the *Measuring Up* conference, this conference also inspired an edited book of best practices, which is the current volume. Many of the chapters in this book are based upon presentations made at the *Taking Off* conference, whereas others are the result of taking a more in-depth look at topics raised at the conference during informal discussions. Having been involved as a co-coordinator for both conferences, I am pleased that not only have we provided an opportunity for over 220 high school, community college, and university faculty to gather and discuss strategies and ideas for enhancing the teaching of introductory psychology, but through the efforts of Dana S. Dunn and Stephen Chew, the editors of this book, the contributors are sharing the latest and freshest perspectives discussed at the conference with a even broader audience.

As an aside, STP is already working with its partner organizations in the development of additional "Best Practice" conferences, the next of which will focus on teaching statistics and research methods in psychology. Not only do I hope we continue to offer these conferences for many years to come, but that we continue to collect the best ideas into additional volumes like this one.

Preface

Introduction to psychology is a ubiquitous and popular course. Not all undergraduate students major in psychology, but many—perhaps most—will take introduction to psychology. Introductory psychology is typically the beginning and the end of a student's education in psychology: an elective choice or a distribution requirement within general education or the liberal arts curriculum. Although relatively few students who enroll in this survey of the discipline will become psychologists, there is a strong sense that whoever teaches the course must nonetheless "get it right," that is, adequately and accurately portray the current state of the discipline, its findings, and insights.

Teaching introduction to psychology is a lot of work. Many psychology teachers believe the introductory course is the critical place to present psychology as science and practice, and that better practices for teaching the course should be available. They are right, of course, on both accounts. The problem teachers face is finding materials that address these twin concerns. We conceived of *Best Practices for Teaching Introduction to Psychology* in order to address these concerns and to present multiple perspectives on how to effectively teach the course.

The genesis of this book was the September 26–27, 2003, conference, *Taking Off: Best Practices in Teaching Introductory Psychology*, which was held in Atlanta, Georgia, under the auspices of Kennesaw State University. Over 200 teachers of psychology attended or presented during the 2-day conference, which was sponsored by the Society for the Teaching of Psychology (STP), the National Institute on the Teaching of Psychology (NITOP), the Kennesaw State Center for Excellence in Teaching and Learning (CETL), and the American Psychological Association (APA). Following the event's success, we invited a group of nationally known teachers, many of whom took part in the conference, to write about key issues in teaching introductory psychology.

This book is aimed at a broad audience: All secondary and postsecondary educators who teach introductory psychology will benefit from reading this book. Why? Virtually all new faculty members in psychology gain experience with this course early in their careers. Similarly, introductory psychology is often the first teaching experience for graduate students in psychology; those with teaching opportunities or graduate assistantships will also be interested in the book. Many instructors end up teaching the course regularly across their careers, revising their approach—from changing textbooks to adding new classroom activities—periodically. Thus, we believe that veterans, those who have taught "intro" since their careers began as well as new teachers, will find much to use, debate, adapt, and adopt herein.

We believe that the book makes for good reading and good teaching because it highlights key issues for better practice, including:

Topical coverage. The book offers a variety of perspectives on the critical issue of coverage in teaching introductory psychology. What topics should be covered in the introductory class? What should teachers do when the material is unfamiliar?

Choosing a text. Introductory instructors routinely struggle to choose the correct text for portraying the discipline adequately while meeting their students' academic abilities. How can instructors make informed and optimal textbook choices?

Effective online instruction. The availability of online introductory courses is increasing, but many teachers worry that students enrolled in such courses will never become fully engaged with the material. How can such nontraditional instruction be made effective and involving?

Assessing learning outcomes and critical thinking, and integrating standards in introductory psychology. The book provides assessment advice to teachers and administrators so they can demonstrate that student learning is indeed occurring in the introductory class. Does introductory psychology live up to its educational goals? How can standards be used, and learning outcomes and critical thinking be assessed?

Choosing pedagogies that work. Introductory psychology courses usually rely on a diverse array of pedagogical tools to promote student learning. Which ones actually help students?

Engaging students in the course. Individual chapters address ways to teach about race, ethics, interdisciplinary issues, student misconceptions, paranormal and nonscientific beliefs, and how personal stories can motivate students.

The contributors to this book have created an indispensable resource for introductory psychology teachers, those beginning their careers, enjoying midcareer stride, or rejuvenating the last stages of their professional lives. Throughout any teaching career, new questions and issues emerge about practice, technique, and coverage. What was once considered good teaching begins to look inadequate, possibly antiquated; pedagogical change and growth are essential. Our book supports teachers committed to the continuous pursuit of best practices in teaching introductory psychology.

The development, execution, and production of this book went smoothly because of the good work of our authors and the professionalism of the Lawrence Erlbaum Associates editorial and production team. We are especially grateful to those colleagues who pulled the *Best Practices* conference together: Jane Halonen, Bill Hill, Doug Bernstein, Maureen McCarthy, Randy Smith, the psychology faculty and CETL staff at Kennesaw State University, and Linda Noble. At Moravian, the project proceeded on time due to the efforts of Jackie Giaqunito, Sarah Dougherty, Jaime Marks, and Paula Saslafsky, and Dunn is also indebted to the Faculty Development and Research Committee for providing necessary travel funds. A Moravian College SOAR Grant underwrote portions of Dunn's efforts in summer 2003. Chew is indebted to Samford University and to Teachers of Psychology in the Secondary Schools (TOPSS) for providing travel funds for the Best Practices conference. He also owes a debt of gratitude to Charlotte Baughn for help in manuscript preparation.

We thank our peers who reviewed and constructively commented on the proposal for this book: Eric Landrum (Boise State University), Herman Huber (College of St. Elizabeth), Kevin J. Apple (James Madison University), and Douglas A. Bersnstein (University of South Florida).

At Lawrence Erlbaum Associates, we thank our editor, Debra Riegert, for her encouragement and vision from the start of the project. We appreciate the organizational efforts of Kerry Breen and the LEA production staff, especially Debbie Ruel.

On the home front, Dunn is grateful to his loving family—Sarah, Jacob, and Hannah. Chew thanks Daisy and Michael for their love, patience, and understanding.

Dana S. Dunn
Stephen L. Chew

Grounding the Teaching of Introductory Psychology: Rationale for and Overview of Best Practices

Dana S. Dunn
Moravian College

Stephen L. Chew
Samford University

Introductory psychology is often the first course—indeed, possibly the only psychology course—that undergraduate students take in the discipline. As a result, students and their teachers harbor great expectations about the course. Students anticipate being exposed to the whole field of psychology, a proverbial Cook's tour in one term. They are curious to learn, but their curiosity is often tempered, if not colored, by prior expectations about what they believe psychology *is*. Many students are surprised to learn that, although important, a mental health service orientation is but one aspect of the discipline. Learning that psychology is a science committed to discovery, as well as application, is often news to undergraduate students, but this message is especially critical in the introductory course.

For their part, teachers want to do justice to the discipline by presenting the necessarily broad survey of psychological phenomena in a rigorous and scientific manner. The matter of coverage immediately becomes a paramount concern: so much material, so little time in the typical term. Teachers wrestle with the inherent trade-off between focusing on breadth or depth, or finding a balance between classic findings and timely results. Each time they teach the introductory class, instructors must distill a wealth of research results into a brief period of time (e.g., "it's class three—time to present the neuron").

This book offers a range of solutions to the challenges and dilemmas of teaching the first course in psychology. The contributions herein are designed to appeal to the needs of students and the consciences of teachers. The authors in this volume advocate that teachers make the commitment to ground their teaching of introductory psychology. A grounded course is one that furnishes students with a real foundation for learning psychological knowledge through the use of best teaching practices. *Grounding*, then, means that teachers must create a coherent justification for the course by using scholarship concerning the teaching of psychology. The justification must be satisfying to both parties, which means that matters of coverage, active learning, assessment and learning outcomes, and teaching philosophy must be articulated. This collection of chapters is meant to help secondary and postsecondary teachers ground the teaching of this essential course in psychology. The remainder of this first chapter identifies key issues in the teaching of introductory psychology and then presents a précis of each section of the text and its contents.

ISSUES IN TEACHING INTRODUCTORY PSYCHOLOGY

Scholarship on teaching the first course in psychology—variously called introductory psychology, introduction to psychology, or general psychology—typically focuses on practical pedagogical issues, including text selection (e.g., Landrum & Hormel, 2002), traditional versus modular presentation (e.g., Nevid & Carmony, 2002), and whether to require a laboratory component (e.g., Berthold, Hakala, & Goff, 2003). Although these are important considerations, especially for the novice instructor, they barely begin to address the complex challenges presented in the introductory psychology course. Veteran psychology instructors are likely to list introductory psychology as the most difficult psychology course to teach well (with the possible exception of statistics), and these teachers report continuing to wrestle with the challenges of the course throughout their careers. Ironically, introductory psychology is typically the first course graduate students and new assistant professors teach, and they usually do it with little or no teacher training.

Teaching introductory psychology raises challenges not found in later psychology courses. Besides the sheer breadth and number of new concepts for students to learn, they must also develop a basic conceptual framework for understanding psychology. Teachers convey the importance of the scientific process in the discipline of psychology (e.g., Miller, 1992), and how to distinguish scientific psychology from popular and pseudoscientific views. Many students come to the course with gross misconceptions about psychology's domains of inquiry and ignorance about what psychologists do. Instructors must confront these mistaken beliefs and correct them accordingly.

Introductory psychology teachers truly need a resource in order to teach the fundamental first course effectively. Until now, outside of periodical pieces (both stand-alone articles and book-length compendiums of previously published work), no single, up-to-date resource on teaching introductory psychology has been available. Instructor's manuals that accompany introductory psychology texts tend to provide practical help tailored to that specific text, such as lecture outlines, previously published class activities, relevant videos, and additional lecture topics. Yet these ancillaries provide little help in improving overall teaching effectiveness in the course, such as overcoming student misconceptions, teaching students with diverse cultural backgrounds, teaching the course in the context of liberal education or improving student learning through assessment.

The contributors to this volume go beyond teaching tips and reviews of the technical aspects of teaching to introduce a more scholarly approach. Halpern et al. (1998) defined the "scholarship of teaching in psychology" as pedagogical research aimed specifically at investigating and improving the learning of psychology. Such scholarship is needed to address issues in teaching the course that have no single best solution for all teachers and all students in all situations. As readers will learn, the term *best practice* implies that, where feasible, there is empirical support for the effectiveness of a teaching technique.

BEST PRACTICES FOR TEACHING INTRODUCTORY PSYCHOLOGY

Basic Issues in Teaching Introductory Psychology

This book is based on the premise that teaching introductory psychology raises challenges in teaching that are both fundamentally different and substantially more complex than teaching subsequent psychology courses. Furthermore, the extent to which these challenges are successfully met is measured in student learning. The opening section of the book deals with basic issues that are particularly relevant to instructors teaching introductory psychology for the first time. More experienced instructors, nevertheless, will also find these chapters of value because they address issues that teachers of psychology must address and resolve multiple times in their careers.

The first critical decision facing any teacher of introductory psychology is selecting a textbook that will complement and enhance classroom instruction. Publishers offer a large array of textbooks pitched for different audiences with different kinds of pedagogical features. Teachers usually select textbooks based on their own preferences, teaching style, and intuition, but without any real evidence about the substantive differences in textbooks or the actual impact of pedagogical aids on learning. Griggs (chap. 2, this volume) did an extensive study on the substantive differences among textbooks and his chapter provides a set of meaningful dimensions that will help instructors make more informed choices.

One challenge facing all teachers of introductory psychology is teaching subjects that they do not know well. Psychology is such a broad and diverse field, and graduate training is typically so narrowly focused, that no new instructor is equally familiar with all aspects of the field. The expedient solution is not to teach those troublesome areas, but Dunn, Schmidt, and Zaremba (chap. 3, this volume) offer better, long-term solutions in their chapter on covering less familiar topics. They focus on both short-term solutions for the new instructor and longer term solutions that will help instructors grow into master teachers of general psychology.

Gurung and Daniel (chap. 4, this volume) subject pedagogical features found in textbooks to empirical tests to determine which aids actually influence student learning and which are mere window dressing. The results turn out to be both surprising and interesting. All instructors who ever wondered if a particular feature of a textbook was designed more to sell books than aid student learning will benefit from reading this chapter.

Appleby (chap. 5, this volume) examines the role of critical thinking in teaching introductory psychology effectively. First, he describes and compares the various extant definitions of critical thinking. He then resolves the issue of which definition is best suited to introductory psychology in a unique and creative way. He assigns a series of critical thinking projects (CTPs) that challenge his students to think about authentic problems in psychology within a framework of critical thinking that they choose as being most applicable to their own educational goals. Appleby describes his method for developing, utilizing, and assessing CTPs, and provides some examples of student learning that demonstrate their flexibility and effectiveness in promoting critical thinking.

At large research universities, much of the responsibility for teaching introductory psychology falls on graduate teaching assistants. In recent years, many universities have increased their emphasis on training teaching assistants for their duties, in part because of external pressures to improve undergraduate courses and in part because such training increases the marketability of graduate students. Hackney, Korn, and Buskist (chap. 6, this volume) describe two successful programs for preparing graduate students to teach introductory psychology. They argue that the foundation of teaching introduction to psychology effectively is not sound technique, but developing a comprehensive philosophy of teaching. All pedagogical choices and approaches then flow from this philosophy.

Alternative Approaches to Teaching Introductory Psychology

The stereotypical introductory psychology class is large, lecture-oriented, and reliant on a big textbook, but this arrangement is becoming less common with the introduction of alternative approaches to teaching the course. A major stimulus for these nontraditional approaches is the increasing ethnic and cultural diversity of students taking the course, especially at community colleges. Another impetus is technology. The second section of the book explores these alternative approaches to teaching general psychology.

Johnson and Carton (chap. 7, this volume) address how to teach introductory psychology without using the traditional, encyclopedic textbook. They argue that large textbooks can be counterproductive to student learning, because they promote skimming, shallow processing of information, and memorization of arcane detail rather than understanding of basic principles. Their solution is to have students read two briefer books that are closer to primary sources. These books focus more on the rationale, method, results, and implications of key studies in psychology, but the studies have been paraphrased to be accessible to introductory psychology students. By reducing the reading load but increasing the depth of focus on key studies, Johnson and Carton argue that students come away with a better understanding of the process of psychological research and application across all areas.

In recent years, the field of psychology has paid increasing attention to the influence of racial, ethnic, and cultural influences on behavior both in terms of research and teaching. The content of introductory psychology textbooks certainly reflects this move toward inclusiveness. Teachers of introductory psychology would likely agree that issues of race, ethnicity, and culture should be considerations both in terms of content and teaching practice. Most teachers, however, are unaware of the history, development, and uses of the constructs of race and ethnicity. Trimble (chap. 8, this volume) addresses these issues in his chapter, reviewing the development of the constructs from biological, anthropological, sociological, and psychological perspectives. He addresses the question of how racial and ethnic diversity are best integrated into the general psychology course through several examples. He recognizes that discussion of racial and ethnic issues often evokes strong emotional reactions among students, but argues that their inclusion can greatly enrich introductory psychology.

Stoddart and McKinley (chap. 9, this volume) describe how they each teach introductory psychology within an interdisciplinary context through the use of literature, narratives, and primary sources. In their chapter, they argue forcefully, using current pedagogical theory, that such an approach can enhance student learning and appreciation of psychology as a scientific enterprise rather than detract from it. They argue that close reading of narratives and literature yields students better equipped to apply psychological concepts to complex situations. Stoddart and McKinley arrived at this teaching approach at their respective institutions independently and through different routes, but the goal of both is to enhance the learning experience of students in introductory psychology through interdisciplinary connections between psychology and other fields. They provide extensive lists of readings and activities for teachers interested in this approach.

Nothing has had a greater impact on course delivery in recent years than advances in technology. Advances in multimedia technology and the emergence of the Internet as a cultural cornerstone have changed the nature of the classroom experience and created whole new ways for teachers to teach and students to learn. Finley (chap. 10, this volume) examines how to teach introductory psychology in an online environment and still keep the students active and engaged in the learning process. Due to the asynchronous nature of student participation, teaching online requires a different way of approaching the course and designing content. What is lost in face-to-face interaction can be compensated for by richer discussions and utilization of web resources. Finley argues that, although the learning goals remain the same, the online environment requires a change in the traditional roles of teacher and student. She examines the advantages and disadvantages of teaching introductory psychology online, and the mechanics of developing, implementing, and assessing learning activities for this environment.

Ludwig and Perdue (chap. 11, this volume) examine how the classroom experience in introductory psychology has changed due to the developments in multimedia and information technology. Most colleges and universities now boast multimedia classrooms with Internet access through networked computers, and the ability to present material through presentation software and digital video. Ludwig and Perdue trace the historical development of multimedia technology in the classroom starting from chalkboards to the current day. They examine ways of using technology to enhance student learning, and how to avoid its perils and pitfalls. Taking lessons from both their personal experience and the research literature, they summarize general principles for the effective use of multimedia for introductory psychology that should apply as the technology continues to evolve.

Psychologists have prided themselves on their emphasis on ethics, but in introductory psychology, this subject is mainly touched on at the beginning of the course with a discussion of research ethics and perhaps again in connection with Milgram's studies on obedience or other controversial research. Handelsman (chap. 12, this volume) argues that ethics is deserving of much more coverage than most instructors give it, either as a major topic on its own or by interweaving ethical considerations throughout the introductory psychology course. He outlines many areas where the study of ethics can complement and enhance discussion of a topic. He looks upon ethics as a way of thinking rather than a content area, and so it can be applied to any topic in the introductory course.

Assessment Issues in the First Course

A major trend in higher education is increased emphasis on the importance of assessment of student learning at all levels of analysis, from the individual student to the course to the whole curriculum. The third section of this book examines the development of course and curricular goals and the approaches different colleges and organizations have taken to assess those goals.

Smith and Fineberg (chap. 13, this volume) describe the development of the *National Standards for the Teaching of High School Psychology*, and how the development and assessment of these standards has strongly influenced how psychology is taught at the high school level. They demonstrate how the standards have been successfully adapted by one college to provide a framework of assessment for its curriculum. Finally, they address the issues and controversies surrounding the development of standards or guidelines for undergraduate psychology programs.

Introductory psychology is commonly taught as part of the general education requirements for students at most colleges. Halonen, Harris, Pastor, Abrahamson, and Huffman (chap. 14, this volume) describe the role that introductory psychology plays in general education at James Madison University. They discuss the assessment approach they developed to measure the impact that taking introductory psychology had on students in relation to the goals of general education. The evolution of their assessment approach nicely illustrates the move toward more authentic assessment and assessment that is explicitly linked to learning goals.

Focusing on Students in Introductory Psychology

If students were empty vessels to be filled with knowledge, then the benchmark of good teaching would be the accuracy and clarity of the presentation. Psychologists know, however, that students come into the introductory psychology course with preconceived notions about both the course and content, and they construct an understanding of psychology based on the interaction of those expectations and what they learn from the instructor and textbook. The benchmark of good teaching, therefore, must be in what students learn from the course. This section of the book focuses on what students bring to the course and how instructors can optimize student learning.

Chew (chap. 15, this volume) examines the common misconceptions and expectations that students bring into introductory psychology and how these factors influence their learning. He reviews research indicating that these preformed beliefs are both common and often highly resistant to correction through traditional instruction. Far from being a minor nuisance, Chew argues that misconceptions can have a major influence on what students learn in introductory psychology, and whether this new learning will be retained once the course is over. He outlines several approaches to overcoming these preconceived notions and provides evidence for their effectiveness.

One subject where preconceived beliefs and misconceptions abound among students is in the area of paranormal claims like ESP and clairvoyance. Benassi and Goldstein (chap. 16, this volume) describe their research in attempting to change these beliefs based on scientific reasoning and evidence. They demonstrate how difficult it can be to alter paranormal beliefs and, if successful, how vulnerable the belief in scientific reasoning is to further "proof" of paranormal abilities. They describe how introductory psychology provides an excellent forum for examining and challenging these nonscientific claims.

Abrahamson (chap. 17, this volume) describes how he engages and motivates students to learn through the use of personal storytelling. The use of stories increases the rapport between students and teacher and personalizes research findings. Presenting material within a narrative story structure makes the material more memorable to students. This approach to teaching introductory psychology is grounded in both a long history of oral narrative and also research on the memorability and persuasiveness of stories.

A Last Word

Myers (chap. 18, this volume), noted author of one of the most highly regarded introductory textbooks in the field, ends by condensing his years of teaching and writing experience into a set of teaching tips that are especially applicable to introductory psychology. The tips Myers offers emphasize both the pragmatic and the interpersonal nature of teaching. New instructors often seek the wisdom of more experienced instructors on pragmatic issues of course content and testing, but they rarely consider the interpersonal dimensions of teaching. Myers provides important guidelines for this often overlooked aspect of teaching. He also reviews research that defines the differences between master and less skilled teachers, which is relevant to teachers at all levels of experience. The wisdom of experience represented in this chapter will aid teachers in reflecting on and evaluating their own teaching practice.

CONCLUSIONS

The enjoyment—often the challenge—of being a student in introductory psychology is discovery of the discipline, of being exposed to a new and critical way of looking at behavior. The challenge—and, indeed, the enjoyment—of teaching introductory psychology is found in the ongoing need to refine, create, and revise the course and its contents—in other words, to ground it. There is a wealth of scholarly and pedagogical material in this book filled with best practices that can only enhance the experience of students and faculty alike.

REFERENCES

Berthold, H. G., Hakala, C. M., & Goff, D. (2003). An argument for a laboratory in introductory psychology. *Teaching of Psychology, 30,* 55–58.
Halpern, D., Smothergill, D., Allen, M., Baker, S., Baum, C., Best, D., Ferrari, J., Geisinger, K., Gilden, E., Hester, M., Keith-Speigel, P., Kierniesky, N., McGovern, T., McKeachie, W., Prokasy, W., Szuchman, L., Vasta, R., & Weaver, K. (1998). Scholarship in psychology: A paradigm for the twenty-first century. *American Psychologist, 53*(12), 1292–1297.
Landrum, R. E., & Hormel, L. (2002). Textbook selection: Balance between the pedagogy, the publisher, and the student. *Teaching of Psychology, 29,* 245–248.
Miller, N. E. (1992). Introducing and teaching much-needed understanding of the scientific process. *American Psychologist, 47,* 848–850.
Nevid, J. S., & Carmony, T. M. (2002). Traditional versus modular format in presenting textual material in introductory psychology. *Teaching of Psychology, 29,* 237–238.

I

Basic Issues

Chapter
2

Selecting an Introductory Textbook: They Are Not "All the Same"

Richard A. Griggs
University of Florida

The importance of choosing an appropriate text cannot be overemphasized. A rather sizeable literature has emerged ... which supports the notion that it is the textbook more than the mode of instruction that affects performance in a course.

—Morris, 1977, p. 21

One of the most important decisions an instructor makes is the selection of a textbook.... Given that textbook selection is crucial, the method of text selection should be comprehensive, reliable, and responsive to learner characteristics and course objectives.

—Chatman and Goetz, 1985, p. 150

There is no substitute for detailed review of the competing texts for the course you are teaching ... research on teaching suggests that the major influence on what students learn is not the teaching method but the textbook.

—McKeachie, 2002, p. 14

The aforementioned quotes denote both the important role of the textbook in a course and the critical nature of informed textbook evaluation and selection to the course's success. Thus, because 98% of teachers use textbooks for the introductory course (Miller & Gentile, 1998), introductory textbooks play a major role in defining psychology for our students. However, with the large number of introductory texts available, it is difficult for a teacher to know many of the books well. A survey of teachers conducted by Weiten (1988) attested to this difficulty. Weiten asked a large sample of professors who taught introductory psychology to rate each of 43 textbooks, but only 4 of 43 textbooks were rated completely by 50% or more of the respondents. Griggs and Jackson (1989) found that introductory psychology text editors and authors, like the psychology teachers, were also not very familiar with many of the available introductory texts.

Much of this difficulty stems from the sheer number of texts available for the introductory course. Although the number has dramatically decreased during the past two decades (Griggs, Jackson, Christopher, & Marek, 1999), there are still 37 textbooks, along with briefer versions of 17 of these texts, currently available for course adoption (Koenig, Daly, Griggs, Marek, & Christopher, 2004). This large number of texts makes the text evaluation and selection process a complex, arduous task if teachers systematically seek to find the best texts for their introductory courses and students. In fact, the task's difficulty has often led to the stereotyping of these texts as "all the same," which is clearly not the case (Griggs & Marek, 2001). Stereotyping these texts will lead teachers to ignore the individual strengths and weaknesses of the various texts and thus not select the best book for their course and students.

My purpose here is twofold. First, I want to make teachers aware of the variance among introductory textbooks on some dimensions directly relevant to the text evaluation and selection process. Substantial variance exists between introductory texts on most textbook dimensions. There is little overlap of reference citations across textbooks. One would tacitly assume that given their introductory, basic nature, these texts would all cite a common core of classic articles and books, but they do not. Analyzing 24 introductory psychology textbooks published between 1985 and 1989, Gorenflo and McConnell (1991) found that out of thousands of bibliographic items, not a single journal article was cited in all of the sampled texts. Only three articles were cited in at least 90% of the texts, and only 14 appeared in at least 75%. Even more surprisingly, Griggs, Proctor, and Cook (2004) found that not even one book was cited in all of the 15 current introductory textbooks that they sampled. Of 3,608 unique book citations, 70% were cited in only one text, and 91% in three or fewer of the 15 sampled texts.

Whereas reference citation is not a critical dimension for text evaluation, it nicely illustrates the nonhomogeneity that pervades introductory textbooks and the dimensions that are more critical to the selection process. As is discussed later, there is not even a substantial common core vocabulary among introductory textbooks (Griggs, Bujak-Johnson, & Proctor, 2004); it appears that there may never have been one (Griggs & Mitchell, 2002). Even the term *psychology* does not appear in all of the text glossaries. As Zechmeister and Zechmeister (2000) concluded, "if psychology has a common language, there are many dialects" (p. 10).

This chapter also provides direction to resource information on current introductory textbooks that can be used in an objective textbook screening procedure to reduce the number of texts that have to be more carefully considered to a smaller, more manageable number. Given their nonhomogeneity and the scarcity of current objective information about these texts and the significant differences between them, Jackson, Marek, Christopher, and I, with the receipt of an inaugural Division Two Office of Teaching Resources instructional research award in 1998, developed a major resource to aid introductory teachers in the text evaluation and selection process. This resource is *A Compendium of Introductory Psychology Texts* (hereafter referred to as the *Compendium*), which is available online at Division Two's Office of Teaching Resources Web site (http://www.lemoyne.edu/OTRP/introtexts.html). The *Compendium* provides individualized narrative descriptions and tabular cross-comparisons on many selection-relevant dimensions, such as percentage of coverage of each of the standard chapter topics, for all of the introductory textbooks copyrighted in the last 4 years. Because the revision cycle for introductory texts is generally 3 years, this set of texts includes all of those currently viable for adoption. The *Compendium* is updated yearly; the current version covers the period from 2001 to 2004 (Koenig et al., 2004).

The chapter discusses various textbook dimensions relevant to the selection process, and explains how the *Compendium* or another resource can facilitate consideration of that dimension, thereby reducing the number of texts to be evaluated in greater detail. It discusses the dimensions in their most logical progression. Thus, some dimensions that are considered less relevant to the text selection process are discussed before some considered to be more relevant. Before beginning these discussions, there is a brief discussion of the importance of some preliminary evaluation–selection considerations.

PRELIMINARY EVALUATION–SELECTION CONSIDERATIONS

As the first step in the text evaluation and selection process, teachers should carefully think about their own individualized versions of the course, especially with respect to course objectives and student abilities. For new teachers or teachers new to the school at which they are teaching the course, the latter may be difficult to assess until they have more experience with their students. Information could be gained, however, from colleagues at the school given their relevant teaching experiences. Students' ability is a critical consideration in deciding what level(s) of text difficulty a teacher would want to consider during the text selection process. Students vary greatly from community college students (who typically need more extensive pedagogical support) to students at more selective colleges and universities (who do not need as much support). Minimally, teachers should decide if their students are above average, average, or below average in ability. This classification will enable a teacher to greatly narrow the initial set of introductory texts under consideration.

Defining course content, structure, and objectives before beginning the textbook evaluation–selection process is also important. As Brewer (2002) so adroitly pointed out, "If you do not know where you are going, the likelihood that you will get there borders on randomness" (p. 39). It is very difficult, if not impossible, to satisfactorily cover all of the topics in a regular introductory text, so a teacher may only want to consider briefer versions of such texts in order to cover more topics. Alternatively, a teacher may want to use a regular text but cover fewer topics, that is, use the "less is more" approach. Regardless of the approach taken, teachers will need to determine which topics they want to emphasize and how they will structure their coverage of them. These content and structure decisions will then allow teachers to identify and compare texts that emphasize these topics and structure their coverage in a manner similar to their own.

Introductory teachers should also be careful to select a textbook whose objectives fit best with their overall course objectives. For example, critical thinking may be an important objective, and introductory textbooks vary greatly in both their emphasis on such thinking and their explicit pedagogical features to develop it. Thus, selecting one of the texts that both emphasizes critical thinking and does so in a manner congruent with a particular teacher's approach should greatly enhance that teacher's chances of achieving this objective. Griggs, Jackson, Marek, and Christopher (1998) provided a review of explicit critical thinking coverage in both introductory textbooks and their ancillaries; and Marek, Jackson, Griggs, and Christopher (1998) reviewed supplementary critical thinking books. Regardless of their specific nature, the teacher's goals should optimally be as congruent as possible with those of the selected textbook so that the teacher and text mesh to facilitate meeting the teacher's course objectives and to create a better learning experience for the students. A teacher at war with the textbook only increases student casualties.

In summary, introductory teachers need to mindfully assess their students' ability and course emphases, organization, and objectives before starting the text selection process. This assessment will greatly facilitate the process by narrowing the search early on, allowing more time to compare a much smaller set of texts on the dimensions that are more important to them and thus selecting the best text for their courses. This beneficial impact of engaging in mindful upfront thinking is similar to the source of differences in problem solving between better and poorer students (Bloom & Broder, 1950). Better students spend more time up front deciding how to solve a problem, thereby facilitating the actual solution process. Similarly, if teachers spend more time up front carefully thinking about their own course, objectives, and students, then they will not only find the evaluation process easier but will likely also make a better text selection. Having completed this preliminary thinking, the first text dimension a teacher should consider is level of text difficulty, because this dimension will allow the teacher to greatly reduce the set of texts to consider further.

TEXT LEVEL OF DIFFICULTY

Considering opinions of textbook authors and editors, Griggs and Jackson (1989) distinguished three levels of text difficulty (high, middle, and low), which reflected breadth and depth of coverage, ties to the experimental literature, the number of pedagogical aids, illustrative programs, and coverage of nontraditional topics. Higher level texts provide great depth and breadth of content coverage and are closely tied to the experimental literature. These texts seem most appropriate for students with above average ability, such as those in honors classes, or possibly for two-term courses in which there is more time to cover the material. Middle level texts usually have the breadth, but not the depth, of the higher level texts. The writing is more engaging for average students, but the treatment is still scientifically rigorous. Lower level texts represent another step down in depth of coverage and, on average, include far more pedagogical aids, are typically more heavily illustrated, and more often provide chapter coverage of nontraditional topics (i.e., sex and gender, industrial-organizational psychology, and applied psychology). This level-of-difficulty differentiation corresponds roughly to the above average, average, and below average student ability classification.

To better familiarize yourself with these three levels of difficulty, try an exercise I use to help the graduate students in my teaching of psychology seminar understand the differences between these levels. I have them do a careful comparison of the three introductory textbooks published by Worth—Gray (2002), Myers (2004), and Hockenbury and Hockenbury (2003). These three texts are prototypes for the three levels of difficulty—high, middle, and low, respectively. I use these texts because, having the same publisher, they share many similar illustrations, which functions to focus a reader's attention on and thereby highlight the differences between the books. Based on my seminar experiences, the biological and sensation/perception chapters are especially good at illustrating the level differences.

Griggs (1999) enlarged this three-level system into a five-level classification scheme by dividing the middle level into three levels (high middle, middle, and low middle). The additional level categories are based on the same defining dimensions. For example, the high middle text would not have as much depth of coverage as the high level text but more than a middle level text. Griggs also provided an objective way to make level classifications. Combining the number of pedagogical aids and nontraditional chapter variables with a measure of author eminence (*Social Science Citation Index* counts for the authors over a 9-year period), he made objective classifications of level for the 37 introductory texts published between 1995 and 1997. These level judgments were then validated through a comparison with independently determined, experientially based level judgments. The fits were excellent. Although Griggs's classification procedure is only a first attempt to objectively quantify level, these data clearly indicate that the texts vary greatly with respect to level—one of the most important dimensions of textbook selection.

Based on Griggs's 5-level classification scheme, the *Compendium* is organized entirely by level of text difficulty. The narrative descriptions and tabular comparisons are arranged from high level to low level, alphabetically within each level. Thus, teachers can easily compare the texts available at the level or levels they want to consider. I recommend that two adjacent levels (e.g., low and low middle levels) be considered to protect against any misjudgments about student ability or miscalculations in text level. If teachers want to challenge their students, then they might go a level higher than their students' ability (e.g., high middle vs. middle for average students). If teachers use one or more supplementary books in their courses, such as a critical thinking book or a collection of primary readings, then they may want to go a level lower (e.g., low middle vs. middle for average students) because they won't be spending as much course time on the text. At present, there are 5 high level, 9 high middle level, 9 middle level, 6 low middle level, and 8 low level textbooks, excluding briefer versions of some of these texts. Thus, if only two levels are considered, the number of texts that have to be considered further drops from 37 to 14, 15, or 18. Once teachers have decided about text level, they might next consider text length.

TEXT LENGTH

Text length can be assessed in different ways; for example, by number of chapters, number of pages, and regular versus briefer text versions. With respect to the first two text length measures, the average number of chapters has decreased over the past two decades, but the number of text pages has increased, leading to an increase in number of pages per chapter (Griggs et al., 1999). Thus, the number of chapters is a deceiving measure, and I do not recommend its use. Griggs et al. found that the texts are definitely much longer compared to Weiten's (1988) data, almost 100 pages of text on the average and more than 100 pages when appendices, indexes, and other back matter are included in the page count. The median number of chapters and total pages for the current set of introductory textbooks are 17 chapters and 746 pages, respectively (based on data in Koenig et al., 2004). Reviewers of introductory psychology textbooks over the past decade or so seem on target when lamenting that texts have become so lengthy that it is impossible to cover an entire text in a one-term course (e.g., Nallan, 1996).

Excessive textbook length would seem to be a serious problem, because about 90% of our introductory courses are only one term in length (Miller & Gentile, 1998). Only 2 of the 37 textbooks are brief: Gaulin and McBurney (2001) and Mynatt and Doherty (2002). Both have fewer than 500 total pages, with nontraditional organizations. The Gaulin and McBurney text uses evolution as its organizing concept and covers those introductory topics most receptive to the evolutionary framework. The Mynatt and Doherty text has 44 short chapters (averaging about 10 pages in length), each concerned with a singular generalization based on psychological research. The organization of these generalizations roughly maps onto the typical order of topics in an introductory text. Thus, although these two texts are relatively brief, they are idiosyncratic with respect to approach and content. However, many of the other 35 texts have been published in briefer traditional versions. At present, this is the case for 17 of them, with 2 texts having two different briefer versions. These "briefer" versions, however, are not always brief in length. Although the median number of chapters and total pages for current briefer versions are 14 and 623 pages, respectively (based on data in

Koenig et al., 2004), a few of these briefer versions are longer than many of the regular textbooks (Griggs & Koenig, 2001). For example, 4 of the current 19 briefer versions are over 700 pages in length (Koenig et al., 2004).

During the selection process, teachers should not eliminate all regular texts and evaluate only briefer versions. The best text for an individual teacher's course may not be available in a briefer version. In addition, all of the chapters or even entire chapters in a regular text do not have to be assigned. Teachers can in effect create their own briefer versions though the particular text pages they assign. A few publishers will even customize their texts in accordance with individual teachers' needs.

The main advantage of a briefer version text is cost. Because it is typically softbound and briefer, it is usually less expensive than its regular parent text. However, the difference in cost is likely not great, and certainly not worth the cost of not selecting the best text for your course. I recommend that teachers first try to identify the best texts for their individual courses; and then if briefer versions of these texts are available, teachers then might opt to use them. Other variables that I do not think should play a large role in the selection process are chapter topics and organization, which are discussed next.

TEXT CHAPTER TOPICS AND ORGANIZATION

Griggs and Marek (2001) concluded that the misperceived homogeneity in introductory textbooks was the product of overgeneralization from two very salient, easily accessible, global text variables—chapter topics and organization. They examined the 41 full-length textbooks copyrighted between 1997 and 2000 and found that only 2 of the 41 texts offered novel topic coverage and organization (the atypical Gaulin & McBurney, 2001, and Mynatt & Doherty, 2002, texts described earlier). There was little variance in the remaining 39 texts (95%). The following sequence illustrates both the standard topics and prototypical organization: introduction/research methods, biological processes (psychobiology, sensation-perception, and consciousness), learning and cognitive processes (learning, memory, thought-language, and intelligence), emotion-motivation, developmental psychology, clinical and health psychology (personality, health psychology, disorders, and therapies), and social psychology. Although some texts do offer chapters on nontraditional topics (mainly sex and gender), such chapters are still uncommon and found only in lower level texts. Other than this, there are no meaningful differences in chapter topics and their organization across text levels.

The chapter topics and their organization are given in the individualized narrative description of each textbook in the *Compendium*. These narrative descriptions are also organized by text level to facilitate text comparisons. I do not recommend that chapter topics and their organization be weighted heavily in the selection process because the chapters can be assigned in a different order without sacrificing much continuity, and any nontraditional chapter topic can be easily added through lectures and assigned reading, especially in smaller classes. Although chapter topics and their organization are relatively standardized in introductory textbooks, such global similarity does not preclude divergence in extent of major chapter topic coverage across texts, which is very relevant to the text selection process.

COVERAGE OF MAJOR CHAPTER TOPICS

What topics do introductory psychology teachers typically cover and think are important? Miller and Gentile (1998) provided some relevant data from their national survey study of introductory psychology teachers. Please note that research methods was not included in the list of topics to be rated. The top 10 most frequently assigned topics from 1 to 10 were: learning, memory, biology, abnormal psychology, personality, social psychology, perception, cognitive development, cognition, and sensation. Teachers may want, however, to add other topics to this list and possibly not teach all 10 of these. Because teachers vary with respect to the chapter topics they choose to cover and the mesh between teacher–textbook topic emphases is an important factor in textbook selection, the percentages of coverage of the standard chapter topics *within* each textbook are provided in tabular comparative format in the *Compendium*.

The extent of coverage for each major topic varies significantly between textbooks. For example, biological psychology ranges from 5% to 11% (median = 7%), developmental psychology ranges from 6% to 14% (median = 8%), social psychology from 5% to 12% (median = 7%), and sensation-perception from 6% to 13% (median = 8%). Thus, having defined a set of topics to be covered and emphasized in their courses, teachers can consult the compendium to compare the extent of coverage of these topics in the available texts. The *Compendium* provides such information for each text, organized by level and given separately for regular texts and briefer versions. For example, if teachers want to emphasize (or deemphasize) the biological processes, they can easily determine which texts at any level more optimally fit such course plans. The topics are also arranged in the prototypical order that they appear in introductory texts so that texts can be directly compared with respect to their emphases on the major sections of the text (i.e., biological processes, learning and cognitive processes, emotion-motivation, developmental psychology, clinical and health psychology, and social psychology), as well as on individual chapter topics.

In addition to topic emphases, introductory teachers may be concerned in their course plan with the learning or pedagogical aid program in their text. This should be congruent with their teaching objectives and testing philosophy and the abilities of their students. Thus, student perception of the usefulness and value of various pedagogical aids and the information available on their use in introductory texts are discussed next.

TEXT PEDAGOGICAL AIDS

Three recent studies (Marek, Griggs, & Christopher, 1999; Weiten, Deguara, Rehmke, & Sewell, 1999; Weiten, Guadagno, & Beck, 1996) surveyed high school, community college, and university students' evaluation of 15 pedagogical aids on three dimensions: familiarity, use, and educational value. The main finding that pervaded all three studies was that use of boldface type, running and chapter glossaries, chapter summaries, and self-tests were reported to be most useful and valued. All of these aids seem to reflect students' concern with test preparation.

Congruent with these results is Landrum and Hormel's (2002) finding that these particular pedagogical aids were rated as important to student learning in their survey of introductory psychology teachers. Some recent evidence (Gurung, 2003; see also Gurung & Daniel, chap. 4, this volume), however, indicates that students' reported use of pedagogical aids and their perceived helpfulness may not be related to student exam performance. This finding may be due, however, to the lack of a relationship between the type of learning (e.g., recalling facts versus application or synthesis) involved in the particular pedagogical aid and the type of learning being assessed on the exams. At this time, there is no good answer to the question of how valuable particular aids are to student learning. Regardless, as with extent of topic coverage, the *Compendium* provides inclusion information on 15 different pedagogical aids, organized by level of text and given separately for regular versus briefer versions. Thus, if there are particular pedagogical aids that teachers definitely want their text to include, they can easily check for their inclusion in the set of texts that they are considering.

There is substantial variance between introductory textbooks with respect to both the type and number of aids used. For the current set of textbooks, the number of pedagogical aids (for the 15 checked) varies from two to ten, median = seven (based on data in Koenig et al., 2004). High level texts use an average of 5.6 aids, whereas the average for low level texts is 8.5 aids. Whereas differences among texts with respect to pedagogical programs might be expected, differences in core vocabulary would not be. Such differences are surprising because if introductory textbooks are describing the basic core knowledge of the discipline, then it should follow that their core vocabularies will have substantial overlap. However, they do not, providing strong evidence that these texts are not all the same.

TEXT CORE VOCABULARY

As mentioned earlier, substantial differences exist across introductory texts with respect to core vocabulary. For example, Zechmeister and Zechmeister's (2000) content analyses of the glossaries of ten introductory psychology textbooks revealed that only 64 of 2,505 different glossary terms appeared in all ten glossaries and that about half of the concepts appeared in only one glossary. Similarly, Landrum (1993) conducted a page-by-page analysis of "important" terms in six introductory textbooks and found that 1,600 of 2,742 different terms were in only one text, and only 126 were in all six textbooks. Analyzing 52 introductory textbook indexes, Quereshi (1993) also found little commonality; only three terms appeared in all of the indexes and only 141 appeared in 75% of the indexes. Thus, three studies, each employing a different type of vocabulary analysis, found that introductory textbooks do not share a very large core vocabulary.

Landrum and Hormel (2002) found that introductory psychology teachers rated highly both a text's definition of terms and its glossary when they selected a text and established goals for student learning. For example, teachers rated these text attributes fourth and seventh, respectively, out of 79 attributes for importance to student learning. Chatman and Goetz (1985) also suggested using the extent to which textbooks cover key concepts as a means of reducing the size of the set of texts chosen for further, more detailed analyses during textbook evaluation. Given this importance of a text's core vocabulary in student learning and text selection and the finding that introductory textbooks do not share a substantial core vocabulary, information on the core vocabulary (regardless of its size) for the set of current introductory textbooks would be helpful. The *Compendium*, however, does not include information on this dimension, but a recent research study does.

Griggs, Bujak-Johnson, and Proctor (2004) analyzed the glossaries of the 44 introductory textbooks, with latest copyright from 1997 to 2003, to identify the set of common core concepts using two criteria, common to more than 50% and to 80% or more of the textbooks. We also computed individual textbook glossary size, percentage of coverage of the common core for both criteria, and glossary uniqueness. Out of 6,269 different terms across the 44 textbooks, only 14 (0.22%) appeared in all 44 glossaries. Over half (3,446; 55%) were unique to only one text glossary, and about 74% (4,654) were in three or fewer text glossaries! Only 155 terms (2.5%) met the commonality criterion of appearing in 80% or more of the text glossaries. Only 415 terms met the other commonality criterion of being in more than 50% of the 44 textbooks.

Griggs et al. (2004) reported the percentage of coverage of both of these sets of core terms as well as the glossary size for each introductory text. Coverage of the set of 155 common core terms ranged from 47.7% to 98.1%, with median coverage of 91.6%; and coverage of the set of core terms appearing in more than 50% of the textbooks ranged from 26.5% to 88.0%, with median coverage of 73.2%. Thus, teachers who are concerned about coverage of introductory psychology's core vocabulary may want to include these data in their text selection process. Even more useful is Griggs et al.'s calculation of each text's glossary uniqueness percentage (the percentage of its glossary terms appearing *only* in that text's glossary). These uniqueness percentages ranged from 1.4% to 29.7%, with a median of 10.6%. This means that for the text with the largest uniqueness percentage (29.7%), almost one out of every three terms appears only in that text's glossary.

Because glossary uniqueness is significantly correlated with size of glossary, teachers should check a text's uniqueness percentage if it has a large glossary. Complete data are provided in Griggs et al. (2004) and should remain current and comprehensive because glossaries do not usually change much with new editions and few new introductory textbooks (not new editions or new briefer versions but rather entirely new texts) enter the market each year. For example, an examination of the last three versions of the *Compendium* revealed that there have been only four new texts published in the last 3 years, with no new texts in 2004 and none projected for 2005. These data fit with the predictions of psychology acquisition editors at 13 publishers about the future of the introductory psychology textbook market (Cush & Buskist, 1997). They predicted that the number of introductory textbooks would decrease because of the shrinking number of publishers of such texts. The number of such publishers has decreased from 20 about 15 years ago (Griggs & Jackson, 1989) to only 10 at present. Even more striking is the fact that three companies (McGraw-Hill, Pearson, and Wadsworth) now publish about 75% of the current introductory textbooks (Griggs, 2003).

EPILOGUE

The suggestions herein are intended to help provide introductory teachers with an objective screening procedure to narrow down the set of textbooks that they need to more intensively compare. Once this is done, Morris (1977) strongly recommended that teachers actually read these texts to compare them. I wholeheartedly agree. I believe there is no better way to make the final selection decision. As Dewey (1995) stressed in his discussion of introductory textbook selection, "there is no substitute for a close reading" (p. 32). Reading the texts allows teachers to make a more informed choice about which texts will best help them to meet their individualized course goals and objectives and will fit best with their course structure and students' abilities. You truly do not know a text until you read it and teach from it. Obviously, the former should precede the latter.

ACKNOWLEDGMENTS

I would like to thank Andrew Christopher, Sherri Jackson, Cynthia Koenig, and Pam Marek not only for valuable comments on an earlier version of this chapter but also for their invaluable contributions to my introductory psychology textbook research program over the past 15 years.

REFERENCES

Bloom, B. S., & Broder, L. J. (1950). *Problem-solving processes of college students*. Chicago: University of Chicago Press.

Brewer, C. L. (2002). Reflections on an academic career: From which side of the looking glass? In S. F. Davis & W. Buskist (Eds.), *The teaching of psychology: Essays in honor of Wilbert J. McKeachie and Charles L. Brewer* (pp. 499–507). Mahwah, NJ: Lawrence Erlbaum Associates.

Chatman, S. P., & Goetz, E. T. (1985). Improving text selection. *Teaching of Psychology, 12*, 150–152.

Cush, D. T., & Buskist, W. (1997). Future of the introductory psychology textbook: A survey of college publishers. *Teaching of Psychology, 24*, 119–122.

Dewey, R. A. (1995, March). Finding the right introductory psychology textbook. *APS Observer, 8*, 32–33, 35.

Gaulin, S. J. C., & McBurney, D. H. (2001). *Psychology: An evolutionary approach.* Upper Saddle River, NJ: Prentice-Hall.

Gorenflo, D. W., & McConnell, J. V. (1991). The most frequently cited journal articles and authors in introductory psychology textbooks. *Teaching of Psychology, 18,* 8–12.

Gray, P. (2002). *Psychology* (4th ed.). New York: Worth.

Griggs, R. A. (1999). Introductory psychology textbooks: Assessing levels of difficulty. *Teaching of Psychology, 26,* 248–253.

Griggs, R. A. (2003, May). *Selecting an introductory textbook: Aren't they all the same?* Invited address at the Teaching Institute, 15th annual convention of the American Psychological Society, Atlanta, GA.

Griggs, R. A., Bujak-Johnson, A., & Proctor, D. L. (2004). Using common core vocabulary in text selection and teaching the introductory course. *Teaching of Psychology, 31,* 265–269.

Griggs, R. A., & Jackson, S. L. (1989). The introductory psychology textbook market: Perceptions of authors and editors. *Teaching of Psychology, 16,* 61–64.

Griggs, R. A., Jackson, S. L., Christopher, A. N., & Marek, P. (1999). Introductory psychology textbooks: An objective analysis and update. *Teaching of Psychology, 25,* 254–266.

Griggs, R. A., Jackson, S. L., Marek, P., & Christopher, A. N. (1998). Critical thinking in introductory psychology texts and supplements. *Teaching of Psychology, 25,* 254–266.

Griggs, R. A., & Koenig, C. S. (2001). Brief introductory textbooks: A current analysis. *Teaching of Psychology, 28,* 36–40.

Griggs, R. A., & Marek, P. (2001). Similarity of introductory psychology textbooks: Reality or illusion? *Teaching of Psychology, 28,* 254–256.

Griggs, R. A., & Mitchell, M. C. (2002). In search of introductory psychology's classic core vocabulary. *Teaching of Psychology, 29,* 144–147.

Griggs, R. A., Proctor, D. L., & Cook, S. M. (2004). The most frequently cited books in introductory texts. *Teaching of Psychology, 31,* 113–116.

Gurung, R. A. R. (2003). Pedagogical aids and student performance. *Teaching of Psychology, 30,* 92–95.

Hockenbury, D. H., & Hockenbury, S. E. (2003). *Psychology* (3rd ed.). New York: Worth.

Koenig, C. S., Daly, K. D., Griggs, R. A., Marek, P., & Christopher, A. N. (2004). *A compendium of introductory psychology textbooks, 2001–2004.* Retrieved April 1, 2004, from http://www.lemoyne.edu/OTRP/introtexts.html

Landrum, R. E. (1993). Identifying core concepts in introductory psychology. *Psychological Reports, 72,* 659–666.

Landrum, R. E., & Hormel, L. (2002). Textbook selection: Balance between the pedagogy, the publisher, and the student. *Teaching of Psychology, 29,* 245–248.

Marek, P., Griggs, R. A., & Christopher, A. N. (1999). Pedagogical aids in textbooks: Do college students' perceptions justify their prevalence? *Teaching of Psychology, 26,* 11–19.

Marek, P., Jackson, S. L., Griggs, R. A., & Christopher, A. N. (1998). Supplementary books on critical thinking. *Teaching of Psychology, 25,* 266–269.

McKeachie, W. J. (2002). *Teaching tips: Strategies, research, and theory for college and university teachers* (11th ed.). Boston: Houghton Mifflin.

Miller, B., & Gentile, B. F. (1998). Introductory course content and goals. *Teaching of Psychology, 25,* 89–96.

Morris, C. J. (1977). Choosing a text for the introductory course. *Teaching of Psychology, 4,* 21–24.

Myers, D. G. (2004). *Psychology* (7th ed.). New York: Worth.

Mynatt, C. R., & Doherty, M. E. (2002). *Understanding human behavior* (2nd ed.). Needham Heights, MA: Allyn & Bacon.

Nallan, G. B. (1996). Introductory psychology textbooks: Two encyclopedic volumes. *Contemporary Psychology, 41,* 690–691.

Quereshi, M. Y. (1993). The contents of introductory psychology textbooks: A follow-up. *Teaching of Psychology, 20,* 218–222.

Weiten, W. (1988). Objective features of introductory psychology textbooks as related to professors' impressions. *Teaching of Psychology, 15,* 10–16.

Weiten, W., Deguara, D., Rehmke, E., & Sewell, L. (1999). University, community college, and high school students' evaluations of textbook pedagogical aids. *Teaching of Psychology, 26,* 19–21.

Weiten, W., Guadagno, R. E., & Beck, C. A. (1996). Students' perceptions of textbook pedagogical aids. *Teaching of Psychology, 23,* 105–107.

Zechmeister, J. S., & Zechmeister, E. B. (2000). Introductory textbooks and psychology's core concepts. *Teaching of Psychology, 27,* 6–11.

Chapter

3

On Becoming a Fox: Covering Unfamiliar Topics in Introductory Psychology

Dana S. Dunn
Michelle E. Schmidt
Stacey B. Zaremba
Moravian College

The fox knows many things, but the hedgehog knows one big thing.

—Archilochus of Paros (flourished 700 or 650 BCE)

Berlin (1993) famously used this poetic fragment in an essay on Tolstoy, suggesting that some authors (foxes) explore a variety of perspectives, whereas others (the hedgehogs) connect everything to a solitary, focused idea. In Berlin's view, Tolstoy very much wanted to be a hedgehog, but given his perceptive gifts, he really was more of a fox. Due to training and erudition, most psychologists aspire to be hedgehogs, that is, specialists, at what they do. It is also true that generalists are in less demand, so contemporary psychology produces few foxes these days.

Yet, if there is one truth about being a teacher of introductory psychology, it is this one: To be effective, even the most scholarly hedgehog must become a fox—or learn to act like one. To adequately portray the discipline's scope, introductory psychology teachers must cover myriad topics. Some topics are familiar, of course, but many are not, especially when teachers recognize that learning about them in a class setting is a much different experience than teaching them to others. The pedagogical hedgehog in all of us wonders, if not worries: How will I cover all those unfamiliar topics in my class?

Most introductory psychology instructors ask this question. Their concern is our concern, and it is well-founded; the question is hardly rhetorical. How, for example, does the psychobiologist learn to teach about attribution theory or Piaget's stages? How does the cognitive psychologist do justice to archetypes in personality or the *DSM–IV*, let alone the intricacies of bipolar disorders? How well can a specialist in visual perception teach about cultural worldviews? In short, how do diligent hedgehogs in the library or lab become emboldened foxes in the classroom? These are no small matters when teachers feel compelled to cover the majority of chapters and topics found in most introductory psychology texts.

Teaching unfamiliar topics, then, is the particular challenge for the teacher of introductory psychology. We—a social psychologist, a developmental psychologist, and a learning psychologist—each have our areas of expertise and interest, as well as what might charitably be called knowledge gaps, or areas of the discipline outside our ken. We believe there is genuine benefit to be found when teachers stretch themselves a bit by teaching about things they know little about. After all, there is a certain virtue (possibly a mandate) associated with continuing to learn about new developments in one's specialty area. The same argument can be made convincingly when the issue is broadening one's intellectual horizons about the wider discipline.

More to the point, however, is the fact that psychology is an integral part of liberal education (McGovern, Furumoto, Halpern, Kimble, & McKeachie, 1991) and introductory psychology is a mainstay of almost any undergraduate curriculum. Teachers of introductory psychology have an obligation to convey the discipline's highlights in a compelling manner to students, most of whom will not further their education in the field. For this reason, especially, teachers of introductory psychology should be willing to challenge themselves by learning and covering unfamiliar material in their classes.

This chapter reviews common instructor concerns about teaching unfamiliar material in the introductory course. It then reviews three categories of strategies for effectively teaching about unfamiliar topics. When reviewing each category, a variety of examples, exercises, and practical tips are provided for teaching unaccustomed topics. The discussion turns to whether avoiding certain topics is ever an option for the introductory instructor.

TEACHING THE UNFAMILIAR: INSTRUCTOR CONCERNS

When facing the prospect of teaching the introductory course for the first time, most instructors probably do a bit of soul searching captured by questions like the following:

Shouldn't I know everything in order to teach an introductory level course? In a word, "No." Although all teachers were probably once students in an introductory course and had exposure to a wide variety of psychological topics, their focus narrowed from that point onward. Most teachers know quite a bit about some issues, precious little or nothing about others. Instructors cannot nor should they be expected to know everything. They can and should teach so as to capitalize on their strengths but also make certain to balance their coverage as much as possible.

Will I overemphasize my expertise and interests? This risk is an obvious one: People are drawn to the familiar, the comfortable, to what they already know— and know well. Teachers of introductory psychology will want to do justice to their area of expertise, but not at the cost of sacrificing other material that general psychology students should learn. No one teaching introductory psychology should turn the course from a general survey of the field into a special topics course. Teachers should consciously, and conscientiously, avoid overemphasizing what they know best.

Will I have to read and prepare extensively? As all teachers know, preparing for one thing means less available time to prepare for another. New teachers are especially conscious of what they do not know and, consequently, they tend to overcompensate by overpreparing (Boice, 2000; see also Boice, 1992, 1996). Ironically, such overpreparation can be counterproductive. When preparing material on an unfamiliar topic, do not read everything available; rather, locate a good review article or text and draw a few key points from it. A good introductory instructor gives a brief but solid overview of a topic, conveying a basic sense of the area, not an exhaustive introduction that is heavy on idiosyncratic details (see Boice, 2000, for suggestions on effective but moderate course preparation).

Will my colleagues and students find out what I don't know? Probably not. In any case, your colleagues are just as subject to knowledge gaps as you are. They are apt to know some topics better than you, but not others. This fact actually provides a useful form of social comparison (Festinger, 1954). No one knows everything, and learning new information is always a possibility. Given the literal explosion of knowledge in psychology and the ever-increasing girth of introductory texts, no scholar, researcher, or teacher knows everything about the discipline any longer. Rest easy where colleagues are concerned.

But what about the students—will they find you out? One way to approach this possibility is by disclosing the number of different divisions currently represented in the American Psychological Association (APA; as of this writing, there are 55 standing divisions), indicating those you either belong to or feel some affinity toward. Discussing divisional diversity is a way to concretely illustrate the field's breadth. No one belongs to all divisions and no one can keep up with all the research developments within the disciplinary areas represented by the divisions. Students will probably be relieved to know that their instructor has limits, because many of them feel overwhelmed by the scope of the discipline. Telling them that you do not know everything would be an honest admission and it would give you a chance to share your enthusiasm for learning new things along with them.

Our recommendation is simple: Students appreciate candor, so admit when you do not know something. There is a caveat to such candor, however; no instructor in an introductory course should claim ignorance of too many subject areas. Such "self-doubters," who communicate information inefficiently and inadequately (Brown, Bakhtar, & Youngman, as cited in Forsyth, 2003), are apt to undermine student confidence. In fact, students who doubt the level of instructor preparation for class are less likely to attend class sessions and acknowledge what the instructor is telling them (Hovland, Janis, & Kelley, as cited in Forsyth, 2003).

Is there a happy medium? Certainly. Admit when you do not know something, but immediately offer to rectify the situation by reporting back on the issue in the next class. (Alternatively, ask a group of students to see what they can find out and have them report back during the next class. Pitch this invitation as a sincere learning opportunity and not a burden, but issue it no more than once or twice a semester). Consult a colleague or a text, but do obtain and then share the information at the very next class meeting. It goes without saying (almost) that promising to find out some fact and then neglecting to do so is not a confidence builder in the eyes of students.

STRATEGIES FOR COVERING UNFAMILIAR TOPICS

There are three categories of strategies that instructors can call on as they prepare to teach unfamiliar topics in introductory psychology: those that primarily aid the instructor, mutually engage the instructor and the students, and focus principally on the students. The move away from traditional lecture methods and toward more active student learning techniques (e.g., Cuseo, 1996) provides an atmosphere in which it is more acceptable for the instructor to share teaching and learning with students.

Instructor-Centered Strategies

In general, instructor-centered strategies are traditional pedagogical practices that help teachers plan and organize class activities. A number of factors contribute to whether one should use these more traditional practices. For example, this practice is more appropriate for an introductory level class, like introduction to psychology, that is more concerned with breadth than depth. Introductory courses also are more likely to have higher enrollments, which makes them more conducive settings for traditional teaching techniques. Instructor-centered strategies are particularly appropriate in large lecture halls where issues of space and time become problematic for group-based activities. This section presents some suggestions for how to deal with unfamiliar content in settings where it is appropriate for instructors to rely on the more traditional lecture method.

Read Up on What You Don't Know. The simplest strategy is to simply acknowledge what you know little about and then go about doing reading related to the topic. In lieu of searches on PsycINFO, a good first strategy is to read review articles that synthesize topical research (e.g., *American Psychologist, Psychologi-*

cal Bulletin) or provide up-to-date, yet encapsulated, summaries. *Current Directions in Psychological Science*, a bimonthly journal of brief scholarly reviews published by the American Psychological Society, is another fine source. Also, a trip to your library's periodical collection to locate a few recent articles from an unfamiliar topical area to share with your class, or a few paper sessions at a professional conference, might be helpful.

Develop an Effective Teaching Style and Classroom Presence.   Each teacher brings some degree of individuality to the classroom, thereby creating (and leaving) an indelible impression in the minds of students. Such impressions influence how well students learn. Halonen (2002), for example, discussed behaviors that teachers can use to display their receptivity—their willingness to connect—to students, including agreeableness and empathy. Developing good rapport and demonstrating concern and consideration for students will enhance the delivery of course material, even unfamiliar course material.

A number of other personal characteristics have been associated with more effective teaching (for reviews, see Forsyth, 2003; Halonen, 2002). Where lecturing is concerned, for example, students associate a clear and loud voice with more expertise (e.g., Gronbeck, German, Ehninger, & Monroe, 1998). Although we do not encourage a boisterous lecture style, mumbling, muttering, or sonorously reading your notes will get you nowhere. We hasten to add, too, that creating meaningful connections with students is not restricted to sections of introductory psychology with relatively low enrollments. Personalizing an introductory class with an enrollment of several hundred students is entirely possible, as well (Benjamin, 1991; Halgin & Overtree, 2002).

Team Teaching.   Psychology departments are typically comprised of a number of faculty members with different areas of specialization. Why not take advantage of individual teachers' strengths? The mix of specializations can work well as a solution to the problem of unfamiliar content; what is unfamiliar to one member of the faculty may be familiar to another member. Beyond providing pedagogical advantages to students, team teaching the introductory class can also serve as a source for enhancing faculty development (Ware, Gardner, & Murphy, 1978).

Team teaching may involve two colleagues or all members of the department's faculty, and any combination in between. At Wheaton College (Wheaton, IL), for example, four of the seven people who teach undergraduate courses (a developmental, social, clinical, and biological psychologist) in the department share the responsibilities for lecturing in the introductory course. Members of the team lecture within their own area of specialization (e.g., the clinical psychologist covers the lectures on clinical psychology, psychopathology, and personality theory). In contrast, all 10 members of the University of Richmond psychology department share responsibility for teaching the introductory course. Each professor is responsible for three lectures over the course of the semester, and exam preparation and grading duties rotate each semester. Team teaching models provide students with thorough coverage of introductory psychology course material and also have the advantage of exposing aspiring majors to multiple members of the departmental faculty.

Developing a team teaching approach to the introductory course obviously requires effort and coordination, as well as the creation of some infrastructure (e.g., Flanagan & Ralston, 1983). If it is to serve both faculty and students, team teaching requires a heavy commitment to detail, especially where individual instructor expectations, grading, testing styles, and other class management issues are concerned (e.g., Buckley, 2000). The rewards can be great, however. Faculty gain respect for one another while learning from each other, and students get an overview of the interests, expertise, and personalities of department faculty.

Guest Lecturers. Although using a large number of guest lecturers in a course is not recommended, they can provide expertise that enhances coverage of the course material. Guest lecturers are found in other departments at your institution (e.g., a member of the biology department might come in to give a lecture on the brain or evolutionary theory), other institutions in your area (e.g., if your department does not have a cognitive psychologist, there may be one at another local school), or the larger community surrounding your institution (e.g., a neonatologist from the local hospital can talk about the newborn for the developmental segment of the course). Invite any guest lecturers to assign a reading associated with their presentations. Although there is little substantive literature on the effectiveness and usefulness of guest lecturers, our experience is that students welcome a different perspective once in a while.

Rely on Media. Occasionally shifting from lecturing to showing a video, DVD, or other form of media can help supplement your lecture and capture students' attention. Publishers often provide videos for the introductory course, and a number of articles have been published suggesting how movies can help supplement lectures. For example, one book discusses movies and mental illness and provides a great resource for those seeking media sources to illustrate concepts within the abnormal psychology section of the intro course (see Wedding & Boyd, 1998). Students usually welcome a shift from auditory verbal information to images and sounds, and may consider the new information a welcome distraction from class routine (Lutsky, 1999). In fact, the diversion may help refocus them on the material at hand. In addition to the media providing a needed distraction to you and your students, this alternate form of presentation requires dual processing, which students report contributes to learning (e.g., Mayer, 1997).

Shared Strategies

The move away from traditional lecture methods and toward more active student learning techniques (e.g., Cuseo, 1996) provides an atmosphere in which it is more acceptable for the instructor to share teaching and learning with students. Taking knowledge from the instructor as well as the student creates new forms of knowledge (Whipple, 1987). Shared strategies encourage instructors to pass some of the educational responsibilities to the students (e.g., Ferguson, 1986). This section presents some strategies that effectively engage the student and the instructor through collaborative goals.

Out-of-Class Writing Assignments and Student Lecturers.   Consider having students write a short literature review paper on a topic not covered in class. Perhaps the topic can come from a skipped chapter in the textbook or from a section of a chapter with which the instructor is less familiar. After researching the topic and writing a short paper, students can share the results of their library research with the class.

Some textbooks have text boxes that include additional information that is not covered within the main body of the chapter (e.g., Mary Calkins, America's first female psychologist, is a perennial favorite). Authors usually present this information as an aside, but it often is among the most interesting material to students. Students can research these sideline topics and then give a 10-minute "mini" lecture to the class. After doing a bit of research and writing on a topic, a student may actually know more about it than the instructor. Students become the experts and their classmates, as well as the instructor, benefit from the learning experience. Such empowerment is intellectually rewarding to students and gratifying to instructors.

Fostering Active Discussion.   The simplest way to deal with unfamiliar topical material may be to ask students to share their opinions, feelings, or even experiences regarding it. However, leading an effective class discussion takes some practice, especially because both the teacher and the students must be comfortable sharing their opinions, and possibly airing disagreements or different perspectives, in the classroom. A teacher can ask either a specific or a general question to start, entertaining answers from the floor and writing them on the board for reference as the discussion proceeds. A second option is to hand out several questions in advance that deal with a day's assigned readings. Students can use the questions to guide their reading and to prepare for the day's discussion. A final option that we will offer is to employ electronic bulletin boards for students to exchange thoughts before class. The online discussion can serve as a prime for beginning to discuss a topic at the next class meeting.

Teachers must learn to be comfortable departing from prepared notes and leading an active, animated, and possibly unstructured discussion. In part, leading a discussion requires teachers to have an effective classroom presence (see Halonen, 2002). One way to begin is to ask specific questions about course topics, with an eye to gauging the students' personal opinions. Students may know little or nothing about some topical area (e.g., intelligence assessment), but lack of knowledge does not preclude them from having strong opinions (e.g., "All IQ tests are biased"). The goal is to move beyond a dialog between an instructor and single students. Instead, the instructor and students should have an actual, sustained intellectual exchange about a topic, one where the introduction of one issue (or controversy) leads to another.

Engaging the Local Community.   The instructor can turn to the local community for student learning opportunities. There are experts outside of the academy; those who practice what we preach are important sources of information for our students in psychology. Two examples of assignments that promote learning and engage the community are investigative projects and taking action projects.

Investigative projects challenge students to learn to apply textbook knowledge in the community. For example, a student could be assigned the topic "schizophrenia." The student would then be responsible for researching best practices related to treatment of schizophrenia, interviewing people in local hospitals, and comparing how written best practices relate to real-world practices. Students become "experts" on the topics and conclude the reports with presentations to the class.

Another way to establish collaborative partnerships between students, faculty, and the community is through more formal service learning projects in psychology. Service learning is a form of experiential learning that provides students with opportunities to use newly acquired skills and knowledge in real-life situations in their communities (Ehrlich, 1996). The service learning project topic can focus on an issue with which the instructor is unfamiliar (e.g., homeless, mental illness). Service learning projects encourage faculty to let the students take on the role of teacher and learner. Students benefit from this work in that it fosters a sense of social responsibility, makes them active learners, and expands the walls of the classroom.

Student-Focused Strategies

There is nothing wrong with straying from the traditional lecture method. Faculty members should not feel responsible for relaying all course content to the students. In fact, in recent years, the college classroom has shifted from an environment of passive learning to one of active learning (McKeachie, Pintrich, Lin, & Smith, 1986). This position encourages students to take on the responsibility of seeking and finding knowledge. By putting students in the driver's seat, they may gain a more thorough understanding of existing information and create new knowledge. Ideally, this student-centered learning approach produces a more engaged student compared to the student who passively listens to a lecture. This approach might not be appropriate for all topics covered in the introductory course, but it can certainly supplement more traditional lectures, particularly those for which instructors have less expertise. A variety of student-centered learning strategies are discussed that can empower students to take an active role in the learning process.

Individual Learning Opportunities: The Case for Focused Freewriting.
A great approach for getting students to think actively and deeply about novel course material, and to respond to it in meaningful ways, is to have them do some freewriting at the start of class (e.g., Dunn, 1994). *Freewriting*, a technique devel-

oped in writing workshops, involves having students continuously write whatever comes to mind in response to some prompt for some period of time, usually 10 minutes or so (e.g., Elbow & Belanoff, 1995). While writing, students ignore the usual stylistic niceties: Correct grammar, punctuation, and spelling do not count. The point is to get students to put ideas, reactions, and thoughts down on paper and to see what they are and how they might be developed later. For example, freewriting is often used as a way for students to create or refine ideas for their papers (Elbow & Belanoff, 1995).

Some teachers claim that focused freewriting at the start of a class allows students to integrate their thoughts and feelings about a topic with what they previously read (e.g., Pennebaker, 1990). When beginning a new topic in introductory psychology, for example, students might freewrite for several minutes about what they think, feel, or know about the topic. Alternatively, they could write about what they hope to learn about the area of psychological research. Minimally, starting a class with a round of freewriting primes students for the lecture or discussion to follow, just as it virtually ensures that they have something to say about the topic (i.e., what they just wrote about). Pennebaker (1990) also found that routine use of freewriting promotes better regular class attendance and higher grades on essay exams (see also S. Hinkle & A. Hinkle, 1990).

Discussion Based In-Class Activities.   Small group, collaborative activities provide interesting examples of active learning (e.g., Giordano & Hammer, 1999). For example, the instructor can present a question to the class, give them a short amount of time to think about it individually, pair students together to discuss their responses to the question, and then ask students to share their discussions with the rest of the class. This technique, termed *think-pair-share* (Lyman, as cited in Ledlow, 2001), is useful for getting students to be more active participants in the learning process. Students can create their own knowledge by reading course material and being challenged to use that information in class. If students expect they will have to "perform" in class, then they are more likely to learn the material in preparation for class.

Alternatively, the instructor can divide the class into groups to debate various issues. Debating is a useful technique that can highlight some of the diverse viewpoints that exist in the field of psychology (Budesheim & Lundquist, 1999). Engaging in a debate, even a brief one, is a good way for students to identify the key issues or controversies in an area of research (e.g., gender differences in math and spatial abilities). It is helpful if the instructor provides background reading materials for preclass preparation but the responsibility of more thorough explanation and exploration is transferred to the students. Alternatively, part of the shift of responsibility can include students researching appropriate information for an assigned viewpoint. Although the instructor may need to provide some ground rules for acceptable and unacceptable debating techniques, monitor the time, and moderate questions between students, debating can be an exciting way for students to engage one another in learning without a lot of interference by the instructor.

A *fishbowl activity* can also foster discussion in the classroom. Students are asked to form an inner and outer "fishbowl." That is, one group of four or five students watches while another similar size group engages in a discussion concerning a day's assigned readings (e.g., REM sleep and dreams). Following this discussion, students in the outer circle then discuss what they learned from the conversation, as well as what else they want to know about the topic.

Finally, students can participate in a *jigsaw project*, a group-based, cooperative learning experience where each student possesses a "piece" of information necessary for creating and completing some final product (e.g., E. Aronson, Stephan, Sikes, Blaney, & Snapp, 1978). In introductory psychology, each member of a group of four students receives a section of a journal article (i.e., introduction, method, results, discussion) concerning a day's topic (e.g., helping behavior in social psychology) to read and then share with the others. After learning from one another, each group can then designate a spokesperson to describe the article's research to the larger class. Although this classroom activity is usually associated with elementary classrooms (e.g., J. Aronson, 2002), the basic idea is easily modified for use in secondary and postsecondary settings (for the literal use of jigsaw puzzles in introductory psychology, see Krauss, 1999). Jigsaw projects obviously benefit students by promoting active and cooperative learning in class, but there is another advantage. Instructors can tackle more complex topics because students have an opportunity to learn about an issue in three ways: *individually* at first when they learn about their piece of the puzzle, then *cooperatively* in the jigsaw group, and finally *as a whole class* during discussion.

Hands-On Experiences.   Some introductory psychology courses have a formal laboratory component. If the department can support this practice, it provides yet another opportunity for active learning. Students can investigate psychological phenomena through hands-on experience. For example, at Drexel University, a lab session devoted to perception (see http://www.pages.drexel.edu/~kld22/index101v.html) gives students the opportunity to investigate the principles of visual perception. At the University of Richmond, faculty members collaborate with student teaching fellows to publish an annual laboratory manual that includes 11 labs for students to complete over the course of the semester (e.g., Newcomb, Bagwell, Goldman, & Popaca, 2000). By designing their own lab manual, instructors can control which material they will cover in lectures and which they will leave for students to learn through hands-on experience in labs (e.g., semantic learning, five factors of personality).

If a department cannot support a formal laboratory component due to staffing, space, or other resource difficulties, then in-class activities can serve as small-scale lab opportunities. The purpose of the lab is to give students hands-on experience that provides active learning opportunities. The classroom environment can support that practice. For topics that are easier demonstrated than spoken about, the instructor can use a portion of class time.

For ideas on classroom "mini labs," consult ancillaries that accompany introductory psychology textbooks. In addition to overheads and lecture outlines (which also can aid in teaching unfamiliar content), instructor's resource manuals have helpful exercises that can serve as "mini labs." For example, the resource manual (Bolt, 2001) that accompanies Myers' (2001) *Psychology: Myers in Modules* offers dozens of great classroom exercises that students find enjoyable and worthwhile (e.g., classroom exercises on eye movements and human earphones supplement the sensation and perception modules; exercises on eyewitness recall and retrieval cues supplement the memory modules). Do not underestimate the usefulness of ancillaries both for preparing lectures on unfamiliar content and helping make students active learners of content for which you are not most comfortable.

OTHER TEACHING RESOURCES FOR COVERING UNFAMILIAR TOPICS

Besides the teaching strategies and techniques presented in this chapter, there are a variety of other resources for preparing to teach unfamiliar topics in introductory psychology. These resources include the teaching literature, course syllabi, the Internet, and newspaper articles.

Search the Teaching Literature

Consult the journal *Teaching of Psychology* or search the ERIC or PsycINFO databases for articles or activities related to teaching introductory psychology. There are also several books covering teaching introductory psychology, including a recent one by Brody and Hayes (1997). Edited compilations of previously published articles drawn from the teaching literature are also available (Benjamin, Daniel, & Brewer, 1985; Griggs, 2002; Hebl, Brewer, & Benjamin, 2000), as is a collection of personal essays written by introductory psychology text authors (Sternberg, 1997). Other perspectives on teaching introductory psychology are spread throughout other books on pedagogy in psychology (e.g., Davis & Buskist, 2002; McGovern, 1993; Perlman, McCann, & McFadden, 1999).

Ask Colleagues for Copies of Their Syllabi

As argued earlier in the discussion of team teaching, departmental colleagues are a great teaching resource. Asking colleagues for a copy of their introductory syllabus is flattering; most teachers are delighted to help or offer advice. Engage your colleagues by asking about what class activities, demonstrations, and discussion topics they find work well (or typically need more work than appears reasonable). Alternatively, consult the Office of Teaching Resources in Psychology (OTRP), which is sponsored by the Society for the Teaching of Psychology (STP). OTRP makes a wide variety of peer-reviewed, downloadable syllabi and other teaching resources available at this web address: http://www.lemoyne.edu/OTRP/teachingresources.html#coursesyllabi

Search the Internet

As long as the introductory instructor is selective and critical, searching the Internet can be an acceptable way to locate additional information for teaching unfamiliar material. Let the buyer (teacher) beware, however; outside of Web sites maintained by and for the members of professional organizations in psychology, there is no guarantee of quality control for web-based materials or their accuracy.

Read the Newspaper and Share Current Stories in Class

Psychology is in the news. Why not supplement lectures and textbook chapters with current research published in local or national newspapers? Thought provoking, relevant, and current information about various subtopics in introductory psychology take students beyond the information in the readings of the day. For example, supplement a lecture on abnormal psychology with a recent *New York Times* article on the use of antidepressants in treating children with depression. Or, follow a discussion of developmental psychology with one concerning day care in the news. Newspaper articles can assist the instructor with additional information on a course topic that may be unfamiliar and students can benefit by expanding their understanding of a course topic and learning more about the applied world of psychology. After all, instructors should go beyond simply restating in class everything the students already read in a text outside of class (see also Rider, 1992).

IS AVOIDING TEACHING AN UNFAMILIAR TOPIC EVER AN OPTION?

Familiarity does breed content, so is it possible to go into greater depth about research areas that you know well if you are planning to skip only a chapter or two? Some instructors do this and explain why they favor some topics over others (e.g., instructor interest, expertise, time available). There is an important caveat to consider, however. There are some canonical topics in the introductory class that cannot be passed over. An instructor might feel ill-prepared to cover the finer points of the brain's physiology, but such feelings are not carte blanche to avoid teaching about or discussing the chapter on brain and behavior. Resources exist and teachers should use them (e.g., Kalat, 2002).

CONCLUSIONS

To know psychology, therefore, is absolutely no guarantee that we shall be good teachers. To advance to that result, we must have an additional endowment altogether, a happy tact and ingenuity to tell us what definite things to say and do when the pupil is before us.   (James, 1899/2001, pp. 3–4)

Centuries after Archilochus flourished, William James (1899/2001) expressed this all too true claim in one of his essays to teachers.[1] He intuitively knew about the scholarly tendency to be a hedgehog and not a fox. Indeed, the writing of the *Principles of Psychology* looks like the act of a hedgehog, but James' love of ideas, his curiosity, wit, and intellectual breadth, suggest he was a restless fox (and that Tolstoy was by no means alone). As James implied, being a psychological hedgehog—one of those specialists who know so much about particular phenomena—is no guarantee that we will be good teachers. We can become good teachers, canny foxes of psychology education, however, by stretching ourselves to teach about unfamiliar topics in the all-important introductory class.

ACKNOWLEDGMENTS

We thank Stephen Chew and Randy Smith for their thoughtful comments on an earlier version of this chapter.

REFERENCES

Aronson, E., Stephan, C., Sikes, J., Blaney, N., & Snapp, M. (1978). *The jigsaw classroom.* Thousand Oaks, CA: Sage.

Aronson, J. (Ed.). (2002). *Improving academic achievement: Impact of psychological factors on education.* San Diego, CA: Academic Press.

Benjamin, L. T., Jr. (1991). Personalization and active learning in the large introductory class. *Teaching of Psychology, 18,* 68–74.

Benjamin, L. T., Jr., Daniel, R. S., & Brewer, C. L. (Eds.). (1985). *Handbook for teaching introductory psychology.* Hillsdale, NJ: Lawrence Erlbaum Associates.

Berlin, I. (1993). *The hedgehog and the fox: An essay on Tolstoy's view of history.* Chicago: Ivan R. Dee.

Boice, R. (1992). *The new faculty member.* San Francisco: Jossey-Bass.

Boice, R. (1996). *First-order principles for college teachers.* Bolton, CT: Anker.

Boice, R. (2000). *Advice for new faculty members: Nihil nimus.* Boston: Allyn & Bacon.

Bolt, M. (2001). *Instructor's resources.* New York: Worth.

Brody, R., & Hayes, N. (1997). *Teaching introductory psychology.* Philadelphia: Psychology Press.

Buckley, F. J. (2000). *Team teaching: What, why, and how?* Thousand Oaks, CA: Sage.

Budesheim, T. L., & Lundquist, A. R. (1999). Consider the opposite: Opening minds through in-class debates on course-related controversies. *Teaching of Psychology, 26,* 106–110.

Cuseo, J. B. (1996). Cooperative learning: A pedagogy for addressing contemporary challenges and critical issues in higher education. [Monograph]. Cooperative Learning and College Teaching. Stillwater, OK: New Forums Press.

Davis, S. F., & Buskist, W. (Eds.). (2002). *The teaching of psychology: Essays in honor of Wilbert J. McKeachie & Charles L. Brewer.* Mahwah, NJ: Lawrence Erlbaum Associates.

Dunn, D. S. (1994). Lessons learned from an interdisciplinary writing course: Implications for student writing in psychology. *Teaching of Psychology, 21,* 223–227.

---

[1] We are grateful to Steve Hobbs for bringing this quote to our attention.

Ehrlich, T. (1996). Foreword. In B. Jacoby & Associates (Eds.), *Service-learning in higher education: Concepts and practices* (pp. xi–xii). San Francisco: Jossey–Bass.

Elbow, P., & Belanoff, P. (1995). *A community of writers: A workshop course in writing* (2nd ed.). New York: McGraw-Hill.

Ferguson, N. B. L. (1986). Encouraging responsibility, active participation, and critical thinking in general psychology students. *Teaching of Psychology, 13*, 217–218.

Festinger, L. (1954). A theory of social comparison processes. *Human Relations, 7*, 117–140.

Flanagan, M. F., & Ralston, D. A. (1983). Intra-coordinated team teaching: Benefits for both students and instructors. *Teaching of Psychology, 10*, 116–117.

Forsyth, D. (2003). *The professor's guide to teaching: Psychological principles and practices*. Washington, DC: American Psychological Association.

Giordano, P. J., & Hammer, E. Y. (1999). In-class collaborative learning: Practical suggestions from the teaching trenches. *Teaching of Psychology, 26*, 42–44.

Griggs, R. A. (Ed.). (2002). *Handbook for teaching introductory psychology: With an emphasis on assessment* (Vol. 3). Mahwah, NJ: Lawrence Erlbaum Associates.

Gronbeck, B. E., German, K., Ehninger, D., & Monroe, A. H. (1998). *Principles of speech communication* (13th ed.). New York: Longman.

Halgin, R. P., & Overtree, C. E. (2002). Personalizing the large class in psychology. In C. A. Stanley & M. E. Porter (Eds.), *Engaging large classes: Strategies and techniques for college faculty* (pp. 290–298). Bolton: Anker.

Halonen, J. S. (2002). Classroom presence. In S. F. Davis & W. Buskist (Eds.), *The teaching of psychology: Essays in honor of Wilbert J. McKeachie and Charles L. Brewer* (pp. 41–55). Mahwah, NJ: Lawrence Erlbaum Associates.

Hebl, M. R., Brewer, C. L., & Benjamin, L. T., Jr. (Eds.). (2000). *Handbook for teaching introductory psychology* (Vol. 2). Mahwah, NJ: Lawrence Erlbaum Associates.

Hinkle, S., & Hinkle, A. (1990). An experimental comparison of the effects of focused freewriting and other study strategies on lecture comprehension. *Teaching of Psychology, 17*, 31–35.

James, W. (2001). *Talks to teachers on psychology and to students on some of life's ideals*. Mineola, NY: Dover. (Original work published 1899)

Kalat, J. (2002). Teaching biological psychology to introductory psychology students. In S. F. Davis & W. Buskist (Eds.), *The teaching of psychology: Essays in honor of Wilbert J. McKeachie and Charles L. Brewer* (pp. 361–368). Mahwah, NJ: Lawrence Erlbaum Associates.

Krauss, J. (1999). A jigsaw puzzle approach to learning history in introductory psychology. *Teaching of Psychology, 26*, 279–280.

Ledlow, S. (2001). *Using think–pair–share in the college classroom*. Retrieved February 18, 2004, from Arizona State University, Center for Learning and Teaching Excellence Web site: http://clte.asu.edu/active/usingtps.pdf

Lutsky, N. (1999). Teaching with overheads: Low tech, high impact. In B. Perlman, L. I. McCann, & S. H. McFadden (Eds.), *Lessons learned: Practical advice for the teaching of psychology* (pp. 67–72). Washington, DC: American Psychological Society.

Mayer, R. E. (1997). Multimedia learning: Are we asking the right questions? *Educational Psychologist, 32*, 1–19.

McGovern, T. V. (Ed.). (1993). *Handbook for enhancing undergraduate education psychology*. Washington, DC: American Psychological Association.

McGovern, T. V., Furumoto, L., Halpern, D. F., Kimble, G. A., & McKeachie, W. J. (1991). Liberal education, study in depth, and the arts and sciences major—Psychology. *American Psychologist, 46*, 598–605.

McKeachie, W. J., Pintrich, P., Lin, Y., & Smith, D. (1986). *Teaching and learning in the college classroom: A review of the research literature.* Ann Arbor, MI: University of Michigan, NCRIPTAL.

Myers, D. G. (2001). *Psychology: Myers in modules* (6th ed.). New York: Worth.

Newcomb, A. F., Bagwell, C. L., Goldman, J. L., & Popaca, C. J. (2000). *Psychological science laboratory manual* (7th ed.). New York: McGraw-Hill.

Pennebaker, J. W. (1990). Self-expressive writing: Implications for health, education, and welfare. In P. Belanoff, P. Elbow, & S. I. Fontaine (Eds.), *Nothing begins with n: New investigations of freewriting* (pp. 157–170). Carbondale, IL: Southern Illinois University Press.

Perlman, B., McCann, L. I., & McFadden, S. H. (1999). *Lessons learned: Practical advice for the teaching of psychology.* Washington, DC: American Psychological Society.

Rider, E. A. (1992). Understanding and applying psychology through the use of news clippings. *Teaching of Psychology, 19,* 161–163.

Sternberg, R. J. (Ed.). (1997). *Teaching introductory psychology: Survival tips from the experts.* Washington, DC: American Psychological Association.

Ware, M. E., Gardner, L. E., & Murphy, D. P. (1978). Team teaching introductory psychology as pedagogy and for faculty development. *Teaching of Psychology, 5,* 127–130.

Wedding, D., & Boyd, M. A. (1998). *Movies and mental illness.* New York: McGraw-Hill.

Whipple, W. R. (1987). Collaborative learning: Recognizing it when we see it. *AAHE Bulletin, 40,* 3–6.

Evidence-Based Pedagogy: Do Text-Based Pedagogical Features Enhance Student Learning?

Regan A. R. Gurung
University of Wisconsin–Green Bay

David Daniel
University of Maine at Farmington

The vast majority of undergraduate psychology courses rely on textbooks as the major source of information. Introductory psychology texts, in particular, contain a plethora of "pedagogical aids" that are offered as tools for the students' mastery of the content, with those aids that are successful in the market (i.e., positively influence sales) becoming integrated in textbooks in other areas of psychology. In fact, the variety and ubiquity of such devices has increased remarkably over the past 10–15 years (Marek, Griggs, & Christopher, 1999).

Despite the growth and popularity of text-based pedagogical aids, little effort has been given to determining which, if any, are actually effective. Particularly in the field of psychology, we find this lack of information to be an intriguing state of affairs. In a field where people who believe in spoon bending and alien invaders are relegated to the realm of misguided, it is, at the least, ironic that the most popular required textbooks are replete with untested "learning aids." Strangely enough, the same group that teaches about the scientific method often fails to utilize the scientific method when developing and selecting effective text-based pedagogy! Although it is clear that students use many of the aids in texts (e.g., Weiten, Guadagno, & Beck, 1996), responsible faculty lack the empirical data needed to develop appropriate teaching techniques and assessment based on the general effectiveness of specific pedagogical aids. Why are these features so popular with instructors? How do pedagogical features affect student learning (if at all)? The potential importance of pedagogical aids compels a thorough understanding of their effectiveness and use. This chapter is an effort to develop a conversation among teachers regarding the most effective and appropriate uses of text-associated learning tools with the goal of developing an arsenal of evidence-based pedagogy for a variety of learning outcomes.

Specific learning goals vary from instructor to instructor, but we all want our students to learn. Whether it is memorizing the basic concepts in the field, understanding the material, or being able to successfully synthesize, evaluate, and apply the material, instructors work hard to modify their teaching styles and techniques to optimize learning. In addition, there are a variety of attempts to improve student learning that take place in and around the normal teaching context (i.e., in the classroom where teaching is principally focused on the material to be taught and not the building of the students' skills or cognitive or metacognitive abilities). Commonly referred to as study skills or study habits, there exists a vast literature documenting such attempts (for reviews, see Hartley, 1986; Pintrich & de Groot, 1990) and recommending the best ones (Al-Hilawani & Sartawi, 1997; Fleming, 2002; Gettinger & Seibert, 2002; Rittschof & Griffin, 2001). There are even meta-analyses that identify the study skills that are successful (Hattie, Biggs, & Purdie, 1996). Attempts to improve study skills were boosted by the advent of pedagogical aids.

PEDAGOGICAL AIDS IN PSYCHOLOGY TEXTBOOKS

Pedagogical aids are designed to enhance learning and provide additional resources and ways to study. Pedagogical aids also emphasize and clarify certain material. Optimally, such devices may serve as metacognitive tools alerting students as to how much they know and how well they know it, as well as giving them the ability to consciously and deliberately monitor and regulate their learning (Hacker, Dunlosky, & Graesser, 1998). Pedagogical aids, then, if used correctly, could alert students to what they know or do not know and enhance their learning. Alternatively, the use of some aids might actually hurt students who use them incorrectly and waste study time memorizing the aids instead of using the aids as a test of knowledge. Unfortunately, many students may use aids only because they get credit for doing so or may memorize the information in an aid because they think those specific items likely to be on exams (Marek et al., 1999).

Pedagogical aids have populated texts for decades (Marek et al., 1999). Every introductory psychology book includes a variety of study aids designed to help students enhance their learning. Certain aids are extremely common. In their examination of 37 full-length introductory psychology textbooks, Marek et al. (1999) found that boldface type and chapter outlines were present in 100% of the books. Chapter summaries (84%) and discussion questions (70%) followed close behind. Other pedagogical aids include the use of italics, running glossaries, chapter glossaries, end-of-chapter review questions, and self-tests. These aids have grown in number and variety over the decades (Weiten & Wight, 1992). The potential importance of pedagogical aids has compelled a number of empirical studies of students' perceptions and use of these aids (Gurung, 2003; Marek et al., 1999; Weiten, Deguara, Rehmke, & Sewell, 1999; Weiten et al., 1996).

Students clearly use many of the aids in texts (Gurung, 2003; Weiten et al., 1996). For example, Weiten et al. (1996) showed that the aids varied considerably in terms of their familiarity to students, their likelihood of being used, and their perceived value. These authors also found that students' educational experiences, as measured by their year in school and their previous academic grade point averages, did not relate strongly to their ratings of pedagogical aids. Weiten et al. (1999) extended these findings, showing that university, community college, and high school students agreed about which learning aids were most useful. Knowing about students' preferences is useful in predicting the extent to which they may use particular aids and to which aids may be helpful, but how much do students actually use these aids? Additionally, does use correlate with standard measures of learning (i.e., exam scores)?

Although students rate a number of pedagogical aids as helpful in mastering the information in the text, few studies exist linking usage with academic performance. In contrast to the studies of aid usage, little is known about their effectiveness. The small amount of extant research testing the effectiveness of pedagogical aids has been conducted relatively recently and in experimental contexts that may not reflect the spontaneous use of students working on their own.

The vast majority of the available research focusing on the potential effectiveness of pedagogical aids has focused on a variety of signaling devices commonly found in textbooks. A number of studies have demonstrated that pedagogical aids that draw attention to the to-be-learned content (e.g., headings, summaries, and overviews) may serve as organizational tools on subsequent recall and summarization tasks (Lorch & Lorch, 1995; Lorch, Lorch, & Klusewitz, 1995; Sanchez, Lorch, & Lorch, 2001). Topic overviews, for example, have been found to encourage both faster reading times and structure recall for expository passages (Murray & McGlone, 1997) and headings have been shown to encourage memory for text topics and text organization (Lorch, Lorch, Ritchey, McGovern, & Coleman, 2001), as well as the manner in which readers searched texts for answers to specific questions (Klusewitz & Lorch, 2000). Headings may be more helpful to a reader when the topic is not familiar or when the topic was only briefly discussed in the text (Lorch & Lorch, 1996). On the other hand, the value of signaling through chapter headers may be limited when it comes to mastering key concepts imbedded in the text. Recently, Nevid, and Lampmann (2003) demonstrated that signaling these key concepts via marginal inserts positively influenced student mastery of the material. However, such signaling did not increase or decrease the reader's recall of nonsignaled content, even though the participants were explicitly encouraged to also attend to the material that was not signaled.

Such studies show great promise and provide a glimpse about usage under ideal conditions. However, to what extent would students not explicitly involved in a study spontaneously use such pedagogy? The next section focuses on students' spontaneous usage of available pedagogy and the effects of such usage on performance.

EMPIRICAL TESTS OF THE EFFECTIVENESS OF PEDAGOGICAL AIDS

Most extant research testing the effectiveness of pedagogical aids has been conducted relatively recently (e.g., Balch, 2001). Effectiveness is important to this chapter, and so consider a recent study that provides a detailed picture of the issue at hand.

Gurung (2003) correlated the use of different textbook aids with students' scores on exams to ascertain the effectiveness of each aid. Data were collected during the course of a semester from two sections of an introductory psychology class. A short survey was added to the end of the first and last of four exams. After 65 multiple-choice questions testing material from class, participants read instructions stating that the remaining questions on the exam sheet would assess how the various parts of the class and the textbook influenced learning. Students were told that participation was voluntary and the answers to the questions would not affect their class grades or exam scores. Instructions also stated that only group-level information from the questions would be discussed and student responses would remain confidential.

Over 200 students completed a survey measuring their use and their perceived effectiveness of six pedagogical aids present in the assigned textbook (i.e., chapter outlines, chapter summary/review sections, boldface terms, italicized terms, key terms, practice test questions). Each aid was defined based on a pedagogical aids survey originally administered by Weiten et al. (1996). Participants first read a brief description of the aid and then used a 4-point scale to indicate the extent to which they used the aid. They then rated the overall value of each aid. The textbook assigned to the class was a brief version of a full-length textbook in the high-middle level of difficulty (Griggs, 1999) and had a large number of common pedagogical aids.

Table 4.1 presents the average reported use and average reported utility data for each textbook pedagogical aid and the percent of students who chose each response option for the use and utility of each aid. Students reported using boldface and italicized terms most often, followed by the practice test questions, the chapter summaries/reviews, the key terms, and the chapter outlines. A series of paired

TABLE 4.1
Descriptive Data for Use and Helpfulness of the Different Pedagogical Aids

	Mean	Use [Frequency (%)]				Helpful [Frequency (%)]			
		Not at all	Little	Moderate	Extremely	Not	Somewhat	Moderate	Extremely
Outlines	1.93	52 (22)	131 (56)	37(16)	10 (4)	36 (15)	102 (43)	79 (34)	1
Summary	2.69	14 (6)	79 (34)	89 (38)	48 (20)	9 (4)	51 (22)	101 (43)	68 (29)
Boldface	3.52	2 (1)	12 (5)	62 (26)	154 (65)	0	17 (7)	63 (27)	150 (64)
Italics	3.12	0 (0)	41 (17)	108 (46)	77 (33)	1	37 (16)	109 (46)	79 (34)
Key Terms	2.22	40 (17)	96 (41)	62 (26)	27 (11)	24 (10)	73 (31)	90 (38)	38 (16)
Review	2.86	42 (18)	46 (20)	48 (20)	90 (38)	25 (11)	20 (9)	71 (30)	110 (47)

Note: Numbers in parentheses represent percent of total.

sample *t* tests showed that students reported using aids to different extents, except for the use of chapter summaries/reviews and the use of practice test questions (both were used to the same extent). Many authors (e.g., Marek et al., 1999) have suggested that students pay more attention to those aids that directly relate to exams, and this claim was mostly true in this sample (60% of the class used the practice test questions *moderately* or *extremely*).

Similar to previous research (e.g., Weiten et al., 1996), the most helpful pedagogical aids were boldface terms, italicized terms, and practice test questions (92% of the sample rated boldface terms as *moderately* or *extremely helpful*). Again, students rated most aids significantly differently in helpfulness from each other. Only the reported helpfulness of the chapter summary/review sections and italicized text aids, and the italicized and practice test question aids, did not differ significantly from each other.

The results of zero-order correlations between the reported use of different aids showed that the students' reported use of one aid did not guarantee the reported use of other aids (see Table 4.2). Most correlations within usage categories were low to moderate. The reported use of chapter summary/review sections correlated with reported use of all other aids except for italics. Students who reported using the chapter summary/review sections were particularly likely to report using the prac-

TABLE 4.2
Correlations Between the Reported Usage and Helpfulness of Different Pedagogical Aids

	1	2	3	4	5	6	7	8	9	10	11
1. Outlines	–										
2. Summary	.27**	–									
3. Boldface	.18*	.27**	–								
4. Italics	.15*	.04	.54**	–							
5. Key terms	.18**	.36**	.25**	.21*	–						
6. Review	.09	.53**	.25**	.12	.13*	–					
7. OutlineH	.58**	.19**	.19**	.08	.24**	.10	–				
8. SummaryH	.13	.68**	.15*	−.06	.19**	.47**	.28**	–			
9. BoldH	.07	.02	.66**	.45**	.14*	.15*	.10	.11	–		
10. ItalicsH	.06	.05	.46**	.74**	.23**	.14*	.09	.05	.62**	–	
11. KeyH	.06	.20**	.28**	.23**	.65**	.04	.20*	.31**	.28**	.31**	–

Note: H = helpfulness.
*p < .05; **p < .01.

tice test questions. Similarly, students who reported using boldface terms were likely to report using italicized terms.

Correlations between the ratings of helpfulness of different aids showed similar results. Most correlations within helpfulness categories were low with some exceptions. Students who found the chapter summary/review sections helpful were particularly likely to find the practice test questions helpful. Similarly, students finding boldface terms helpful were extremely likely to find italicized terms helpful. The correlations between reported usage of aids and their helpfulness were moderate to strong. For example, as would be expected, students reporting use of boldfaced terms also rated them as being very helpful.

Did the reported use of pedagogical aids predict exam scores? Zero-order correlations assessed whether or not the reported use of different aids and their perceived helpfulness related to performance on exams in class. In general, the reported use and the perceived helpfulness of the different pedagogical aids were not significantly associated with exam scores. Only one correlation was significant. Student ratings of the helpfulness of key terms was negatively related to their exam scores, $r(237) = -.20, p < .01$. A closer look at this finding with an analysis of variance (ANOVA) showed that students who reported the key terms as being more helpful had significantly lower exam scores, $F(3, 228) = 4.35, p < .01$. Students who did not find key terms at all helpful achieved a mean of 85 points as compared to students who found key terms most helpful, who scored 77 points on average, $t(225) = 2.63, p < .01$. These findings were replicated in a second study (Gurung, 2004) that controlled for both student effort and ability, and also measured usage and helpfulness at two points of the semester. Thus, all but one of the pedagogical aids evaluated demonstrated no effect on exam scores, with the use of key terms associated with lower exam scores.

The fairly robust findings that the most commonly available pedagogical aids have no negative effects on exam performance are, at first, disconcerting. It seems that the results obtained in more controlled experiments may not reflect the results using those same pedagogical aids as students spontaneously use them. One potential resolution to this dilemma may be to provide instructions on proper usage to students. In fact, despite the best of intentions, providing such instructions does not seem to affect the way students use pedagogical aids (Brothen & Wambach, 2001).

Balch (2001) provided students in an introductory psychology course both a handout and in-class instructions on how to use study strategies to optimize performance on exams. These study tips included strategies on getting the most from review quizzes (see Carlson & Buskist, 1997), strategies for effective note-taking, and instructions on elaborative encoding, as well as tips on charting performance, forming study groups, and using friends to question the student on class material. These efforts produced no overall effect on course performance with the students admitting to slightly less than moderate usage of the study tips. The lack of effect on performance may be because, on their own, students are generally not very good at recognizing areas where they need to improve (Dunning, Johnson,

Ehrlinger, & Kruger, 2003) or they tend to gravitate toward study techniques that require less time and effort.

Another potential solution to this dilemma may be to provide some structure and contingencies for students. Instead of just having students complete an aid, provide an adequate context and instructions on how to complete it and also how long they have to complete it and how many times they can attempt to complete it. In fact, the search for the most effective structure and contingencies for the use of pedagogical devices is a very fruitful area for future research. One aid that lends itself to such refinement is online quizzing, the use of short quizzes available on the Internet at a textbook Web site or on a university computer server.

Variations on a Theme: Online Quizzes

A number of studies have provided evidence that routine in-class quizzing increases student performance on exams (e.g., Connor-Greene, 2000; Grover, Becker, & Davis, 1989; Taraban, Maki, & Rynearson, 1999). In-class quizzing, however, consumes valuable contact time as well as time for grading and providing feedback. The amount of class time needed, as well as the increased effort required from the instructor for grading, diminishes the practical utility of quizzing as class size increases. Thus, quizzing is not often used in larger courses where the positive impact may be most appreciated.

Alternatively, Web-based quizzing may allow teachers to incorporate the benefits of quizzing without sacrificing valuable class time (Brothen & Wambach, 2000; Peat & Franklin, 2002). This system also allows the quizzes to be automatically scored and recorded for the instructor. However, students left to their own devices may interact with quizzes differently and less effectively when done outside of class.

Spontaneous use of online quizzes, like those supplied by most publishers, has not demonstrated positive effects on exam scores (Brothen & Wambach, 2001; Gurung, 2003). Brothen and Wambach (2001) provided students with the opportunity to take unproctored online quizzes. Surprisingly, their results demonstrated a negative relation between the number of quizzes taken and exam scores! However, students given access to online quizzes in a proctored setting did seem to benefit (Brothen & Wambach, 2000). Of course, students probably approach these quizzes differently. It is likely that students left to their own devices are focusing on quizzes as ends in themselves and not as a check on their level of mastery. Thus, students employed strategies to optimize their score rather than guide their learning.

The adoption of different strategies is evident in a study by Daniel and Broida (2004). Each of three different sections of a child and adolescent course were assigned to either a no quiz, an in-class quiz, or an unproctored, online quiz condition. Results at midsemester showed a positive effect on exams for the in-class quiz group, but no effect for online quizzing relative to the no-quiz group (see Table 4.3). We were intrigued by the results. Because the quizzes were the same for both the in-class and online groups, we hypothesized that the online quiz group must be employing quizzing strategies that, although allowing them to

TABLE 4.3
Overall Results: Group by Mean Exam Score and Percent Change

Group	Mean score Exams 1 and 2	Mean score Exams 3 and 4	Percent Change	N
No quiz	48.95	46.45	5%	44
Web-based quiz	49.75	60.90	18%	39
In-Class Quiz	59.45	61.60	3%	42

Note: Exam scores out of 75.

score well on the quizzes, did not mirror those employed by the students taking in-class quizzes.

So, we empirically tested this question by assessing student opinions. Students in the online group had, almost universally, employed a variety of "cheating" strategies. Most prominent were using the text while taking the quiz, copying and/or printing the quiz to share with other students (they were allowed multiple attempts), using a publisher-provided online glossary, and working in groups (see Table 4.4). For the second half of the semester, we took steps to minimize cheating. These "fixes" are outlined in Table 4.4. In addition to making the online glossary unavailable, we timed the quiz to discourage searching the text and increased the pool of questions so that each quiz contained different questions for each attempt and each student. We hoped that this would minimize the utility of printing and sharing the quiz as well as the effectiveness of working in groups.

The results after the changes were dramatic. By the end of the semester, indeed on the next exam, the online quiz group's exam performance had risen to the level

TABLE 4.4
Summary of Issues and Changes to Online Quizzes at Midsemester

"Cheating" strategies	"Fixes"
Printing and Sharing Quizzes	Increase Pool from 10 to 100 Questions
(10 question quiz from 10 question pool)	Randomly Assign 10 Questions from Pool
Searching Text for Answers During Quiz	Decreased Time Allowed to
(open book)	Take Quiz (from 15 to 7 minutes)
Opening Online Glossary in Adjacent Window site	Remove Glossary Option from web

Note: Strategies reported by web-based students, fixes represent midsemester changes in quiz settings.

of the in-class group (see Table 4.4). These results argue both for caution and for hope. Students in the web-based quiz group quickly discovered strategies to optimize their quiz performance without mastering the text. Efforts to discourage these strategies, however, were very effective. So, whereas quizzing is generally effective, unproctored online quizzing may not be: Success is accomplished under very specific conditions (see also Brothen & Wambach, 2004).

To test whether or not there is a "best way" to prepare for and take the online quizzes, Gurung (2004) compared the students who read the chapter and then took an online quiz with those students who just took the quiz with the book open looking for the answers for each question (students who guessed, copied, or took the quizzes in any other way were excluded). Students who read the chapter before taking the quiz had significantly higher exam scores, scoring a mean of 85 points, as compared to students who took it without reading the chapter first, who scored an average of 77 points. It is very plausible, then, that the conditions described encourage students to read the text more carefully, resulting in increased mastery of the material.

Will This Formula Work in Introductory Psychology?

Many psychology departments struggle to develop a credible introductory psychology course capable of serving the large number of students who enroll in it every semester. We tried mandatory study guides with visits to teaching assistants at the end each section to verify completion. We also tried to make available a number of pedagogical aids and extra credit for using them via a course management system. Although the study guides were more effective tools than optional web-based activities, we felt that we could do better (see Daniel & King, 2003). Given the impressive results with online quizzes already described, the second author applied the quizzing formula to a 200+ student general psychology course while everything else remained unchanged. By simply using the online quizzes structured in the same fashion as described above (see also Daniel & Broida, 2004), students' performance had dramatically increased. The mean scores for all exams were significantly higher for the web-quizzing group than the scores from both the study guide and the optional web activity (Daniel & King, 2003). In a subsequent study examining student characteristics and online quizzing, Daniel, Broida, and Hearns (in preparation) found that the positive effects of online quizzing did not discriminate on the basis of gender, age (traditional vs. nontraditional aged college students), history with and anxiety toward computers, or learning style. The positive effects of online quizzing are, indeed, very robust. We have no way of knowing, however, if these benefits are due to the quizzing itself, or to the fact that quizzes encourage reading. Whereas more research is needed to tease these issues apart empirically, the practical effect of quizzing is noteworthy.

It seems, then, that when properly constructed and evaluated, certain types of pedagogy can be used with great success in our classes. In particular, the difference between performance on proctored as opposed to unproctored online quizzes may be in the simple act of holding students accountable for interacting appropriately with the quizzes and creating an appropriate interactive structure. Previously, for example, we demonstrated that study guides had little effect on exam scores when the method of checking their use was an end of section verification. However, Flora and Logan (1996) required students to use online study guides in preparation for two exams, but not for the other two exams. These online study guides were sent to the instructors when completed and checked. The results showed that there was an increase in exam scores when these study guides were used. Furthermore, a majority of students thought they were helpful and enjoyed using them in their exam preparation. Thus, determining which pedagogical tools will be most effective and holding students accountable for properly interacting with them may be necessary in order to obtain the maximum benefits.

RECOMMENDATIONS FOR TEACHERS

From our review of the data, it is clear that the mere availability, or even use, of pedagogical aids does not guarantee improved student performance. Students who are not held accountable for interacting with specific types of pedagogy may not interact productively with those tools. The reviewed data also imply that developing a system for obtaining feedback regarding the effectiveness of pedagogical devices and making changes based on the results can have positive effects on student performance and course evaluations.

Do Not Judge a Textbook by Just Its Pedagogical Aids

Pedagogical aids are often used as a valid criterion to compare textbooks (Griggs, 1999; Griggs, Jackson, & Napolitano, 1994). Should adoption of a certain textbook depend on whether or not it has the well-used aids? A review of the literature suggests that the absence of aids should not be grounds for avoiding a text. The number of pedagogical aids in a textbook influence how a book looks, in terms of visual appearance, size, and perceived ease of use. Instructors expect pedagogical aids to increase the elaboration of material, test understanding, and enhance learning, but there is little evidence to support this assumption. It is no surprise, then, that a large number of aids do not always mean a book is pedagogically sound. Weiten (1988) showed that the use of italics, a common pedagogical aid, predicted instructors' beliefs in a textbook's capacity to engage student interest and their awareness of a book, although the aids did not relate to professors' evaluations of a text's overall pedagogical quality. Unfortunately, pending the development of better ways to get students to use pedagogical aids and additional empirical tests of their effectiveness, most pedagogical aids presently may serve as mere window dressing. Having many aids conveys the impression of a strong textbook written to better serve students, but in reality this serves no real function. In fact, the misuse of some aids might actually hurt students who take time to use them instead of spending their time in a more productive way. Based on our review, we do not feel that choosing a textbook primarily based on available technology or type of pedagogical aids is warranted.

Assess the Effectiveness of Your Assignments

Selecting a text that incorporates the appropriate set of features is only the next step. Each instructor is encouraged to evaluate the effectiveness of pedagogical aids within the context of their own course structure and goals along with their means of assessment. As suggested in the *backward design* method of instruction and class planning, teaching techniques should be guided by first setting clear desired goals and standards, then designing accurate performance measures of the goals, and finally planning learning experiences and instruction to match (Wiggins & McTighe, 1998). Multiple-choice exams are one of the most common assessment methods used in large introductory psychology classes, but they often assess only limited forms of learning. For example, most multiple-choice exams are not written to assess student's ability to analyze, synthesize, evaluate, or apply their knowledge (Sternberg, 2004). It is possible that different assessment measures could reveal different pedagogical aids that enhance learning. A better assessment of the effectiveness of aids and other instructional techniques could be achieved by an examination of different outcome measures (e.g., content of group exercise discussions, quality of critical thinking demonstrated in the papers). Similarly, whereas the online quizzing reviewed earlier seems to have positive effects on performance on multiple-choice exams, they may not be productive for a course primarily using essay exams or emphasizing writing (Daniel & Broida, 2004). At this point, evaluating your own efforts is key. Far too little is known about whether and under what circumstances pedagogical aids are helpful, much less what kinds of learning results from different pedagogical aids. More research, either formal research or in-class studies, on what kinds of learning are obtained from different pedagogical aids and activities is needed before we can broadly match aids to assessment and outcomes.

Well-Used Aids Could Benefit Learning

Some textbook pedagogical aids, if used optimally, can be particularly important in large introductory classes where the standard lecture is often the most common and most practical way of interacting with students. Many instructors do not have the time or training to conduct in-class exercises to engage different levels of understanding and different types of learning styles in the way that many pedagogical aids can. Having effective pedagogical aids can benefit both the instructor and the student. We feel that the potential utility of pedagogical aids is best determined by instructors of a course based on their learning objectives, teaching style, and the demonstrated impact of specific aids within the context of a particular course.

Can Using Some Pedagogical Aids Actually Hurt Exam Performance?

Longitudinal data suggests that, although the extent of damage is low (i.e., only the use of a few aids early in the semester were related to lower scores later in the semester), overuse of some aids can be dangerous (Gurung, 2004). Many students spend too much time on some aids (e.g., key terms) at the expense of studying other important material or working on elaboration and understanding of the material. Students are selective in what aids they use and find helpful. We need to realize that students will not always use the aids available or use them correctly. Further research and developmental efforts should be aimed toward optimizing ways to ensure the adequate use of aids. If a different form of learning results from different kinds of aids, then we need to be able to better measure it and also ask if it is the kind of learning we strive for in our courses. Just having more aids is not the answer. Just telling students to use them may not work either. We need to be cognizant of situations that make pedagogical aids effective.

Teaching Is Still Paramount

Textbooks and technology, although powerful tools in their own right, do not replace a good teacher. The teacher provides the context, goals, and contingencies necessary for a successful and productive journey through a course. Despite the ubiquity and possible overabundance of pedagogical tools associated with textbooks it is still up to the responsible teacher to select the proper activities and provide appropriate contingencies to encourage students to attain the appropriate learning objectives. Therefore, careful examinations of your learning objectives, a review of which pedagogical tools best encourage progress toward those goals, and the development of a system where the student is accountable for using the tools are essential.

REFERENCES

Al-Hilawani, Y. A., & Sartawi, A. A. (1997). Study skills and habits of female university students. *College Student Journal, 31*(4), 537–544.

Balch, W. R. (2001). Study tips: How helpful do introductory psychology students find them? *Teaching of Psychology, 28*, 272–274.

Brothen, T., & Wambach, C. (2000). The effectiveness of computer-based quizzes in a PSI introductory psychology course. *Educational Technology Systems, 28*, 253–261.

Brothen, T., & Wambach, C. (2001). Effective student use of computerized quizzes. *Teaching of Psychology, 28*, 292–294.

Brothen, T., & Wambach, C. (2004). The value of time limits on internet quizzes. *Teaching of Psychology, 31*, 62–64.

Carlson, N. R., & Buskist, W. (1997). *Psychology: The science of behavior* (5th ed.). Boston: Allyn & Bacon.

Connor-Greene, P. A. (2000). Assessing and promoting student learning: Blurring the line between teaching and testing. *Teaching of Psychology, 27*(2), 84–88.

Daniel, D. B., & Broida, J. P. (2004). Using web-based quizzing to improve exam performance: Lessons learned. *Teaching of Psychology, 31*(3), 207–208.

Daniel, D. B., Broida, J. P., & Hearns, J. H. (in preparation). *Learner characteristics and the effectiveness of web-based quizzing.* Unpublished manuscript, University of Maine at Farmington.

Daniel, D. B., & King, J. (2003, January). *What works in general psychology? The differential effects of study guides, web-based activities and web-based quizzing on exam scores.* Poster presented at the meeting of the National Institute of the Teaching of Psychology, St. Petersburg Beach, FL.

Dunning, D., Johnson, K., Ehrlinger, J., & Kruger, J. (2003). Why people fail to recognize their own incompetence. *Current Directions in Psychological Science, 12,* 83–87.

Fleming, V. M. (2002). Improving students' exam performance by introducing study strategies and goal setting. *Teaching of Psychology, 29*(2), 155–119.

Flora, S. R., & Logan R. E. (1996). Using computerized study guides to increase performance on general psychology examinations: An experimental analysis. *Psychological Reports, 79,* 235–241.

Gettinger, M., & Seibert, J. K. (2002). Contributions of study skills to academic competence. *School Psychology Review, 31*(3), 350–366.

Griggs, R. A. (1999). Introductory psychology textbooks: Assessing levels of difficulty. *Teaching of Psychology, 26,* 248–253.

Griggs, R. A., Jackson, S. L., & Napolitano, T. J. (1994). Brief introductory psychology textbooks: An objective analysis. *Teaching of Psychology, 21,* 136–140.

Grover, C. A., Becker, A. H., & Davis, S. F. (1989). Chapters and units: Frequent versus infrequent testing revisited. *Teaching of Psychology, 16*(4), 192–194.

Gurung, R. A. R. (2003). Pedagogical aids and student performance. *Teaching of Psychology, 30*(2), 92–96.

Gurung, R. A. R. (2004). Pedagogical aids: Learning enhancers or dangerous detours? *Teaching of Psychology, 31*(3), 164–166.

Hacker, D. J., Dunlosky, J., & Graesser, A. C. (Eds.). (1998). *Metacognition in educational theory and practice.* Mahwah, NJ: Lawrence Erlbaum Associates.

Hartley, J. (1986). Improving study skills. *British Journal of Educational Research, 12,* 111–123.

Hattie, J., Biggs, J., & Purdie, N. (1996). Effect of learning skills interventions on student learning: A meta-analysis. *Review of Educational Research, 66,* 99–136.

Klusewitz, M. A., & Lorch, R. F., Jr. (2000). Effects of headings and familiarity with a text on strategies for searching a text. *Memory & Cognition, 28*(4), 667–676.

Lorch, R. F., & Lorch, E. P. (1995). Effects of organizational signals on text-processing strategies. *Journal of Educational Psychology, 87*(4), 537–544.

Lorch, R. F., & Lorch, E. P. (1996). Effects of headings on text recall and summarization. *Contemporary Educational Psychology, 21*(3), 261–278.

Lorch, R. F., Lorch, E. P., & Klusewitz, M. A. (1995). Effects of typographical cues on reading and recall of text. *Contemporary Educational Psychology, 20*(1), 51–64.

Lorch, R. F., Jr., Lorch, E., Ritchey, K., McGovern, L., & Coleman, D. (2001). Effects of headings on text summarization. *Contemporary Educational Psychology, 26*(2), 171–191.

Marek, P., Griggs, R. A., & Christopher, A. N. (1999). Pedagogical aids in textbooks: Do college students' perceptions justify their prevalence? *Teaching of Psychology, 26,* 11–19.

Murray, J. D., & McGlone, C. (1997). Topic overviews and processing of topic structure. *Journal of Educational Psychology, 89*(2), 251–261.

Nevid, J. S., & Lampmann, J. L. (2003). Effects on content acquisition of signaling key concepts in text material. *Teaching of Psychology, 30,* 227–230.

Peat, M., & Franklin, S. (2002). Supporting student learning: The use of computer-based formative assessment modules. *British Journal of Educational Technology, 33,* 515–523.

Pintrich, P., & de Groot, E. (1990). Motivational and self-regulated learning components of classroom academic performance. *Journal of Educational Psychology, 82,* 33–40.

Rittschof, K. A., & Griffin, B. W. (2001). Reciprocal peer tutoring: Re-examining the value of a cooperative learning technique to college students and instructors. *Educational Psychology, 21*(3), 313–322.

Sanchez, R. P., Lorch, E. P., & Lorch, R. F., Jr. (2001). Effects of headings on test processing strategies. *Contemporary Educational Psychology, 26*(3), 418–428.

Sternberg, R. J. (2004). The CAPS model: Assessing psychology performance using the theory of successful intelligence. In D. S. Dunn, C. M. Mehrotra, & J. S. Halonen (Eds.), *Measuring up: Educational assessment challenges and practices for psychology* (pp. 111–124). Washington, DC: American Psychological Association.

Taraban, R., Maki, W., & Rynearson, K. (1999). Measuring study time distributions: Implications for designing computer-based courses. *Behavior Research Methods, Instruments & Computers, 31*(2), 263–269.

Weiten, W. (1988). Objective features of introductory psychology textbooks as related to professors' impressions. *Teaching of Psychology, 15,* 10–16.

Weiten, W., Deguara, D., Rehmke, E., & Sewell, L. (1999). University, community college, and high school students' evaluations of textbook pedagogical aids. *Teaching of Psychology, 26,* 19–21.

Weiten, W., Guadagno, R. E., & Beck, C. A. (1996). Students' perceptions of textbook pedagogical aids. *Teaching of Psychology, 23,* 105–107.

Weiten, W., & Wight, R. D. (1992). Portraits of a discipline: An examination of introductory psychology textbooks in America. In A. E. Puente, J. R. Matthews, & C. L. Brewer (Eds.), *Teaching psychology in America: A history* (pp. 453–504). Washington, DC: American Psychological Association.

Wiggins, G., & McTighe, J. (1998). *Understanding by design.* Alexandria, VA: Association for Supervision and Curriculum Development.

Defining, Teaching, and Assessing Critical Thinking in Introductory Psychology

Drew C. Appleby
Indiana University-Purdue University Indianapolis

Critical thinking is an almost universally valued outcome in American higher education (Halpern, 2002). Even a cursory online search of college and university Web sites reveals that the majority of colleges and universities list critical thinking as one of the skills they want students to acquire. Unfortunately, the popularity of critical thinking is not matched by its semantic clarity. Although it is often mentioned, it is almost never defined. This situation can produce frustration in introductory psychology when instructors are required to teach their students how to think critically and determine whether or not their students have accomplished this task. It can also leave introductory psychology students puzzled when they are required to think critically. The challenge of this situation is compounded by the fact that introductory psychology classes are often taken to satisfy general education requirements and are therefore filled with students whose majors span the full gamut of academic disciplines. This chapter describes a strategy that can enable introductory psychology faculty to *define* critical thinking in a clear and practical manner for all their students, use that definition to *teach* their students what critical thinking is, and *assess* their students' ability to think critically.

DEFINING CRITICAL THINKING

Critical thinking has been defined in many ways, including those definitions in Table 5.1. Faculty want their students to think critically, but defining and assessing this skill can be problematic because it can be approached in so many ways from so many disciplinary perspectives, for example:

- a philosopher can teach her students to think critically by requiring them to logically analyze formal syllogisms in order to determine their validity

TABLE 5.1
Definitions of Critical Thinking

- "Critical thinking is a process that emphasizes a rational basis for beliefs and provides procedures for analyzing, testing, and evaluating them" (Barry, 1984, p. 9).
- "Critical thinking is the careful and deliberate evaluation of ideas or information for the purpose of making a judgment about their worth or value" (McWorter, 1988, p. 97).
- "Critical thinking is defined as the result of the following steps. Step 1: Decide what you think and why you think it. Step 2: Seek other views and more evidence. Step 3: Evaluate the various views. Step 4: Construct the most reasonable view" (Ruggierro, 1989, p. 86).
- Critical thinking is "our active, purposeful, and organized efforts to make sense of our world by carefully examining our thinking and the thinking of others in order to clarify and improve our understanding" (Chaffee, 1988, p. 29).
- "The highest level of understanding is the critical level. Here, you judge what you learn in terms of standards you have set for yourself. You determine the credibility of the author and the text. You attempt to distinguish between an author's opinions and facts. You search for bias and propaganda" (Longman & Atkinson, 1988, p. 84).
- "Critical thinking is disciplined, self-directed thinking that exemplifies the perfections of thinking appropriate to a particular mode or domain of thought. It comes in two forms. If disciplined to serve the interests of a particular individual or group, to the exclusion of other relevant persons and groups, it is sophistic or *weak sense critical thinking*. If disciplined to take into account the interests of diverse persons or groups, it is fair-minded or *strong sense critical thinking*" (Paul, 1990, p. 51).
- "Critical thinking is thinking that is purposeful, reasoned, and goal directed. It is the kind of thinking involved in solving problems, formulating inferences, calculating likelihoods, and making decisions. When we think critically, we are evaluating the outcomes of our thought processes" (Halpern, 1989, p. 5).
- Critical thinking is "the conscious direction of mental processes toward representing and processing information, usually in order to find thoughtful solutions to problems. In critical thinking, we consciously direct our mental processes to reach particular goals, such as problem solving, making judgments or decisions, and reasoning. In everyday thinking, these three kinds of goals overlap somewhat. Nonetheless the goal of thinking differs for each one. The goal of problem solving is to overcome obstacles (e.g., not having enough money to buy a car) in order to reach a solution. The goal of judgment and decision making is to evaluate various possibilities and to choose one or more of them (e.g., choosing the car that would please you most for the amount of money you have to spend). The goal of reasoning is to draw conclusions from evidence (e.g., infer the relative safety of a model after reviewing the safety records of various cars)" (Sternberg, 1997, p. 224).
- "When you use critical thinking, you decide what to believe and how to act after you carefully evaluate the evidence and the reasoning in a situation" (Matlin, 1995, p. 22).

- a psychology teacher can teach his students to think critically by requiring them to examine and comprehend both sides of an argument (e.g., the nature–nurture issue) in an unbiased manner before they reach an informed conclusion
- a music teacher can teach her students to think critically when they are required to explain why a late Beethoven symphony is classified as an example of early Romantic music (i.e., because it deals with harmonies, phrasing, rhythms, and forms that are accepted as part of the style of early Romanticism)
- an education teacher can teach her students to think critically by requiring them to examine different teaching methods and to select those methods that are most appropriate in different content areas and with different levels of students
- a chemistry teacher can teach her students to think critically by requiring them to use data they have collected in the laboratory to draw conclusions, look for patterns, detect similarities (e.g., determining what acid molecules have in common), and come to a conclusion as to the nature of what the word "acid" means

I teach introductory psychology, which many students take to satisfy a general educational requirement. One of the six principles of undergraduate learning that guide the curriculum at my institution is critical thinking, which is defined as the ability to "analyze carefully and logically information and ideas from multiple perspectives" (Indiana University-Purdue University Indianapolis, 2002, p. 15), and one of the most important goals of my introductory psychology course is to "think critically about the contents of this course" (Appleby, 2004, p. 1). Because the vast majority of my introductory psychology students major in disciplines other than psychology—and their academic advisers place them in my class so they can gain broad academic skills rather than to become psychology majors—I decided several years ago (when I was at my former institution, Marian College) that it would be inappropriate for me to restrict their critical thinking to the type used by psychologists. Faced with this challenge, I resolved to construct a model of critical thinking that is both interdisciplinary (i.e., based on input from many academic departments) and useful as a foundation from which to construct assignments that teach and assess both the acquisition of course content and the development of critical thinking skills.

After a great deal of thought, I devised and sent a questionnaire to each of my 18 Marian College department chair colleagues (and myself), which asked them to define critical thinking from their particular discipline's perspective and to explain how they teach critical thinking to their students. I performed a content analysis of the results of my questionnaire by identifying the verbs (e.g., to evaluate) or action-related words (e.g., evaluation) in my colleagues' responses and then categorizing these words in an attempt to discover the existence of some sort of conceptual pattern or framework.

Approximately half way through my analysis, I realized I had rediscovered the categories of the cognitive domain of educational objectives first described by

Bloom, Englehart, Furst, and Krathwohl (1956) in their *Taxonomy of Educational Objectives: Cognitive Domain* (i.e., knowledge, comprehension, application, analysis, synthesis, and evaluation). My colleagues' specific responses, and my subsequent categorization of these responses, are presented in Table 5.2. (Please note that I used the word "retention" in place of Bloom et al.'s term "knowledge" to maintain the parallel semantic structure of the list of critical thinking skills.) After the initial categorization, I constructed a definition of critical thinking based on these skills and then developed a set of characteristics of each of these skills in terms of how they could be used in a college classroom (see Table 5.3). This definitional model, which appears in my class syllabus, has three basic strengths. It is *interdisciplinary* because it reflects input from all academic disciplines, it has *strong theoretical support* because it is based on established educational theory, and it is a *very practical* because it can be used to create assignments that assess both the acquisition of course content and the development of cognitive skills.

TEACHING CRITICAL THINKING

I spend the first two days of introductory psychology thoroughly orienting my students to the nature and value of the class, what they will be required to do in the

TABLE 5.2
Frequencies of Verbs and Action-Related Words Denoting the Use or Products of Cognitive Abilities Listed in 19 Departmental Explanations of How They Define and Teach Critical Thinking

Evaluation (47)

evaluate (8), judge (7), compare (4), contrast (3), test (2), decide (2), conclude (2), support (2), validate, justify, prove, assess, question, critique, criticize, challenge, decide, determine, select, defend, eliminate, prioritize, choose, determine, find weaknesses"

Analysis (26)

analyze (13), use logic (5), distinguish (2), examine (2), differentiate, reason, conclude, infer

Application (19)

apply (9), solve (8), modify, refine

Retention (18)

recognize (3), identify (3), define (2), read (2), listen (2), observe (2), know, ask, assimilate, be informed

Synthesis (15)

synthesize (3), organize (3), discover (2), derive (2), create, unify, develop, suggest, connect

Comprehension (10)

discuss (2), interpret (2), comprehend, explain, understand, reflect, review, reflect

Note: The number of instances of each skill named more than once follows that skill in parenthesis.

TABLE 5.3

The Model of Critical Thinking That Appears in the Course Syllabus

A. The *Definition* of Critical Thinking: Critical thinking results from the use of a set of cognitive skills that enables an individual to reach intelligent decisions about what they should believe and how they should act.

B. The *Skills* of a Critical Thinker
  1. Retention
     a. definition: the ability to *remember* specific information
     b. required tasks: to remember facts, principles, and steps in sequences
     c. in psychology: to acquire and retain specific psychological terms, definitions, facts, principles, and sequences
     d. questions it helps to answer: Who, what, where, and when?
     e. sample question: What is the definition of psychology?
  2. Comprehension
     a. definition: the ability to *understand* the meaning of material
     b. required tasks: to explain, translate, or interpret to a new form or symbol system
     c. in psychology: to grasp the meanings of basic psychological principles, concepts, methods, and theories
     d. questions it helps to answer: How and why does this happen?
     e. sample question: Why is Wilhelm Wundt known as the founder of empirical psychology?
  3. Application
     a. definition: the ability to use learned material to *solve* problems
     b. required task: to use concepts, principles, and theories to finds solutions to problems
     c. in psychology: to use psychological principles and methods to change behaviors and mental processes
     d. questions it helps to answer: "How can this problem be solved?"
     e. sample question: How can parents use extinction to decrease tantrums in their children?
  4. Analysis
     a. definition: the ability to *separate* complicated wholes into their parts and organizational relationships
     b. required tasks: divide complex entities into their component parts and determine the relationship among these parts
     c. in psychology: to break down complex psychological concepts, theories, and methods into their parts and relationships
     d. questions it helps to answer: "Of what is this complex whole composed and how are its parts related to each other?"
     e. sample question: Describe Freud's three major parts of the personality and explain how they interact.
  5. Synthesis
     a. definition: the ability to *combine* separate parts into new and creative wholes
     b. required task: combine previously learned materials in order to produce new ideas
     c. in psychology: to produce unique and creative psychological ideas, solutions, hypotheses, and theories
     d. questions it helps to answer: What new ideas or conclusions can you reach on the basis of what you have learned?

(continued on next page)

TABLE 5.3 (continued)

    e. sample question: Use the results of empirical research described in your text to answer the question: Does watching violent television cause children to behave more aggressively?

6. Evaluation
    a. definition: the ability to *judge* the value of material for a given purpose
    b. required tasks: make judgments, rate ideas, and accept or reject materials based on valid criteria
    c. in psychology: to identify and use valid criteria and methods during the processes of assessment, diagnosis, and research in order to distinguish between fact and fiction, education and propaganda, relevant and irrelevant information, and rational and irrational beliefs about psychology
    d. questions it helps to answer: Determine the validity of a principle, theory, or method.
    e. sample question: Use the concepts of reliability, validity, and standardization to support or oppose the use of SAT scores as criteria for college admission.

class, and how I will evaluate their performance and assign their final grades. I explain that my most fundamental goal is to provide them with "the experience and understanding they will need to make the world a better place in which to lead productive and fulfilling lives" (Brewer et al., 1993, p. 180). I state that the first way in which I will attempt to help them to accomplish this goal is to provide them with a basic understanding of the fundamental concepts, principles, theories, and methods of psychology and to facilitate their understanding of the value of this information to their current and future lives. I then explain that my second strategy to enable them to accomplish this goal is to help them to become aware of the nature of critical thinking, to strengthen their critical thinking skills, and to develop an understanding of how critical thinking is crucial to their personal, social, and professional development.

Once I have fully explained my definition and model of critical thinking, I then bring my students' attention to the nature and purpose of the six critical thinking projects (CTPs) they will be required to perform in the class. I emphasize that these projects will require them to use all six of their critical thinking skills to retain, comprehend, apply, analyze, synthesize, and evaluate the specific psychological concepts, principles, theories, and methods that the class will cover. The following set of CTP instructions appear in the syllabus:

1. You will write six CTPs worth a maximum of 10 points each.
2. You will submit these CTPs at the beginning of the class on the days designated on the Daily Class Schedule contained in this syllabus. Please note that 20% of your grade on each CTP is determined by the timeliness of its submission.
3. You may drop your lowest CTP score, so the total possible CTP points will be 50.
4. Each CTP will conclude with the answers to the following four questions: What critical-thinking skill did you use in the project? What is the defini-

tion of that skill (in your own words)? How did you use the skill to success-fully complete this CTP? How can you generalize this skill (give a specific example not used in your CTP) to help you in situations outside or after this class (e.g., in your other classes, your personal life, or your future career). These questions will require you to think critically about your criti-cal-thinking skills, which is a reflective activity characteristic of a well-ed-ucated person.

5. Your set of six CTPs must include an example of each of the six criti-cal-thinking skills described in this syllabus (i.e., retention, comprehen-sion, application, analysis, synthesis, and evaluation). It will be your responsibility to do this.

6. All CTPs must be word-processed on one side of one sheet of 8½ × 11 pa-per. Use wide margins and small font if necessary.

7. Each CTP will be worth a maximum of 10 points, which will be awarded on the basis of the following six criteria:

    a. 2 points for timely submission (Did you submit it at the beginning of the class during which it was due?)

    b. 1 point for correct format (Does your CTP use exactly the same format as the sample CTP contained in this syllabus?)

    c. 2 points for completeness and correctness (Does your CTP answer all the parts of a multiple-part question, and is the information in your CTP accurate and correct?)

    d. 2 points for the use of relevant and accurate course material to support your answer (Did you use appropriate information from the text or lec-ture to support your answer or did you rely on common sense or personal opinion?)

    e. 2 points for comprehension of the critical-thinking skill used in the CTP (Were you able to clearly describe how your thought processes resemble those given in the model of critical thinking contained in this syllabus?)

    f. 1 point for writing skill (Does your CTP contain fewer than two gram-matical, punctuational, spelling, or capitalization errors?)

I then answer any questions my students have about how their CTPs are to be written and how they will be evaluated. The next step is to bring my students' at-tention to the page in the syllabus that contains the following assignments for their six CTPs and their final CTP. (Please note that the assignments given are merely representative samples of CTPs that have worked well for the author in his class. The advantage of this type of assignment is that faculty can target any type of content from their classes as long as the CTPs they create allow their stu-dents the opportunity to fully engage in at least one of the critical thinking skills as they create their answers.):

CTP #1: Project yourself into the future. You are a college graduate and you have a job. Identify your job, and briefly explain what it will require you to do. Give a specific example of how your job will require you to use each of the six skills of a critical thinker. Explain a specific negative consequence if you were unable to use each of these critical thinking skills on your job. (Although you will discuss all six skills, be sure you choose only one—the primary one you used to answer the entire question—for the "Critical Thinking Skill" section of your CTP.)

CTP #2: Explain a specific characteristic (i.e., a behavior or mental process) that sets you apart from the majority of other people (one that Gordon Allport would call a cardinal or central trait). Suppose you were curious about how you acquired this characteristic, and you went to five different psychologists, each of whom represents a different approach to explaining human personality (i.e., psychoanalytic, behaviorist, cognitive, humanistic, and biological). What would be their answers to the following two questions? (a) How did I acquire or develop this characteristic? (b) Why do you believe I acquired or developed this characteristic?

CTP #3: You are a psychologist who has been hired by the principal of an elementary school that recently experienced a tornado, which injured several children. The first thing the principal did when his school re-opened after it was repaired was to stage a tornado drill, but the results were not what he expected. When the first alarm rang—just as it had immediately before the tornado hit the school—many of the children began crying hysterically or froze in panic, and the drill was a complete disaster. The news of the tornado drill's failure spread fast, and the principal suddenly found himself under a great deal of pressure from the members of the PTA and the school board, all of whom seemed to be blaming him for the panic and unpreparedness that exists in his school. Use the information that you gained from the learning chapter in your textbook to help the principal accomplish the following tasks. (a) Prepare a short report that he can present to the school board and the PTA that will help them to understand why the children are now so frightened of the fire alarm (Hint: Use the terms unconditioned stimulus, unconditioned response, conditioned stimulus, and conditioned response in your report). (b) Devise a strategy to warn the children of an impending tornado that does not frighten them so much that they become unable to take appropriate precautionary actions (Hint: Use the terms extinction and stimulus discrimination in your strategy).

or

A psychologist who is an expert in operant conditioning has been hired by our college to help our faculty increase their teaching effectiveness. Her first step is to survey students to determine how they feel about their instructors' teaching methods. As one of the participants in her survey, you have been asked to prepare a brief report describing the teaching methods of each of your instructors. Take a moment to consider the classes you are currently taking, and use the following terms to describe the methods your instructors use effectively, ineffectively, or not at all: positive reinforcement, negative reinforcement, schedules of reinforcement, punishment, and shaping. Complete your report with suggestions that you would like your teachers to read so they can help you learn more effectively in their classes.

CTP #4: Choose four aspects of your identity that are in various stages of progress and/or completion (e.g., major choice, career choice, religious beliefs, etc.), and then use a different example of Marcia's (1980) four identify statuses to describe your current status in regard to each of these aspects.

CTP #5: Explain the last stressful situation you experienced. Use specific information from the textbook to describe the coping mechanisms you used to deal with your stress, evaluate how successful these methods were in helping you to cope with this situation, and explain at least two other mechanisms that may have helped you to improve your ability to cope with this situation.

CTP #6: Reflect upon a person you know whose behaviors or mental processes cause you and/or others to consider her/him to be odd, strange, or abnormal. How can you use the specific information presented in your textbook about mood disorders, somatoform disorders, anxiety disorders, schizophrenia, dissociative disorders, or personality disorders to (a) understand this person's behavior or mental processes better and (b) treat her/him in a more humane and understanding manner in the future.

Final CTP

The final CTP is composed of four parts. This last project provides students with an opportunity to reflect on the impact that the course has had on their ability to think critically. In essence, it requires them to engage in the metacognitive task of thinking critically about their critical thinking skills. It also provides me with an opportunity to assess the degree to which they have attained the second major goal of the course (i.e., to become aware of the nature of critical thinking, to strengthen their critical thinking skills, and to develop an understanding of how critical thinking is crucial to their personal, social, and professional development). One of the most important parts of this final CTP is #3 in which students must explain how they have used their experiences in the course to change themselves in a positive way. For me, my students' answers to #3 are often the most enlightening aspect of my course. It is one thing for teachers to tell their students how they expect them to change as a result of completing a class on the first day of class. It is a very different thing for students to tell their teachers how the class has actually changed them on the last day of class. The following are the four parts of the final CPT:

1. Define the six critical thinking skills in your own words. Show me you fully comprehend their meaning; do not simply copy the definitions from the syllabus.

2. After each of your definitions, choose one of your CTPs in which you used that critical thinking skill and cite specific information from this CTP to explain how you used this assignment as an opportunity to think critically about the material you have learned in this course.

3. Give a specific example of how this class enabled you to develop each of the six critical thinking skills. Explain these examples fully by answering the fol-

lowing question completely for each skill: What did you do in the course, and how did this activity, experience, and/or assignment change you from what you were before you enrolled in the course (e.g., At the beginning of this class, I had a difficult time understanding complex information) to what you have become at its completion (e.g., I am now more capable of understanding complex information because I have learned how to use analysis to break it down into smaller, more understandable pieces). Examples of these activities could be—but are not limited to—the multiple-choice tests, the CTPs, the text book, the lectures, the term paper, the class discussions, the study guide, and the extra credit opportunities. Be sure you give—and fully explain—an example of each of the six critical thinking skills in your answer.

4. Your final CTP should be longer than one page. Your final CTP and your six supporting CTPs must be stapled together. I will retain your final CTP; if you would like to keep a copy, please make one before you submit your original to me.

I often write a CTP with a particular critical thinking skill in mind. A good example of this is provided in the CTP written by one of my students (Noelle Moore) that appears in Table 5.4. I wrote this CTP with the thought that most students would choose analysis as the primary critical thinking skill because they would have to separate their own complex identity into four of its parts and then give ex-

TABLE 5.4
A Sample Critical Thinking Project

Critical-Thinking Project 4   Noelle Moore
Question

Choose four aspects of your identity that are in various stages of progress and/or completion, and then use a different example of Marcia's four identity statuses to describe your status in regard to each of these aspects.

Answer

I am a unique individual, but I am still in the process of becoming that individual and fine-tuning the aspects of my identity that I will eventually possess. The four aspects of my identity that I will address in this CTP are my double major selection, career goal, religious practices, and a future family goal.

When I came to IUPUI, I decided that I wanted to major in Spanish, because I possessed a great love for the language, but I did not know what would go with that major. My older brother told me that Communication Studies is an area in the business world growing as fast as Public Relations and Advertising. I decided to look into it as an option. The more I investigated, the more I discovered it was the best match for me. I went through the crisis of switching my major to secondary Spanish Education, only to find out that I did not want to teach, and I finally decided to commit to my double major in Spanish and Communication Studies. Marcia would classify this stage as *identity achievement* because I experienced a crisis, and I am actively in the process of making a commitment.

I was confirmed as a Roman Catholic about four years ago. I attended Catholic elementary school when I was younger, and Catholicism was all I knew growing up. It is only logical that when the time came for me to go through the confirmation rites, I would not oppose the process. I am happy with the decision I made, but I never explored any other options for my religious beliefs. According to Marcia, I was in *identity foreclosure* because I accepted my parents' beliefs as my own. I made a commitment without experiencing a crisis. Fortunately for me, I am happy with the decision.

The next stage of identity is called *identity moratorium*, and Marcia classifies this as someone who is still experiencing crisis, but has not yet made a commitment. This is where my career goal comes into play. I am still trying to decide all the options that I will have because of my double major, more specifically, my Spanish major. I have toyed with several ideas like working for the Department of Natural Resources or for an advertising agency, but I am not yet able to make a clear commitment as to what I want to do. I am also in the process of securing an internship for the upcoming fall semester to help me in my decision.

The fourth stage of identity development that Marcia identifies is *identity diffusion*. This occurs when a person has neither experienced a crisis nor made a commitment. My plan for having a family falls into this category. I have thought about having a family in the distant future, but as far as experiencing a crisis or even making a commitment, I have done neither. In the future, this will more than likely change from diffusion into achievement. But at this point in my life, it is at the diffusion stage.

Critical Thinking Skill

1. In this assignment, I used the critical-thinking skill of analysis to answer the question.
2. Analysis requires an individual to take a complex whole, break it down into understandable parts, and figure out how these parts come together to create the complex entity.
3. I used analysis in this assignment to take myself apart and find four aspects of my identity. These four aspects, while they are all small parts of me, help to form my identity. I was forced to look at myself as a complex person and to find four separate, understandable parts of my identity in order to study them from Marcia's perspective and find out why I am the way I am.
4. In my Spanish pronunciation and diction class, I use analysis. I have to look at the area that includes the mouth, nose, throat, and lungs and I have to break each part into a separate part. I have to determine how each body part works in relation to the production of a sound. Within each body part such as the mouth, there are smaller parts that can be broken down into different categories such as the teeth, tongue, palate and uvula. All of these small parts then work together to produce the sounds that compose the words we hear in conversations.

---

amples of these parts to answer the question. This is how Noelle chose to craft her answer, which she made very obvious when she wrote:

> I used analysis in this assignment to take myself apart and find four aspects of my identity. These four aspects, while they are all small parts of me, help to form my identity. I was forced to look at myself as a complex person and to find four separate, understandable parts of my identity in order to study them from Marcia's perspective and find out why I am the way I am.

However, other students have selected other equally relevant critical thinking skills to write this CTP, such as the following:

- *comprehension* to understand the meaning of each of Marcia's stages and use this understanding to explain the status of four specific parts of their identity
- *application* to solve the problem of identity (i.e., "Who am I?") through the investigation of four important aspects of their current being
- *synthesis* to combine the four different stages into one developmentally coherent identity
- *evaluation* to determine if they are "where they want to be" in one or more of the aspects of their identity (e.g., Should they be engaging in some serious career exploration if the fact that they are in the identity diffusion stage of choosing a major and/or career is beginning to worry them?).

ASSESSING CRITICAL THINKING

I assess the ability of my students to think critically in their first six CTPs by using a rubric consisting of the scoring criteria for CTPs listed in the syllabus:

1. They can earn 2 points by *retaining* the correct day when their CTP is due and submitting it on that date.
2. They can earn 1 point by *comprehending* the required format and *applying* it correctly when they write their CTPs.
3. They can earn 2 points by *analyzing* a complex assignment into its individual parts, *evaluating* the appropriateness of specific course contents to the parts of the assignment, and then *synthesizing* this content into a complete and coherent CTP.
4. They can earn 2 points by *evaluating* the relevance and accuracy of the course material they include to support the contentions contained in their CTPs.
5. They can earn 2 points for *comprehending* the principal critical thinking skills they used to craft their CTP.
6. They can earn 1 point for *applying* college-level writing skills in their CTPs.

I assess my students' metacognitive abilities with the final CTP in which they must reflect on their critical thinking experiences in the class and convince me that the following outcomes have occurred as a result of completing the class:

1. They used *retention* by remembering the definition of each of the critical thinking skills and demonstrated their *comprehension* of these definitions by creating an original definition of each skill in their own words.
2. They used *evaluation* to select appropriate information from their CTPs to use as evidence to support their contention that they learned how to think critically about the course content.
3. They used *analysis* to divide the class into its separate elements (e.g., lectures, CTPs, and tests) so they could describe how they used these opportunities to strengthen their critical thinking skills.

4. They used *application* when they cited specific examples of how they utilized the elements of the course to increase their critical thinking skills.
5. They used *synthesis* to integrate all of the information in their final CTP into an organized and coherent intellectual product.

CONCLUSIONS

Teachers of introductory psychology often find critical thinking to be a difficult skill to define, a challenging concept to teach, and an elusive outcome to measure. This predicament is exacerbated by the fact that introductory psychology is a component of general education at many colleges and universities. This means that faculty who teach it must craft their courses so that enrollees from all disciplines, not just psychology majors, are provided with opportunities to develop the kinds of critical thinking skills that will help produce successful performance in their majors and the various careers to which they aspire. This chapter has presented a multifaceted strategy designed to enable teachers of introductory psychology to create an interdisciplinary model of critical thinking at their own institution and then use this model to define, teach, and assess their students' ability to think critically.

REFERENCES

Appleby, D. C. (2004). *Introductory Psychology as a Social Science syllabus*. (Available from Indiana University-Purdue University Psychology Department, 401 North Blackford Street, Indianapolis, IN, 46202–3275)

Barry, V. E. (1984). *Invitation to critical thinking*. Chicago: Holt, Rinehart & Winston.

Bloom, B. S., Englehart, M. D., Furst, E. J., & Krathwohl, D. R. (1956). *Taxonomy of educational objectives: Cognitive domain*. New York: McKay.

Brewer, C. L., Hopkins, J. R., Kimble, G. A., Matlin, M. W., McCann, L. I., & McNeil, O. (1993). Curriculum. In T. V. McGovern (Ed.), *Handbook for enhancing undergraduate education in psychology* (pp. 161–182). Washington, DC: American Psychological Association.

Chaffee, J. (1988). *Thinking critically*. Boston: Houghton Mifflin.

Halpern, D. F. (1989). *Thought and knowledge: An introduction to critical thinking*. Hillsdale, NJ: Lawrence Erlbaum Associates.

Halpern, D. F. (2002). Teaching for critical thinking. In S. F. Davis & W. Buskist (Eds.), *The teaching of psychology: Essays in honor of Wilbert J. McKeachie and Charles L. Brewer* (pp. 91–105). Mahwah, NJ: Lawrence Erlbaum Associates.

Indiana University-Purdue University Indianapolis. (2002). *IUPUI campus bulletin 2002–2004*. Retrieved May 11, 2004, from http://www.bulletin.iupui.edu

Longman, D. G., & Atkinson, R. H. (1988). *College learning and study skills*. St. Paul, MN: West.

Marcia, J. E. (1980). Identity in adolescence. In J. Adelson (Ed.), *Handbook of adolescent psychology* (pp. 159–187). New York: Wiley.

Matlin, M. W. (1995). *Psychology*. Fort Worth, TX: Harcourt, Brace.

McWorter, K. T. (1988). *Study and thinking skills in college*. Glenview, IL: Scott, Foresman.

Paul, R. W. (1990). *Critical thinking: What every person needs to survive in a rapidly changing world*. Rohnert Park, CA: Center for Critical Thinking and Moral Critique.

Ruggiero, V. R. (1989). *Critical thinking*. Rapid City, SD: College Survival.

Sternberg, R. J. (1997). *Pathways to psychology*. Fort Worth, TX: Harcourt, Brace.

Chapter
6

Learning to Teach Introductory Psychology: Philosophy and Practice

Amy Hackney
Georgia Southern University

James H. Korn
St. Louis University

William Buskist
Auburn University

Perhaps for many of you, the circumstances surrounding your opportunity to teach introductory psychology for the first time were not ideal. Consider the experience of one of the authors (AH), when she was a graduate student. Three weeks before the start of the fall semester at Saint Louis University, a professor approached and asked her if she would like to teach a section of Psychology 101. She said yes immediately. It was not until a few hours later that reality hit her— she didn't know how to teach! It had been almost a decade since she was last inside an introductory psychology classroom, and that was as a bewildered 18-year-old freshman at Indiana University.

Fortunately, AH had already registered to take a "teaching of psychology" course with another author (JK) that fall semester, and he guided her through her first attempt at teaching. Since that first semester, she has continued to try to learn and implement the best practices of teaching introductory psychology.

This scenario is all too familiar in introductory psychology. Although this course is one of the most difficult in the psychology curriculum to teach, if for no other reason than the sheer range of content that forms its subject matter, it often is assigned to graduate students and new PhDs (and sometimes those veteran professors who must take their turn teaching outside their specialty area for the "good of the department"). Thus, one of the goals of this chapter is to encourage the design and implementation of a "teaching of psychology" course within the graduate curriculum and to relate that curriculum to teaching the introductory course. It also illuminates some of the issues faced by new teachers of introductory psychology, including graduate students and faculty who may be teaching the course for the first time.

CORNERSTONES OF THE TEACHING OF PSYCHOLOGY COURSE

Our model for the teaching of psychology course is based on two overriding principles. First, having a well-developed philosophy of teaching provides the foundation for the practice of teaching. Second, teaching is composed of many activities; teaching well involves the successful integration of these activities.

Philosophy

All teachers have an implicit philosophy of teaching that drives their decisions about course objectives, methods, and other aspects of teaching. The foundation of the teaching of psychology course is the explicit statement of that philosophy, which describes, among other things, a teacher's beliefs and assumptions about teaching, conceptions of what learning is and how it occurs, and the goals that underlie the daily teaching routine. A philosophy is implemented in the context of a particular course in a particular college, and is continually reshaped by experience. Thus, a teaching philosophy is unique in that there is no single "correct" philosophy.

Integration

Becoming an effective teacher is more than simply disseminating information to students. It involves advanced planning, selecting textbooks and other media, developing a course syllabus, preparing lectures and group activities, planning and conducting assessments of learning, grading tests and papers, dealing with problem students and academic dishonesty, and assessing teaching quality, to name several aspects of the teaching enterprise. A successful teacher learns to do all these activities well, integrating them so that the class becomes a single, coherent event.

How does a new teacher come to develop a philosophy of teaching? How does a new teacher learn to integrate the activities involved in teaching so that students learn effectively? The traditional answer has been through the school of hard knocks, which is the way many college professors learned to teach. The new teacher is simply told to "go teach" and given very little, if any, genuine guidance in the process. The process is painfully slow and arduous and often accompanied by a heavy toll of student casualties along the way. Our answer is to provide graduate students with explicit training in the teaching of psychology, using the introductory psychology course as a teaching laboratory.

TWO MODELS FOR THE TEACHING OF PSYCHOLOGY COURSE

The teaching of psychology course, like any other content course in the psychology curriculum, may take many forms and involve many different components. Two models are described here. Both courses are PhD level courses that have proven to be effective in helping graduate students acquire valuable teaching skills. The components of these models can also be utilized by faculty teaching the introductory course for the first time.

The Saint Louis University Model

The teaching of psychology course at Saint Louis University consists of a set of modules that provide analysis of, and experience with, the various areas of teaching. Connections between (among) these areas are made explicitly and frequently during the course. For example, the decision to use small group discussion is related to a particular course objective, which in turn is based on the course context and the individual's teaching philosophy. Although these connections are presented as a logical, linear model, the course recognizes that teaching is a dynamic process.

The module on the development of a philosophy of teaching (see Korn, 2003, for a guide to writing a teaching philosophy) is followed by the art and science of course planning, including the selection of a textbook and the writing of a syllabus. Next, there is a set of modules on delivery: lecturing, managing discussions, and varieties of active learning. These modules include presentation style, incorporating small group discussions and whole-class discussions, demonstrations, videos, and guest speakers.

The next two modules concern assessments of students and of teaching, focusing on quiz and test design, including the development of short-answer, multiple-choice, and essay questions. The assessment of teaching includes the use of student evaluations and peer observation. The next module covers ethics, values, and common problems like cheating and disruptive student behavior. In the final module, participants develop a teaching portfolio and consider career development strategies.

Another format for training graduate students how to teach that has been used at Saint Louis University is an intensive summer institute (six 5-hour class meetings spread over 2 weeks) accompanied by follow-up meetings and activities during the summer semester. Having this much time allows the inclusion of reading (e.g.,

B. G. Davis, 1993; Forsyth, 2004), homework, and the practice of teaching skills with feedback to participants. Among the follow-up activities are reviews of revisions of the philosophy statement, critique of course plans, and consultation with on-campus teaching mentors. Each student is assigned another faculty person as a mentor, who provides supervised experiences in the class. Students are also provided with additional supervision in a group that meets biweekly.

The Auburn University Model

The Teaching of Psychology course at Auburn University is a year-long course that meets twice a week (1 hour per meeting). All first-year graduate students who have teaching assistantships are required to take this course. These students serve as graduate teaching assistants (GTAs) for Auburn's Introductory Psychology course, which is a three-credit course that meets twice a week in large sections (200 or more students) led by a faculty member and once a week in a discussion section led by the GTAs (25–30 students per section). In essence, these discussion sections serve as practica for the teaching of psychology course.

The Auburn course is centered on the theory and empirical research in the teaching of psychology and, more generally, in higher education. Students read texts on teaching (e.g., S. F. Davis & Buskist, 2002; McKeachie, 2002) as well as articles from *Teaching of Psychology*. Students also subscribe and contribute to the Society for the Teaching of Psychology listserv (www. teachpsych.org) and frequently present posters and papers at regional conferences (e.g., Southeastern Teaching of Psychology, SEToP conference).

The course also involves a substantial amount of writing. Students write their statements of teaching philosophy and respond to written feedback in subsequent versions of it. These statements then become part of their teaching portfolios, a key component of the course, which must be completed by the end of the second semester of the course. This teaching portfolio will become an important means for reflecting on one's teaching development and will serve as an essential tool in future job searches and tenure reviews. Students write a moderately lengthy essay on some aspect of theory or empirical research in the teaching of psychology. Students also write a syllabus, develop and present a class demonstration on a concept they are covering in their discussion section, and create a scenario that describes a difficult teaching situation or dilemma, which is presented and discussed in class.

Finally, students receive live classroom teaching experience and receive ample feedback in the process. In the teaching of psychology course, all students present one 10-minute PowerPoint and one 10-minute "note and prop free" minilecture over a topic they will cover in their discussion sections. Immediately following each presentation, they receive written and verbal feedback from the teaching of psychology instructor. This instructor also visits each GTA in the actual discussion section and provides similar immediate feedback.

Similar to the Saint Louis University Teaching of Psychology course, the Auburn course helps students develop a teaching philosophy and provides a support network for learning to teach *in situ*. In addition, the Auburn course provides GTAs firm grounding in current theory and research in college and university teaching.

PHILOSOPHY OF TEACHING APPLIED TO THE INTRODUCTORY PSYCHOLOGY COURSE

Having a well-developed philosophy of teaching seems particularly relevant to the introductory course. Three important differences distinguish the introductory course from all other psychology courses, and these differences figure centrally in creating and developing a philosophy of teaching.

The first difference is the breadth of content knowledge demanded of the teacher. No one can have done extensive study in all the areas typically included in this course. Indeed, many introductory psychology teachers may not ever have had a course, undergraduate or graduate, in some of the specialty areas covered in the introductory psychology course. Thus, a problem arises when teachers hold the philosophy that the "teacher is the expert" (see Dunn, Schmidt, & Zaremba, chap. 3, this volume). Following this line of reasoning, some introductory psychology teachers simply will not teach topics with which they are not familiar, or worse, that they do not consider relevant to "true" psychology. For example, we know of one professor, whose specialty is animal learning, who refuses to teach social psychology in his introductory psychology course. His reasoning is simply that he has never had a course in social psychology, he does not like social psychology, and thus he will not teach social psychology in the course.

For obvious reasons, this is not the sort of philosophy that GTAs should be encouraged to develop in a teaching of psychology course (see the APA Board of Educational Affairs Task Force on Psychology Major Competencies, 2002). Instead, the teaching of psychology course might instill the idea that the introductory course will stimulate student interest in psychology in general. That is, as a teacher or GTA of introductory psychology, it is more appropriate to base a philosophy of teaching on the idea that in this course a teacher is not an all-knowing expert, gatekeeper, or sentry, but rather a guide or explorer who provides opportunities for students to learn about, and appreciate, psychology's many subfields. This philosophy will guide course goals and objectives, which then guide teaching methods.

A second difference that distinguishes the introductory psychology course from other psychology courses is the diverse makeup of the students taking the course, and the fact that the majority of students in the course are freshmen, most of whom are not likely psychology majors. Thus, an important consideration in teaching GTAs to teach introductory psychology goes beyond the subject matter and directly to the audience. Students' attitudes and expectations may affect their abilities to learn and thus a teacher's methods of teaching. In particular, GTAs often find it difficult to teach students who lack the motivation to earn good grades and have difficulty realizing that many introductory students do not place the same value on education as they do. Thus, in training GTAs to become competent teachers, instructors of the teaching of psychology course must be mindful of this problem, present alternative means of addressing it directly, and model effective methods of encouraging unmotivated students to do well in their coursework.

The third major difference of the introductory course is the size of the enrollment; there are certain things you can or cannot do—or do less easily—in large classes relative to smaller ones. Most introductory psychology courses have larger enrollments than advanced courses, and some of those enrollments can be quite large at 500 or more students. Although the goals expressed in a philosophy of teaching statement will not be affected by class size, how those goals are realized is likely to be. Suppose, for example, that a GTA's philosophy of teaching has a focus on teaching students to think critically through active learning activities such as writing. This goal can be achieved regardless of class size or level, but the means may be different. Essay exams work well in smaller classes, but in larger classes the sheer number of students makes grading a daunting task. However, GTAs can use in-class activities such as the 1-minute paper in which students respond to a question or issue, or summarize a lecture point in a short essay (Angelo & Cross, 1993). The essays are then collected and a small sample is read aloud to the class, or students may exchange papers to compare answers.

In short, having graduate students write a statement of their philosophy of teaching prompts their thinking about developing realistic goals for teaching the introductory course, given its unique place in the psychology curriculum. In addition, writing such a statement prompts graduate students and new professors to think critically about their own roles as teachers in the context of their academic values and training as specialists in a subfield of psychology.

SPECIAL CONCERNS FOR TRAINING GRADUATE STUDENTS TO BECOME EFFECTIVE TEACHERS

Most graduate students have never taught a class—on any topic or at any level—prior to graduate school. This lack of experience creates interesting challenges for anyone who teaches the teaching of psychology course. For example, Buskist (2000) discovered that new GTAs tend to make the same mistakes, such as posing vague questions, talking while faced away from the class, and giving ambiguous demonstrations in their teaching. Thus, it is important for teachers of the teaching of psychology course to be aware of their students' tendencies so that at least a portion of the class can be devoted to addressing—and correcting—these sorts of mistakes.

Along these lines, it is also useful to know what the new GTAs themselves might perceive to be the major issues that confront them in their teaching roles. To address this matter, one of the authors (WB), along with a colleague, Bryan Saville, recently conducted a short study involving 11 graduate students (9 women, 2 men) near the end of their first year of serving as GTAs in an introductory psychology course. We asked these GTAs to describe individually, in writing, and "in as much detail as possible, the most difficult and pressing issues that you have faced so far in your first year as a GTA." After 20 minutes, he collected the anonymous responses, edited them for conciseness and clarity, and organized them into appropriate categories. One week later, he returned the edited descriptions to the GTAs to discuss as a group and to revise. After 50 minutes, he collected the revised responses, and again, sorted them according to category.

By consensus, the GTAs agreed that four issues were the most difficult problems they faced during their first year of teaching: being fair, presenting course material effectively, dealing with problem students, and adjusting to being both student and teacher (see Table 6.1 for GTAs' descriptions of these issues). Experienced teachers would probably agree that the first three issues are endemic to teaching and are problems with which they occasionally wrestle. Buskist, Sikorski, Buckley, and Saville (2002) found that fairness and the ability to present material effectively are characteristics representative of master teachers (see also McKeachie, 2002, pp. 52–68, 313–314). In addition, Veenman (1984) noted that both new and established high school teachers experienced problems with classroom discipline. Similar problems are likely to occur in college classrooms and may continue to be problematic for even experienced teachers (see, e.g., McKeachie, 2002, pp. 348–360).

The fourth issue, adjusting to being both a graduate student and teacher, is an issue that may be unique only to those persons beginning their teaching careers. This problem genuinely has more to do with the small age gap that may separate traditional graduate students from traditional undergraduates in terms of physical age and appearance, cultural similarities and values, and to a certain extent, behavior (e.g., frequenting bars and engaging in other "night-life" activities) than it does with pursuing knowledge as a student per se (see Table 6.1). On the positive side, the combination of these physical and cultural similarities allows GTAs or young professors to identify with the needs of their students, thus appearing "down to earth" and "in touch." On the negative side, however, this identification makes it difficult for young teachers to establish themselves as authority figures.

These four issues can be quite stressful for the new teacher and do not have easy solutions. One strategy used to rectify these problems at Saint Louis University is a teaching of psychology discussion group that meets biweekly. This discussion group provides an open forum for GTAs to share their concerns, identify problems, and generate potential solutions. Helpful suggestions to these other common issues are also available in several excellent sources, including B. G. Davis' *Tools for Teaching* (1993), Forsyth's *The Professor's Guide to Teaching* (2004), Lowman's *Mastering the Techniques of Teaching* (1995), and McKeachie's *Teaching Tips* (2002). Clearly, these are not the only issues that new GTAs are likely to encounter in the classroom. These issues do, however, provide a useful starting point from which to contemplate the challenging teaching situation in which GTAs find themselves, and to develop strategies and tactics for preparing the next generation of psychology teachers.

CONCLUSIONS

The introductory course may be the most difficult to teach of all psychology courses. It presents special challenges because of the typical class size, the charac-

TABLE 6.1
Graduate Students' Descriptions of the Four Most Difficult Teaching Problems During Their Initial Year as GTAs

Problem	GTAs' description
Being fair	Grading consistently across students, determining whether certain excuses are legitimate, deciding when to be lenient regarding course policies, learning how to trust students, and not showing favoritism toward some students.
Presenting materials effectively	Integrating course concepts so that students can understand; keeping students interested during the class period; presenting information at an appropriate level, presenting relevant outside materials, being aware of sensitive issues surrounding some topics, and effectively teaching course material to students whose major is seemingly unrelated to that material.
Problem students	Rude and obnoxious students; students who challenge the GTA's authority; students who attempt to get by with as little effort as possible, and trying to stay personally motivated to teach when many of students do not seem to care about their education.
Adjusting to teacher's role	Managing the dual responsibilities of being both a graduate student and GTA, trying to find more time to develop better teaching skills, learning all of the students' names, and learning how to be more organized with all of the paperwork involved in teaching.

teristics of the students, and the breadth of content knowledge required of the instructor. Thus, it is particularly important that the instructors have had the education and training necessary for teaching. It is all too common, however, for graduate programs to emphasize research productivity to the exclusion of training teachers, and to assign graduate students or new faculty to the introductory course even though they never have been taught how to teach. Systematic training in teaching, as is provided in the teaching of psychology course, is critical to preparing a new and stronger psychology professoriate that will introduce the field of psychology to literally millions of college students. Indeed, our ethical sensitivity should be aroused whenever we sense such systematic training is not provided.

REFERENCES

Angelo, T. A., & Cross, K. P. (1993). *Classroom assessment techniques: A handbook for college faculty* (2nd ed.). San Francisco: Jossey-Bass.
APA board of educational affairs task force on psychology major competencies (2002, March). Available at http://www.apa.org/ed/pcue/reports.html
Buskist, W. (2000). Common mistakes made by graduate teaching assistants and suggestions for correcting them. *Teaching of Psychology, 27,* 280–282.

Buskist, W., Sikorski, J., Buckley, T., & Saville, B. K. (2002). Elements of master teaching. In S. F. Davis & W. Buskist (Eds.). *The teaching of psychology: Essays in honor of Wilbert J. McKeachie and Charles L. Brewer* (pp. 27–39). Mahwah, NJ: Lawrence Erlbaum Associates.

Davis, B. G. (1993). *Tools for teaching.* San Francisco: Jossey-Bass.

Davis, S. F., & Buskist, W. (Eds.). (2002). *The teaching of psychology: Essays in honor of Wilbert J. McKeachie and Charles L. Brewer.* Mahwah, NJ: Lawrence Erlbaum Associates.

Forsyth, D. R. (2004). *The professor's guide to teaching: Psychological principles and practices.* Washington, DC: American Psychological Association.

Korn, J. H. (2003, July). Writing a philosophy of teaching. *E-xcellence in Teaching, 5,* *PsychTeacher* listserv. Available at http://teachpsych.lemoyne.edu/teachpsych/eit/index.html

Lowman, J. (1995). *Mastering the techniques of teaching* (2nd ed.). San Francisco: Jossey-Bass.

McKeachie, W. J. (2002). *Teaching tips: Strategies, research, and theory for college and university teachers* (11th ed.). Boston: Houghton Mifflin.

Veenman, S. (1984). Perceived problems of beginning teachers. *Review of Educational Research, 54,* 143–178.

II

Alternative Approaches to Teaching Introductory Psychology

Chapter
7

Introductory Psychology Without the Big Book

Elizabeth Johnson
John Carton
Oglethorpe University

Imagine a student named Jill. It is 10:00 PM on a Tuesday night. Volleyball practice finished at 7:00, her dinner was pizza and soda during the sorority rush event, and she just received a message from her supervisor who needs her to work an extra shift the next day. She is assessing her homework situation and finds she has calculus problems due for her 9 AM class, an English paper worth a quarter of her grade is due on Friday, she has a history exam also on Friday, and they are starting chapter 3 "Human Development" in introductory psychology tomorrow. The psychology professor encourages her class to read the chapters by administering 5-point quizzes over the 30 or so pages of reading each week. Knowing that it will take her 2 or 3 hours to read the entire chapter (3 hours if she counts time lost to telephone calls and nodding off at her desk), Jill spends the next 30 minutes skimming through the long chapter and makes a list of all the terms and definitions that appear in boldface font. She hopes to get a few quiz questions correct with this approach. She promises herself she will go back and read the full chapter this weekend. Of course, she promises herself that every week and it has yet to happen.

How common is the previous scenario? How often do your students actually come to class having read the chapter you will cover that day? Teaching introductory psychology usually means choosing a heavy, expensive volume that is packed with information, including psychological trivia that students attempt to memorize just prior to exams. The question here is whether or not traditional introductory textbooks, with their lengthy and dense reading loads, promote or inhibit student learning in the introductory psychology class. Are there other reading assignments that might result in better student outcomes? This chapter discusses the problems with traditional textbooks and the advantages to be gained from using alternative reading materials. It then describes how we teach the introductory psychology course at Oglethorpe University and suggests ways the approach could be adapted to a variety of settings. Finally, it summarizes the benefits this approach offers to both students and teachers.

LIMITATIONS OF BIG BOOKS

Do not get us wrong, big books can be wonderful. Introductory psychology texts contain an incredible amount of information, much of which we, as teachers, find fascinating. These texts introduce students to a wide range of theory and research from every subfield of psychology. However, as many of us warn our students, psychology is a large and diverse field. For this reason, most introductory psychology texts have evolved into veritable encyclopedias of facts, terms, and conclusions. At Oglethorpe, the goal is not to fill students' heads with lists of memorized facts, but to help them appreciate how psychological science is done. Unfortunately, textbook authors rarely have the freedom to discuss how researchers designed a study, chose the methodology, operationally defined constructs, controlled for confounds, or addressed questions concerning the internal or external validity of an experiment.

Most introductory texts relegate research design to its own chapter or sometimes only to an appendix. As with other topics, authors define important terms and give examples, but research design rarely reaches the level of a central unifying theme of the text. With these limitations in mind, we have to ask ourselves how well such texts serve our students. Later it is argued that traditional large textbooks may limit students' attempts to remember information by making unrealistic reading demands, promoting shallow cognitive processing, encouraging massed practice study sessions, and using boldface type for key terms in the chapters that may impair reading comprehension.

First, as our introductory vignette illustrates, large texts place heavy reading demands on today's students. Although many of us in the field would thoroughly enjoy spending the evening wrapped up with a good psychology book, the fact is that our students are busier than ever. A majority of students, for example, hold part-time or full-time jobs while enrolled in school (American Council on Education, 1999). Competing demands from work, other courses, and personal lives too easily push aside the assignments we wish would top students' priority list. Furthermore, class discussions tend to be more productive when students have completed a short reading assignment compared to when they have failed to complete a long reading assignment. But, shorter reading assignments do not mean offering a less academically rigorous course. On the contrary, we have extremely high expectations for the quality of questions and discussion we expect from students and the level of competence they must demonstrate regarding sophisticated psychological concepts. The number of pages we assign is essentially guided by a preference for quality of the academic experience over quantity of pages read.

Second, when students have limited time to study they are likely to engage in a superficial reading of their text, often with highlighter in hand. At this point, we are concerned with the depth of cognitive processing students use when reading. Cognitive psychologists have found that, in order to remember material, it is important that students engage in deep or elaborative processing (Craik & Lockhart, 1972). This finding is the basis for study techniques such as the *SQ3R* method (i.e., survey, question, read, recite, review) and the *PQ4R* method (i.e., preview, question, read, reflect, recite, review), which instruct readers to ask, answer, and reflect on questions during the course of their reading (see Anderson, 1990, for a description of these techniques.) In contrast, when students use a marker to turn entire paragraphs of a textbook bright yellow while the words fly across their retinas, they are probably using a shallow processing technique and are therefore less likely to retain what they are reading (Craik & Lockhart, 1972). Also, if students do devote their limited study time to reading a chapter in its entirety, then they may not be likely to spend additional time reflecting or thinking about the reading, which is a predictor of their likelihood to remember the material (Benton, Glover, & Bruning, 1983).

Third, the amount of time required to read a 30-page chapter is likely to reduce how much information students retain by encouraging massed instead of distributed study sessions. In support of the age-old warning we give students about the evils of cramming for a test, Dickinson, O'Connell, and Dunn (1996) found that students who earned higher scores distributed their studying over more episodes. Dempster and Farris (1990) pointed out that the benefit of distributed study is a robust finding in cognitive psychology, yet it remains underemployed in classrooms. Long reading assignments probably make it less likely students will review their reading material on multiple occasions, especially if it requires a long study session to read one chapter.

Aside from the emphasis on distributed and not massed studying, there may be another advantage to avoiding long reading assignments. Reder and Anderson (1982) found that students were significantly better able to retain the central ideas of a textbook chapter by only studying the chapter summaries. They pointed out that most college texts contain a far greater number of details than any instructor would expect a student to remember. They ask, if texts are meant to train students in particular reasoning skills for a given field, and we do not expect them to remember every fact supporting the central points, then why are these details included? They determined that full-length chapters contained details that distracted students and impaired their test performance.

At this point, we need to clarify our earlier critique of large texts for their lack of detail. In fact, the kinds of details we are advocating are those that directly help students develop the particular reasoning skills for psychological science. Some balance must therefore be sought, and readings should be chosen for their treatment of major themes and concepts and not for the number of research studies, facts, and details a book contains.

The next drawback of traditional texts is related to students' habit of memorizing long lists of key terms often found in boldface print within the texts. Although such busywork might be good preparation for tests that measure rote memorization, we question the usefulness of this approach for providing either college graduates or future psychologists with an appreciation for how psychology asks and answers questions about human behavior. Moravcsik and Healy (1998) reported that students who read text with key terms printed in boldface type (a standard practice in introductory psychology texts) performed worse on comprehension tasks and took longer to read passages than students who read passages with either all or none of the text printed in bold. These effects were somewhat attenuated when the researchers told participants that bold terms in the reading passages were important. Nevertheless, the authors concluded that boldface terms encouraged readers to engage in less active, or deep, cognitive processing and distracted them from other words that were important for extracting the meaning of the text (Moravcsik & Healy, 1998). These results need to be replicated using passages from college level textbooks, but it is ironic to think that instead of helping students learn, publishers who print key terms in boldface may be making the task more difficult. Gurung (2003) reported that introductory psychology students listed bold terms as the number one pedagogical feature of the textbook that they use (see also Gurung & Daniel, chap. 4, this volume). We are concerned that students may rely on this aid and engage in memorizing terms when the goal for this course at Oglethorpe is comprehension and critical thinking skills.

Our final concern is that, for many topics in an introductory text, readers are presented with study results and are not challenged to ask how psychologists obtained those results. Typically, authors introduce a topic by giving examples, defining key terms, and citing the results of some notable research. It is less common to see any explanation of the details of the research cited, including the number of participants and their demographic information, operational definitions of variables, statistical tests used, and the resulting effect sizes. These are questions a person knowledgeable in research design would ask and questions we would like our students to think to ask. Instead, the "results only" approach found in many texts encourages students to learn by deference to authority and may not help them develop critical thinking skills.

We are certainly not alone in recognizing that what cognitive psychologists know about learning and memory does not always match how material is presented in college textbooks. David Myers, a well-known author of introductory and social psychology textbooks and a contributor to this volume, expressed relief that a publisher allowed him to depart from the traditional textbook format and asked him to write a text consisting of 30 short modules on social psychology (Myers, 2000). According to Myers (2000),

This is the book I secretly wanted to write. I have long believed that what is wrong with all psychology textbooks (including those that I have written) is their over-long chapters. Few can read a 40-page chapter in a single sitting, without their eyes glazing over and their mind wandering. So why not organize the discipline into digestible chunks—say forty 15-page chapters rather than fifteen 40-page chapters—that a student *could* read in a sitting, before laying the book down with a sense of completion? (p. xv)

AN ALTERNATIVE APPROACH TO USING BIG BOOKS

Our goal in the introductory course at Oglethorpe University, called Psychological Inquiry, is to teach students to think like psychologists. We accomplish this goal by our focus on research design. Independent and dependent variables, confounding factors, methods of data collection, and issues concerning internal and external validity become second nature to our students by the end of their first psychology course. Not only does this approach produce psychology majors well prepared for their electives, but it means that students who only take one psychology course in their career come away with valuable critical thinking skills and the ability to be competent consumers of science. Because we choose to focus on research design, we are better able to accomplish the objectives of our course using two short texts, *Forty Studies That Changed Psychology: Explorations into the History of Psychological Research,* by Hock (2005), and *Obedience to Authority: An Experimental View,* by Milgram (1974). Both volumes avoid the limitations described earlier because they require fewer pages of reading per week, cover a limited number of experiments in depth, do not present students with an endless list of facts likely to be forgotten, and neither book contains any boldface terms. Instead, students are invited to explore 40 classic experiments that, when combined, demonstrate most of the methods used by psychologists to ask and answer important questions.

Forty Studies That Changed Psychology

The Hock (2005) book has 10 chapters devoted to the various subfields of psychology, often in the same order as conventional textbooks. The volume begins with biological foundations of behavior, moves through learning, cognition, developmental psychology, personality theory, and clinical psychology, and ends with social psychology. Each chapter includes a short introduction to the subfield and then proceeds to discuss four seminal studies in the area. For each study, it covers the theoretical framework, research design, interpretation of results, applications of the findings, and any criticisms or recent research that bear on the interpretation of the data. Whereas the original research articles are often too demanding for an introductory student, this volume presents the research in a thought-provoking format that allows students to see how psychologists choose their questions and how data are collected to answer those questions. The book is extremely readable and many instructors use it to supplement their main introductory text.

In a typical class discussion we ask students to identify the independent and dependent variables and potential confounds of each study. We then move to topics that allow students to elaborate on the material and incorporate it into their existing knowledge. They may be asked for their critical opinion about a study, in what ways are the results applicable to their own life, and have they ever had an experience related to the area under study? For example, after reading about the Thematic Apperception Test (TAT) developed by Murray (1938), students are asked to decide how this test would fare on measures of reliability and validity, what factors might change a person's answers from one day to the next, and how this test should be used today. After reading Rosenhan's (1973) classic article, *On Being Sane in Insane Places*, students talk about their own reactions toward people who are diagnosed with mental disorders and how situational factors may bias our interpretations of events. Rosenthal and Jacobson (1966) found that teacher's expectations of pupils' ability significantly affected young students' performance on an intelligence test. This reading never fails to stimulate a frank discussion about how students' behavior relates to professors' expectations and course grades. Darley and Latané's (1968) experiments on diffusion of responsibility and the bystander effect gets the class talking about their own behavior in an emergency situation or when someone asks for help. Again, when students find ways to connect the readings to their own experiences, they are engaging in elaborative processing and are much more likely to remember the material (Craik & Lockhart, 1972). Finally, students are asked if they agree or disagree with the authors' interpretations of the data and to support their answer with relevant methodological and theoretical concepts. They often go further and suggest future studies that would resolve conflicting explanations of the data. Now our students are thinking like psychologists—our goal all along.

Like conventional texts, we still rely on a secondary source to learn about classic experiments. Why not ask our students to read each of the 40 studies Hock (2005) cited in their original format? The primary reason for not taking that approach is because some studies are too difficult for beginning psychology students. In addition, Hock nicely placed each study in context within the field of psychology and he discussed research inspired by the original work. We do recognize the value of students having exposure to original research articles, however, so we ask students to choose one of the 40 studies from the Hock book, locate it in the library, read it, and answer some questions about the original article. On the day we discuss the article, the student provides additional information about the participants used in the study, talks about the original interpretation of the results and whether or not the author predicted the research's subsequent impact. Students also share any unusual or interesting information from the original article that was not included in the description prepared by Hock. While we expose students to the original writing style of the research, they can also see how it is translated into a secondary source. Because many of our introductory students are in their first year of college, this assignment is also a wonderful way to introduce them to our campus library and to encourage public speaking during class.

As mentioned earlier, *Forty Studies That Changed Psychology* is already a popular supplement to the main text in many introductory courses. However, due to the objectives of the course at Oglethorpe, it is not only sufficient but wonderfully suited to serve as our main text. We can afford to do this because in order to not sacrifice breadth of coverage when using Hock, we spend one or two class meetings lecturing on the usual material covered in most introductory texts. In this sense, our course is quite typical. Students are exposed to the terminology, phenomena, and key findings within each subfield. They experience many of the quick and easy demonstrations that have become the hallmark of the introductory course. It may be one day in a week that we devote solely to discussion.

Obedience to Authority

Milgram's (1974) account of his research program on obedience, carried out at Yale University, is a social psychology classic. We use this text for the last 2 weeks of the course. Before starting the book, we watch the original movie Milgram (1962) produced that describes his research program and shows real trials of the experiment. Once students start reading the book, they enjoy the realization that some of the participants described in the chapters appeared in the movie. Students are provided with a list of reading questions that they answer while reading a few short chapters for each class. We then discuss the answers to the reading questions, and the issues the book raises, during class. At the end of the course, we randomly select some of these questions to make up the last exam.

One strength of this book is that it allows students to see not just how one experiment is designed and conducted, but how an entire research program evolves. They begin to appreciate why the results of one experiment produce new questions to be answered. They also see that even the best laid plans for an experiment might, in hindsight, contain a confound or two and that additional testing becomes necessary to rule out alternative explanations for the data.

The Milgram text also serves as a case study for many issues previously discussed during the semester. For instance, it provides authentic examples of participant recruitment, sampling bias, informed consent, deception, debriefing, questions surrounding internal and external validity, the role of theory in science, the difference between basic and applied science, and, most memorably, the kinds of ethical issues that arise when using human subjects in research. In addition, many social psychological phenomena are evident in the participants' behavior, including diffusion of responsibility, the fundamental attribution error, self-serving bias, conformity, compliance, and deindividuation (Myers, 2000). Instead of memorizing these terms from a study sheet, students see these phenomena in action as the experiments unfold in Milgram's account of his research program.

Other Possible Texts

Although we currently use these two texts and occasional supplements, our course originally included a reading of the *Age of Propaganda* by Pratkanis and Aronson (1991). That text worked well, but was dropped because it too focuses on social psychological research and the Milgram text is already so rich in content that we decided one in-depth case study was enough. Obviously, there are many texts that would work well for the approach described in this chapter, some of which are discussed by Stoddart and McKinley (chap. 9, this volume).

COULD YOU BE TEACHING WITHOUT THE BIG BOOK?

By now you may have guessed that we have the privilege of teaching at a small liberal arts college. The emphasis in all courses is to assign original source material and to use discussion in the place of lecture whenever possible. Our classes are capped at 25 students. It is reasonable, therefore, to wonder how this approach might fare with larger sections. We have met faculty at other schools who successfully engage up to 40 or 50 students in discussion at one time. Alternatively, we have had the class break into groups of 3 or 4 to discuss the day's questions and then asked students to share their comments on one of the questions with the rest of the class. At universities where a class may enroll hundreds of students at once, it is common for graduate student teaching assistants to hold weekly discussion or review sessions. The first author's experience as a graduate teaching assistant for the introductory course at a large state university consisted of meeting with students each Friday to administer and review the answers for a weekly quiz. How much more stimulating it would have been for both student and teaching assistant if we used that time to discuss the appropriate chapter of Hock's (2005) text! Technology may be useful as well. Students could be required to engage in discussion electronically using discussion boards available through teaching software (e.g., Blackboard, WebCT, Yahoo Groups).

Of course, the approach we describe may not be amenable to all situations. Very large classes may be especially difficult because we advocate the use of exam questions that ask students to apply, analyze, synthesize, or evaluate their knowledge, which are all higher order abilities on Bloom's (1956) taxonomy. Although essay and short answer exams are the norm for our small sections, faculty with very large classes more typically rely on publisher provided test banks that allow automated grading of exams. Certainly one can write multiple-choice exams that require higher level thinking, but the time it would take to write these exams, especially multiple versions for multiple sections and semesters, could be prohibitive. In these cases, consider how teaching assistants might be used more effectively to accomplish some of the course objectives discussed in this chapter.

CONCLUSIONS

Miller (1992) put forth similar arguments to those made here in a keynote address he delivered upon receiving the Outstanding Lifetime Contribution to Psychology award from the American Psychological Association. In the address, he argued that many nonpsychologists, including future civic leaders, take introductory psychology courses and, although facts may be forgotten or become obsolete, the use of the scientific method to study behavior will never change (Miller, 1992). Training students in the scientific method provides them with a skill that will outlive their memories of psychological trivia. Miller also recommended using the case history method of teaching, which allows students to see "how new knowledge was discovered, errors were detected and corrected, and how sometimes completely unexpected practical results were secured" (Miller, 1992, p. 849). We believe the Milgram text provides an excellent example of the case study approach.

We hope this chapter sparks a few of you to experiment with alternative texts when it comes to teaching introductory psychology. We both remember our first reactions when arriving at Oglethorpe and discovering that things were done a little differently than is the case at many other schools. We both felt reluctant to let go of the traditional approach to the class because it *felt* tried and true. We are the only faculty members who teach the introductory course and the position of our department, containing four psychologists, is that we have free reign to design the course as we see fit. Nancy Kerr, a social psychologist who taught at Oglethorpe University for many years, designed the course described here. Now, having experienced the benefits of this teaching method, we are both strong advocates.

We need to emphasize that our course was not designed to avoid using a traditional textbook; rather, it was designed to reach particular goals and objectives. We want students to think like psychologists. We want them to understand the scientific method and research design. We appreciate that most of them will not remember hundreds of terms and scores of results in the next few years. As it happens, shorter, more concise readings appear to help us accomplish these goals.

We see the results of our approach in several ways. For example, the second author started receiving more questions about the material after switching from a traditional textbook to the readings discussed here. In addition, when students take their psychology electives, their firm grasp of research design makes them good students of psychology, even though most do not take our experimental design course sequence until the junior year. Seniors who take the psychology subject test for the GRE report that they do not feel they are disadvantaged. We advise students to read a traditional introductory textbook to review for the psychology GRE, but this is sound advice for anyone who is about to be tested over material they learned 3 or 4 years prior to the test. Finally, students report that they like these short texts and find them more interesting and thought provoking than traditional textbooks.

In conclusion, we encourage you to design your introductory class not around the text you choose but the specific goals you have for your students. Consider that, instead of simply introducing students to tidbits of psychology, the introductory course can be a rigorous training ground for critical thinkers. Once students are equipped with the knowledge of how psychological researchers engage in their work, and develop the skills to evaluate this work, they can then excel in their upper level psychology courses where content of the field is a primary goal. Students who do not continue in psychology courses will also take away real skills from this class. Students' understanding of research design can be applied in any field of study where they must evaluate how authors arrive at conclusions and ask themselves on what evidence people base their opinions. They will also appreciate that psychology is a continuing, dynamic field of study, and does not only pertain to the realm of abnormal behavior. They will also retain, and have a deeper understanding of, some famous experiments in the field, those most nonpsychologists still remember from their days in introductory psychology.

REFERENCES

American Council on Education (1999, November 8). *Enrolling part-time and working jeopardize the success of students, ACE report show.* Retrieved April 30, 2004, from http://www.acenet.edu/hena/issues/1999/11_08_99/money_matters.cfm

Anderson, J. R. (1990). *Cognitive psychology and its implications* (3rd ed.). New York: Freeman.

Benton, S. L., Glover, J. A., & Bruning, R. H. (1983). Levels of processing: Effect of number of decisions on prose recall. *Journal of Educational Psychology, 75*(3), 382–390.

Bloom, B. S. (Ed.). (1956). *Taxonomy of educational objectives: The classification of educational goals.* New York: McKay.

Craik, F. I. M., & Lockhart, R. S. (1972). Levels of processing: A framework for memory research. *Journal of Verbal Learning and Verbal Behavior, 11,* 671–684.

Darley, J. M., & Latané, B. (1968). Bystander intervention in emergencies: Diffusion of responsibility. *Journal of Personality and Social Psychology, 8,* 377–383.

Dempster, F. N., & Farris, R. (1990). The spacing effect: Research and practice. *Journal of Research & Development in Education, 23*(2), 97–101.

Dickinson, D. J., O'Connell, D. Q., & Dunn, J. S. (1996). Distributed study, cognitive study strategies and aptitude on student learning. *Psychology: A Journal of Human Behavior, 33,* 31–39.

Gurung, R. A. R. (2003). Pedagogical aids and student performance. *Teaching of Psychology, 30*(2), 92–96.

Hock, R. R. (2005). *Forty studies that changed psychology: Explorations into the history of psychological research* (5th ed.). Upper Saddle River, NJ: Prentice-Hall.

Milgram, S. (1974). *Obedience to authority: An experimental view.* New York: Harper & Row.

Milgram, S. (Writer/Director). (1962). *Obedience* [Motion picture]. (Available from Penn State University Media Sales, 118 Wagner Building, University Park, PA 16802)

Miller, N. (1992). Introducing and teaching the much-needed understanding of the scientific process. *American Psychologist, 47*(7), 848–850.

Moravcsik, J. E., & Healy, A. F. (1998). Highlighting important words leads to poorer comprehension. In A. F. Healy & L. E. Bourne (Eds.), *Foreign language learning: Psycholinguistic studies on training and retention* (pp. 259–272). Mahwah, NJ: Lawrence Erlbaum Associates.

Murray, H. A. (1938). *Explorations in personality.* New York: Oxford University Press.

Myers, D. G. (2000). *Exploring social psychology* (2nd ed.). Boston: McGraw-Hill.

Pratkanis, A., & Aronson, E. (1991). *The age of propaganda: The everyday use and abuse of persuasion.* New York: Freeman.

Reder, L. M., & Anderson., J. R. (1982). Effects of spacing and embellishment on memory for the main points of a text. *Memory & Cognition, 10*(2), 97–102.

Rosenhan, D. L. (1973). On being sane in insane places. *Science, 179,* 250–258.

Rosenthal, R., & Jacobson, L. (1966). Teacher expectancies: Determinates of pupils' IQ gains. *Psychological Reports, 19,* 115–118.

Chapter

8

Enriching Introductory Psychology With Race and Ethnicity: Considerations for History of Psychology, Biopsychology, and Intelligence Measurement

Joseph E. Trimble
Western Washington University

The existence of any pure race with special endowments is a myth, as is the belief that there are races all of whose members are foredoomed to eternal inferiority.

—Boas (1945, p. 20)

Academic discussions about race generate a wide range of opinions. Some voices emphatically argue that the timeworn construct is vacuous, inaccurate, obsolete, and laden with prejudicial overtones. Other voices are more pedantic, reasoned, and reflective where the emphasis is placed on the scientific value of the construct for classifying hominids. And other voices are dangerously self-centered, ethnocentric, and lacking in any logical and substantive evidence whatsoever. Indeed, the esteemed cultural anthropologist Franz Boas was emphatic in his stance on the use of the construct because he considered it a myth.

There is another important context that merits mentioning. In teaching various psychology courses for over three decades, I have noticed that whenever I introduce the topic of race, many students respond through use of a variety of interesting telling gestures, postures, and facial expressions that often unwittingly reveal their attitudes about the topic. Euro-American students often will sigh, roll their eyes, squirm a bit in their seats as if to say "do we have to talk about this again," whereas visible ethnic minority students (i.e., students of color) often will turn their heads, hide their heads in their hands, or turn to a kindred spirit next to them as if to say, "I hope he doesn't call on us to provide our classmates with personal accounts of our unique racial experiences." Occasionally, I will ask many of them why they reacted in their idiosyncratic manner to the introduction of the topic; their cautiously worded replies are varied and often very guarded, suggesting that the topic makes them feel somewhat uncomfortable.

Boas' quotation, the preceding observations, and the broad title frame the theme and contents of this chapter. Growing from the theme, the chapter's purposes are threefold: to provide an overview of a range of various definitions and perspectives on the definition of race and ethnicity in the social and behavioral sciences; to provide classroom exercises and materials for the inclusion of race and ethnicity in the teaching of sections on the history of psychology, biopsychology, and measurement; and to provide numerous reference citations for use in following up on the various treatises and arguments written about the two disputatious constructs.

A GENERAL VIEW

Use of race as a construct to classify hominids is not without controversy; that is certainly the case in the annals of the history of psychology. The constructs, ethnic, culture, or ethnic group, also are often used to refer to classifications of hominids. The latter constructs are less controversial and seem to spark less virulent discussions than the use of race. The psychologist, Janet E. Helms (1994), for example, argued that "ethnicity is often used as a euphemism for race" (p. 297) and consequently the exchange often softens the contentiousness associated with use of race. Helms went on to add that "neither culture nor ethnicity necessarily have anything to do with race as the term is typically used in U.S. society or psychology" (p. 292). Nonetheless, many scholars use the constructs interchangeably to imply, at minimum, the sameness of a band or nation of people who share common customs and traditions often marked by common physiognomic features, skin pigmentation, hair textures, and ancestral heritages. In making a further distinction between the constructs, Perlmann and Waters (2002), in writing about the use of race in U.S. census forms, maintained that "races are usually discussed, in demographic terms, as a special subset of ethnicity, in that race relates to classifications of ancestral origins for groups treated in especially distinct ways in the American past" (pp. 1–2). Although seemingly interchangeable constructs, they vary in meaning and implication. The history of the variations in meaning and use can provide wonderful material for use in introductory psychology courses in large part because they refer to how people appraise, characterize, judge, categorize, label, abuse, oppress, exclude, assess, and respond to both themselves and others.

A PLEA FOR INFUSING RACE AND ETHNICITY IN INTRODUCTORY PSYCHOLOGY COURSES

Understanding and teaching the meaning of race and ethnicity is a challenge that requires the balanced and reasoned use of conceptual, methodological, and pedagogical tools. Despite the findings of the Human Genome Project that race does not appear to have a biological basis, race is a construct that continues to be an integral constituent of our social and psychological fabric. Racial and ethnic categories, for example, are used to establish political and social structures, and these categories in turn are the result of social, historical, and political processes that continue to influence and define the experience of people from all corners of our planet (AAA, 1998; Allen & Adams, 1992; Guthrie, 1998; Jones, 2003). As one scans the literature in popular and scientific publications, it is sometimes difficult to separate discussions about ethnicity and race from socioeconomic status, migration experiences, acculturation, and discrimination. Thus, at times, use of race and ethnicity appear to serve as proxies for other variables such as identity, acculturation, racism, discrimination, and so forth. The challenge is to move away from simplistic categories of race and ethnicity, and toward clearer definitions of these constructs.

In recent years, several studies have pointed to the serious neglect given to the richness and depth of coverage of race and ethnic topics in introductory psychology textbooks (APA, 1998; Hogben & Waterman, 1997; Kowalski, 2000; Trimble, Stevenson, & Worell, 2004; Whitten, 1993). Given the paucity of coverage, scholars recommend that the constructs and their corresponding topics be given appreciable attention in various topical areas in the introductory course.

Incorporating race and ethnic topics in introductory psychology courses is not a matter of political correctness. To ignore the topics may lead to the accusation of "cultural malpractice" (Hall, 1997), because the current U.S. population is more ethnically diverse than ever. The U.S. Bureau of the Census (2001) predicts that, by 2050, the U.S. population will reach over 400 million, about 47% larger than in 2000. The primary ethnic minority groups—namely, Latinos and Latinas, African Americans, Asian Americans, American Indians and Alaska Natives, and Pacific Islanders—will constitute almost 50% of the population.

Changes in North American ethnic and cultural demographic distributions and patterns call into question the relevance of psychology that historically has not been inclusive of ethnocultural and diverse populations (Guthrie, 1998; Holliday & Holmes, 2003). Given the population changes and the historical distortions and misrepresentations about race and ethnicity, the infusion of ethnocultural topics in psychology's curriculum is a matter of scientific and professional responsibility. Race and ethnicity are important to psychology at almost all levels of inquiry.

Psychologists have a responsibility to provide accurate and useful information about race and ethnicity to avoid unknowingly perpetuating harmful myths, stereotypes, and assumptions that may not have a valid basis. Consequently, it is the responsibility of the educator to seek out and challenge these assumptions and conventional modes of action and thought. Incorporating race and ethnicity into introductory psychology courses can serve this purpose, thus providing not only a reactive perspective, but a perspective that encourages equality and fairness of representation across populations typically not represented in classrooms today (Trimble et al., 2004). In order to advance the instructional process and facilitate the enrichment of course material, the next section provides useful information on the historical background of race and ethnicity in psychology and related academic disciplines and provides material for discussion on the meaning and implications of the two constructs.

DEFINING RACE AND ETHNICITY

Race and ethnicity have become commonplace words in our vocabulary so much so that their casual use is put forth without anyone fully understanding their origins and meanings. The constructs are distinctive and hence it may be helpful to explore their origins, similarities and differences, misleading representations, and portrayal of human character or personality. Considerable information on the race construct is available on the Internet; an especially thorough historical review can be obtained from the following Internet address: http://www.yourencyclopedia.net/Race.html.

What Does Race Mean?

As a widely used construct to refer to types of people, race has multiple meanings and therefore is not an easy term to define. The poet and writer, Jean Toomer (1996) asserted that "it may be well to note that no serious student of race claims to know what race really is; nor do we know" (p. 172). The word has roots in a number of European languages and dialects. Although the word's origins are in some dispute, some dictionaries indicate that "race" is related to the French word *race,* or the Old French word *rasse;* these words are similar to the Italian *razza,* the Spanish *raza,* and the Portuguese *raça,* all of which could mean "lineage" in their literal forms. Race also may have multiple meanings, as suggested by Helms (1994). She observed that race could include the following definitional categories "(1) quasi-biological, (2) sociopolitical-historical, and (3) cultural. Each type may have relevance for how race becomes one of an individual's collective identities" (p. 297).

The notion of race likely has it origins in the writings of ancient Greek historians and philosophers (see Sollors, 1996). According to Honigmann (1959), for example, Herodotus used the term *ethnea* to refer to humans who belonged to different groups; Herodotus, however, did not base his classifications of humans according to physical traits, thus it is likely his term was closer to the term *ethnic group*. Use of physical traits and characteristics to define humans began in the 19th century when, for example, the term *Aryan Races* was first coined by Joseph de Gobineau (Honigmann, 1959).

Young (1999) traced the origin of the construct to Carolus Linnaeus, who maintained that human beings come from four types: *"Americanus, Asiaticus, Africanus, and Europeaecus"* (p. 219). Following Linnaeus, at some point physical anthropologists in the early 20th century initiated a classification system where humans were grouped into one of four races: Mongoloid, Negroid, Australoid, and Caucasoid. The classification system prevailed for the majority of the 20th century. However, in the latter quarter of the 20th century, the fourfold system fell from use due to problems associated with blood-gene groupings, race mixtures, and the inability to group humans into four or more discrete categories (Yee, Fairchild, Weizmann, & Wyatt, 1993). Moreover, speaking about the eccentricities of race, Allport (1958) emphasized that "(1) except in remote parts of the earth very few human beings belong to a pure stock; and (2) most human characteristics ascribed to race are undoubtedly due to cultural diversity and should therefore be regarded as ethnic, not racial" (p. 111).

Although there are calls from the social and behavioral science community for the elimination of the use of race as a labeling construct, there are compelling reasons for its continued use in the study of identity development and formation (Allen & Adams, 1992; Yee et al., 1993). Few would seriously question that racism and all of its ugly and oppressive forms no longer exist. To eliminate the use of the race construct would obscure if not disclaim the racist experiences of millions of people who are subjected to it on a constant basis. To merely classify these experiences with the terms *prejudice* or *discrimination* takes away or obfuscates the painful sting of racism. Hence, in order to forcefully confront racism headlong, race must be kept at the forefront of our vocabulary when discussing intergroup and interpersonal relations (Jones, 2003).

Similar to ethnicity, race is a social construction and although it has little if any use in classifying humans from a biological or anthropometrical perspective, it does have use as a social-political category (see Root, 1999, 2000). Helms and Cook (1999) emphasized the significance of the continued use of race because "we want to encourage consideration of the differential environmental significance of the various racial classifications as communicated through powerful societal socialization messages" (p. 30). Helms (2001) also firmly maintained that "racial identity theories do not suppose that racial groups in the United States are biologically distinct but rather suppose that they have endured different conditions of domination or oppression" (p. 181). As an alterative to race, Helms (1996) recommended using *sociorace* to acknowledge "the fact that typically the only criteria used to assign people to racial groups in this country are socially defined and arbitrary" (p. 147). To emphasize her point, she contended that there are least nine characteristics that differentiate sociorace from ethnicity.

The U.S. Bureau of the Census (2000) has developed its own criteria for defining racial heritage; in fact, the bureau has been assessing racial backgrounds in some form or another as far back as 1790. To capture the racial information, for example, from 1850 to 1970, the census bureau asked for one's birthplace, the birthplace of parents, and language preferences (one's "native tongue"). In 1890, Congress added racial items like "quadroon" and "octoroon" to tap mixed African American ancestry (to assess the "one drop" of the Black blood rule); the term *mulatto* was used in the mid-19th century. The term is still used in Puerto Rico to refer to people of mixed African and Euro-American ancestry. Eventually, after much protest, these offensive terms were eliminated from the forms. Beginning in 1900, the census forms used White, Chinese, and Japanese as the primary racial categories. In 1970, a Hispanic origin question was added and, in 1980, four racial designations were added to include Black, Asian American and Pacific Islander, American Indian, White, and an "other" category.

In 2000, the census bureau asked individuals to indicate all of the races of which they considered themselves a part. An individual could choose to indicate one race alone or could mark other *races* along with the single race category. Results from the survey showed that 2.4% of the U.S. population identified with two or more racial groups.

Use of the multiracial item has created an array of contentious debates and problems for all who rely on use of census outcomes (Perlmann & Waters, 2002). The addition of the multiracial category presents complex tabulation and reporting problems for the health care profession, economists, demographers, social and behavioral scientists, and others who use racial categories for their work. In the research domain, if an investigator is interested in attributing an outcome to something about the culture of a racial or ethnic group, then the multiracial or multiethnic category presents formidable attribution problems. For example, if a respondent claims they are of White, American Indian, and African American background, then what culture or ethnic group is most influential in forming and shaping their affective styles, behavior, and cognition? In the words of Prewitt (2002), the addition of multiracial category represents a "turning point in the measurement of race ... and that the arrival of a multiple-race option in the census classification will so blur racial distinctions in the political and legal spheres and perhaps also in the public consciousness that race classification will gradually disappear" (p. 360). No doubt the debate on the census bureau's use of the "check all that apply" question and its continued use of the race construct will continue well into the 21st century.

In closing out this section, the reader may be interested in the stance taken on the race construct by the American Anthropological Association (AAA). Over the decades, anthropologists have produced several documents attesting to the multiple meanings of the construct and approaches that should be taken on its study and use; in effect, not all anthropologists subscribe to the notion that race is a meaningless construct. Nonetheless, after much debate and thoughtful reflection, on May 17, 1998, the AAA issued a formal statement on race predicated on the assertion that "with the vast expansion of scientific knowledge in this century ... it has become clear that human populations are not unambiguous, clearly demarcated biologically distinct groups" (p. 1). The authors concluded that "the 'racial' worldview was invented to assign groups to perpetual low status, while others were permitted access to privilege, power, and wealth. The tragedy in the United States has been that the policies and practices stemming from this worldview succeeded all too well in constructing unequal populations among Europeans, Native Americans, and peoples of African descent" (p. 3). The AAA's statement is not the final word on the construct as other disciplines such as biology have a different take on its use and relevance for scientific inquiry. Now we turn to a discussion on the meaning and definition of ethnicity, a construct often used as a substitute for race but with slightly different overtones and implications.

What Does Ethnicity Mean?

The term *ethnic* has Latin and Greek origins in *ethnicus* and *ethnikas,* which both mean "nation." It can and has been used historically to refer to people as heathens. *Ethos,* in Greek, means "custom, disposition, or trait." *Ethnikas* and *ethos* taken together, therefore, can mean "a band of people (nation) living together who shares common customs."

Sociologists, anthropologists, and historians have written extensively on the topic (see Sollors, 1996; Steinberg, 1981; Thompson, 1989; van den Berghe, 1981). The theoretical positions embraced and advocated range from those that are lodged in one's experiences and worldview to those formed from a sociobiological perspective. Barth's (1969) perspective represented the former where it is the native's worldview that defines relationships, boundaries, lifeways, and thoughtways. The sociobiological perspective is most fervently represented by van den Berghe (1981), who maintained that "ethnic and racial sentiments are extensions of kinship sentiments" (p. 18) and "descent ... is the central feature of ethnicity" (p. 27).

A review of the various treatises written about ethnicity leads one to the inevitable conclusion that it is complex and there is little theoretical agreement on its use in the social and behavioral sciences. In its broadest form, it refers to "any differentiation based on nationality, race, religion, or language" (Greeley, 1974). At a slightly more precise level, some theorists prefer the definition where ethnicity is viewed as "a collectivity within a larger society having real or putative common ancestry, memories of a shared historical past, and a cultural focus on one or more symbolic elements defined as the epitome of their peoplehood" (Schermmerhorn, 1969, p. 123). Yinger (1986) pointed out that "ethnicity has come to refer to anything from a sub-societal group that clearly shows a common descent and cultural background ... to persons who share a former citizenship although diverse culturally ... to pan-cultural groups of persons of widely different cultural and societal backgrounds who ... can be identified as 'similar' on the basis of language, race or religion mixed with broadly similar statuses" (p. 23). Although the many components of Yinger's definition are inclusive and indeed comprehensive as a starting point, he preferred to distinguish between groups by appealing to their unique social and biological characteristics. To form a more concise understanding of the influences of the two characteristics, we must find a shared generic cohort of descendants who share recognizable and acknowledged geopolitical boundaries.

The growing interest and seemingly thriving enthusiasm associated with the ethnic construct also brought out the critics. The "new ethnicity," as some preferred to call it, was criticized as divisive, inegalitarian, and racist (Morgan, 1981). Patterson (1977) affirmed that ethnicity was an artifact created by hidebound intellectuals who preferred to live in a mythical past. Assimilationists and pluralists added the argument that true ethnic identities vanished as group after group internalized an elusive American norm; and the longer the intergroup contact, so the argument went, the greater the likelihood that all homogeneous ethnics would blend into the mainstream of American society. Continuing the argument, some critics acknowledge that as ethnic segregation diminished, so would the saliency of the importance of ethnic identity and group solidarity. Still others maintain that the cultural specific behaviors, values, and lifestyles claimed by ethnic groups were manufactured contrivances and amalgams that had no real factual substance.

The debates and arguments continue, as demonstrated by the abundant increase in journal articles and books devoted to the subject. Few doubt that ethnicity is a controversial topic. Sollors (1989) asserted that "the study of 'the invention of ethnicity' is an interdisciplinary field ... [that gives] ethnic debates such a virulent centrality in the modern world" (p. xx). The mere mention of the construct in many academic circles sparks discussions about segregation and that without it ethnicity would not survive. Sometimes the discussion often turns to the possibility that Americans tend to overemphasize and exaggerate the existence and usefulness of ethnicity (Yinger, 1986). Phrases such as "imagined ethnicity" and "pseudo-ethnicity" are used interchangeably to refer to those who introduce surreptitiously some ethnic factor to justify an action. Similarly, when it comes to conducting research on ethnic factors, Gordon (1978) protested that "students of ethnicity run the risk of finding ethnic practices where they are not, of ascribing an ethnic social and cultural order where they do not in fact influence the person" (p. 151). Consequently, critics often argue about some fanciful line that somehow or another separates ethnic influences from nonethnic ones. The argument begs the questions: When can behavior, personality, values, attitudes, and so on, be attributed to ethnic factors? If an ethnic attribution is not possible or discernible, then what sociocultural and psychological influence can account for the phenomenon?

Indeed, the information provided for the definitional materials for race and ethnicity is not exhaustive of what has been published and distributed in the literature; many of the reference citations point to a rich body of resources for use in further research (Trimble, Helms, & Root, 2002). My intent here was to provide the reader with sufficient material to guide discussions on the topics as they appear in introductory psychology courses. More important, use of the information can assist an instructor in discussing what "humans" the field includes in our body of research and scholarship. It would be helpful to point out that, since 1988, the American Psychological Association has been publishing a series of annotated bibliographies focusing on the gradual accumulation of ethnic literature citations. The series' topics include African Americans, Hispanics, Asians, and North American Indians. Students should be aware that numerous nationalistic and ethnic groups are represented in the literature.

ENRICHING COURSE CONTENT WITH ACTIVITIES AND DEMONSTRATIONS

This section invites readers to consider the use of materials and classroom exercises that enhance student learning and teaching effectiveness, especially as it bears on this chapter's topic and themes. Instructional examples and suggestions are included to cover sections in the history of psychology, biological bases of behavior, and intelligence testing and cultural measurement equivalence; with additional research and a bit of imagination, an instructor can generate examples for infusing race and ethnicity content in other topics in their courses (see Bronstein & Quina, 2003; Trimble et al., 2004).

Getting Started

As mentioned earlier, teaching race and ethnicity topics can create an uncomfortable classroom climate. However, there are a few activities that are useful in easing students into the topics. Many of my colleagues are reluctant to discuss race in their classrooms for fear that they might offend certain ethnic students, because it is a delicate topic considering its virulence and the squabbling that often occupies discussions (especially academic ones). It can be, as Young (2003) called it, a "difficult dialogue," which "occurs when differences in perspectives are challenged or judged to be offensive—often with intense emotions aroused among participants and observers" (p. 348). Hence, one way to avoid these dialogues is to provide documented information in an unbiased and restrained manner where the instructor carefully cites bona fide sources—that is, making it clear that the material does not represent the instructor's opinions but those of the sources cited in the presentation. "Difficult dialogues," however, have a place in classroom settings and reading Young's recommendations about the technique is strongly recommended.

I initiate my discussions on race and ethnicity at the first or second meeting of the course. I start off by introducing students to the changing demographics and ethnic composition of students across the United States. To substantiate the demographic changes each term I administer the short form of the U.S. 2000 census form where respondents are asked to provide information about their race and ancestral background (see Perlmann & Waters, 2002, pp. 42–43). On average, I note with extreme interest that I can have at least 20 different ethnic groups represented in my courses. Not surprisingly, around 35% of my students will indicate a mixed ethnic background as asked for on the census form. I create slides and overhead transparencies of the classroom survey results and match them against national ethnic demographic patterns. The procedure usually leads to active and vibrant discussions about the variety of language use patterns, religious orientations, folkways, mores, and related cultural concepts that might exist in the classroom.

Use of the "difficult dialogues" approach and the ethnic identity activity usually provides a nice background to the teaching of other topics.

History of Psychology

The eugenics movement in Europe and North America in the late 19th century and early 20th century marked a time in the history of psychology where race and genetic determinism dominated the academic worlds more than any other doctrine. Heated debates occurred between those who argued that genes dictated human character and those who argued for the importance of environmental and cultural influences on molding human nature. Sir Francis Galton, Karl Pearson, and Cyril Burt represented the stance that all "of the differences between 'savage' and 'civilized' societies could be explained by the 'innate character of different races'" (Freeman, 1996, p. 8). Boas—together with his former students, Alfred Kroeber, Robert Lowie, and Margaret Mead—represented the cultural determinism camp that almost excluded any reference to the influence of biological variables on human character. Early American psychologists were influenced by the debates as they struggled with the nature–nurture question; that is, who are we and how did we come to be who we are? It is an age-old, controversial question social and behavioral scientists have argued for years.

Consider putting the following question before students during the first week of class: Is it our genes or our environment that determines our personality and behavior? Put another way, is it "nature and not nurture" or "nurture and not nature" that determines who and what we are? Let the discussion unfurl and at the end of class ask students to write a "one-minute essay" on the question on a 3 × 5 index card. Collect the cards and sort them into theme piles and provide the students with the sorting tabulations results in the next class; at that time, give them the opportunity to discuss the topic in more detail.

At the beginning of a course, usually with the section on the history of psychology, I ask students to approach the course with guided skepticism and encourage them to approach theories and research findings with critical thinking skills. That is, I ask them to develop their perspective toward creating or exploring beliefs, arguments, or theories; evaluating the credibility of sources of information; questioning, raising, and pursuing significant questions; and analyzing or evaluating arguments, interpretations, beliefs, or theories. To initiate the process, I rely on the acknowledged accomplishments of a few early American psychologists, particularly G. Stanley Hall, about whom questionable assertions have been made by critics and historians. The eugenics movement serves as an anchor for my presentations and discussions. I preface the presentation with the following quote typically conveyed on an overhead transparency: "The tragedy is not that so many people got the facts wildly wrong; it is that in the mentally lazy and anti-intellectual world we live in today, hardly anyone cares enough to think about trying to determine what the facts are" (Pullum, 1991, p. 171). In reviewing the quotation, I place a strong emphasis on the second sentence; I refer to the quotation on numerous occasions in my courses to promote and advance student critical thinking. After a brief discussion of Pullum's strong words, I use the following example to illustrate the point.

A number of well-known early American psychologists were heavily influenced by the nature–nurture controversy, most notably Hall, founder and first president of the American Psychological Association. Ross (1972), one of Hall's biographers, claimed he was a moderate on eugenics and backed up her claim. Because of his leanings and pronouncements about eugenics and the influence of nature on the human character, a number of contemporary writers have suggested that Hall might have been a racist in his thinking and writings; the assertion may be unfounded and unwarranted.

In a number of textbooks, the following quotation is attributed to Hall, where he allegedly said "that Africans, Indians, and Chinese were members of adolescent races and in a stage of incomplete development." In all instances, the authors did not cite a page number, but in every case say it is Hall's tome on adolescence. I wrote to the textbook authors and asked them where they came up with their unreferenced quote; all indicated they found the quote in someone else's text and decided the sources were reliable and so they inserted the quotation and reference the way they read it in other texts. In an effort to locate the exact page of the quotation, I pored over Hall's *Adolescence* text at least three times and I was not able to find it. Also, I conducted an extensive Internet search and have come up empty there, too. Eventually, I asked a noted psychologist on the history of psychology to put the question out to his listserve subscribers.

We received lots of hints and suggestions, but no one seems to know the actual quote or its location in Hall's 1904 publication. For example, it could be that someone constructed the quotation from the subtitle of *Adolescence* is chapter 18, "Ethnic Psychology and Pedagogy, or the Adolescent Races and Their Treatment." Another possibility could be the liberal interpretation of Hall's statement, "Most savages in most respects are children, or, because of sexual maturity, more properly, adolescents of adult size" (vol. 2, p. 649). Hall made this statement in the last chapter of volume 2 where he included ethnographic and historical accounts of numerous tribal and nationalistic groups, including "Red Indians of Newfoundland," Chinese, Tasmanians, Maori, Native Hawaiians, Eskimos, Africans, Hopi, Sioux, and indigenous cultures of Mexico and Peru among others. Right now, absent a complete and thorough search of all of Hall's publications, I suspect Hall did not make such a claim as cited in the quotation that initiated this discussion. However, I suspect that someone contrived the statement and others picked up on it, embellished it, and made claims that Hall was a racist coupled with his belief in eugenics by making reference to the alleged quote that is not a quote.

After reading Ross' biography on Hall and poring over his many accomplishments, I have come to the conclusion that Hall was not a racist and the attributions are unfair and unfounded. Indeed, as psychological historian David Baker stated,

"Hall was a complex man that must be considered in the context of his time. My own read is that he held typical stereotyped and pejorative beliefs about race and gender. He found individuals who were exceptions (like Sumner) and that tempered some of his immediate behavior" (D. Baker, personal communication, December 23, 2003; Benjamin & Baker, 2004).

After providing the summary of my research on the alleged Hall quotation and reading Pullum's quotation to the class, I show them some of Hall's accomplishments, as follows: In 1910, Hall along with George Blakeslee founded the *Journal of Race Relations* that eventually became the *Journal of International Relations*. Hall titled the last chapter in *Adolescence* "Ethnic Psychology," thus becoming the first psychologist to coin the phrase and give appropriate attention to selected ethnic groups in a major psychological treatise. Additionally, he was an advocate for the inclusion of culture and ethnic topics in psychological inquiries. In *Adolescence*, Hall (1904) stated unequivocally, "Students of the soul should be students of the man, and the unanthropological character of American psychology is not only un-American, but scientifically so unnatural that it must be transient" (p. 52). Among the six African American students who received advanced behavioral science degrees at Clark University between 1916 and 1920 were Howard Long, with a master's in psychology in 1916, and Francis Sumner, with a doctorate degree in 1920. Sumner was the first African American to receive an earned doctorate in any American university. He worked closely with Hall during his time at Clark, and his dissertation—published in *Pedagogical Seminary,* which later became the *Journal of Genetic Psychology*—focused on "Psychoanalysis of Freud and Adler." And, although unsubstantiated, it is alleged that Hall's personal psychoanalyst was an African American (Janet E. Helms, personal communication, May 14, 2002). At the end of the presentation, I provide students with a reading list of works written by and about Hall and ask them to submit a paper at the end of the term on some aspect of the materials that bear on the topic of eugenics and race influences in early American psychology; I remind them about Pullum's words and encourage them to keep in mind as they conduct their research; in effect, I urge them to check and recheck their sources for accuracy.

Biological Bases of Behavior

Biologists, geneticists, and some biopsychologists continue to use "race" to distinguish and characterize human populations on the basis of physical characteristics such as facial features, skin color, hair texture, and other distinguishable features. Most scientists, however, agree that a certain identifiable set of genes does not fit with social and psychological constructions of race. "The classic arguments of biological determinism fail," the biologist Stephen Jay Gould (1981) asserted, "because the features they invoke to make distinctions among groups are usually the products of cultural evolution" (p. 325). Nonetheless, a few geneticists studying polymorphisms have concluded that a certain group of humans can be distinguished from others according to their geographic locale and origin (see Bamshad

& Olson, 2003). Additionally, resources obtained from the Human Genome Project (HGP) are being used to trace people's ancestral heritage; DNA signatures apparently provide enough evidence for researchers to identify common genetic polymorphisms that are present in distinct human populations (see Smith & Sapp, 1997). Studies generated from the HGP provide new and exciting scientific insights into the race concept from a biological level of analysis and thus provide useful information for discussion in class.

In this unit I present a short history of the eugenics movement in early American psychology to illustrate the influence it had on theory and practice especially in research and testing development. I provide students with summary critiques of the early research by Cyril Burt, Paul Broca, Cesar Lombroso, Arthur Jensen, and Lewis Terman (see Gould, 1981). Following the historical presentation, I introduce students to the controversial work and writings of selected contemporary sociobiologists, including Rushton (1984), Tiger (1969), and Wilson (1975) on the influence of heredity on social and intellectual behavior. For a writing exercise, I ask students to select one of the scientists espousing one of the positions and write a brief literature review summarizing their collected works. At the end of the review, I ask students to provide a brief critique of the scientist's writings.

Intelligence Testing and Cultural Measurement Equivalence

Most students of psychology are keenly aware of the influence that the race construct and biological determinism had on the assessment of intelligence. The 20th century beginnings of the field are well documented in a number of sources (see Gould, 1981; Guthrie, 1998) and thus there are numerous sources of information for classroom use. However, few psychologists write or talk about cultural measurement equivalence and its profound influence on testing and assessment.

Cultural measurement equivalence refers "to the problem of whether, on the basis of measurements and observations, inferences in terms of some common psychological dimension can be made in different groups of subjects" (Poortinga, 1983, p. 238). Most cross-cultural researchers agree that cultural equivalence can be examined by giving attention to the following concepts: functional equivalence, conceptual equivalence, stimulus equivalence, linguistic equivalence, and metric equivalence.

Debates abound on the influence of one's worldview in understanding and interpreting standardized tests and psychosocial scales (see Dana, 2000; Irvine & Carroll, 1980; Van de Vijver & Leung, 1997). Moreover, many cross-cultural psychologists contend that "comparing elements from differing societies leads to inadmissible distortions of reality" (Kobben, 1970, p. 584). Ethnic comparative research using intelligence measures may be fraught with problems of "incomparability" and thus may lead researchers to draw conclusions about a finding that may not be valid or justified. Indeed, with some exceptions, most intelligence measures cited in the literature have not factored in cultural equivalence and cultural item bias possibilities. To avoid these possibilities, attention must be given to the concept of cultural equivalence and item bias in measurement studies.

Embedded in the notion of equivalence is the fundamental principle that comparisons between ethnocultural groups require that a common, if not identical, measurement and assessment processes exist (Berry, 1969); stretched to the extreme, the principle holds that a universal process must be developed to demonstrate and assess ethnocultural group comparability (Van de Vijver & Poortinga, 1997). I emphasize this point over and over in class, as well as provide students with several examples of the five kinds of equivalence. Additionally, I distribute selected intelligence test items from old, outdated tests and have students critique them for their cultural equivalence (e.g., the Alpha and Beta sections of the Army Mental Tests developed by Robert M. Yerkes) (see Gould, 1981; Guthrie, 1998). Finally, I ask students to identify two other students to form a small study group and then ask them to conduct a small library research study on the meaning of intelligence from different cultural and ethnic worldviews. Then I ask them to devise some technique for assessing intelligence that would follow the worldview of a particular ethnocultural group and defend their choice.

CONCLUSIONS

The fundamental purpose of this chapter is to provide sufficient material for the enrichment of an introductory psychology course or even advanced course with material concerning the history and influence of the race and ethnicity constructs in psychology. Use of race in psychology has had a far more pervasive influence than ethnicity. Classroom instructional examples are provided for the teaching of the history of psychology, the biological bases of behavior, and intelligence and intelligence testing. Hopefully, instructors can find uses for the information with respect to other topics and units in their courses. Considerable reference citations are provided to provide direction in following up on the information and to assist in developing classroom materials based on scholarly and authoritative publications.

Use of the race construct in psychology aided in establishing a basis for the contention that human behavior and character had a biologically determined foundation. The influence of this belief on the historical development of the field is staggering considering the wealth of research on testing and its subsequent influence on public policy and general public beliefs and attitudes toward people from different "racial" groups. Cultural determinism entered the debate in the early 20th century, but the majority of those advocating this perspective were not psychologists. In fact, the discipline ignored cultural and ethnic influences on behavior and cognition right up to the 1960s; the absence of that influence and psychology's denial of its importance makes for a noteworthy discussion indeed.

We must be mindful of the efforts of scientists to explain human behavior solely from a biological determinist perspective. To accomplish this, most resorted to the race construct to sanction the objective. But the race construct that was and is being used by some has been seriously challenged; it is a myth as stated in the opening quotation from Boas. But we also must be mindful that the concept of pure cultural determinism (*tabula rasa*) as advocated by radical behaviorists is a myth, too, and thus the nature–nurture controversy is open for speculation and debate. We must recognize that there is a biological bases to human behavior and that culture and all that it represents plays a role, too, in shaping who and what we are. But we must not build the doctrines by using the race construct as the foundation. On this note, it is only fitting that we close out the chapter with another quotation from Boas (1924), who maintained that "the fundamental differentiation between what is inherent in bodily structure, and what is acquired by the cultural medium in which each individual is set, or, to express it in biological terms, what is determined by heredity and what by environmental causes, or what is endogene and what is exogene" (pp. 163–164). There is, Boas (1931) maintained, "a fundamental need for a scientific and detailed investigation of hereditary and environmental conditions" in order to fully understand the human character (p. 1).

ACKNOWLEDGMENT

The author wishes to extend his gratitude and appreciation to Hillary Caryl, one of his psychology research assistants at Western Washington University, who assisted him in compiling many of the materials and providing him with guidance on the use of a multitude or resources in various sections of the chapter.

REFERENCES

American Anthropological Association (AAA). (1998). American Anthropological Association statement on "race." Retrieved July 6, 2004, from http://www.aaanet.org/stmts/racepp.htm

Allen, B. P., & Adams, J. Q. (1992). The concept of "race": Let's go back to the beginning. *Journal of Social Behavior & Personality, 7,* 163–168.

Allport, G. W. (1958). *The nature of prejudice.* Garden City, NY: Doubleday Anchor.

APA Task Force on Diversity Issues at the Precollege and Undergraduate Levels of Education in Psychology. (1998, March). Enriching the focus on ethnicity and race. *APA Monitor, 29*(3), 43.

Bamshad, M., & Olson, S. (2003). Does race exist? *Scientific American, 289*(6), 78.

Barth, F. (Ed.). (1969). *Ethnic groups and boundaries.* Boston: Little Brown.

Benjamin, L. T., Jr., & Baker, D. (2004). *From séance to science: A history of the profession of psychology in America.* Belmont, CA: Wadsworth.

Berry, J. (1969). On cross-cultural comparability. *International Journal of Psychology, 4,* 119–128.

Boas, F. (1924). The question of racial purity. *American Mercury, 3,* 163–169.

Boas, F. (1931). Race and progress. *Science, 74*(1905), 1–8.

Boas, F. (1945). *Race and democratic society.* New York: J. J. Augustin.

Bronstein, P., & Quina, K. (Eds.). (2003). *Teaching gender and multicultural awareness.* Washington, DC: American Psychological Association.

Dana, R. H. (Ed.). (2000). *Handbook of cross-cultural and multicultural personality assessment.* Mahwah, NJ: Lawrence Erlbaum Associates.

Freeman, D. (1996). *Margaret Mead and the heretic.* Ringwood, Victoria, Australia: Penguin.

Gordon, M. M. (1978). *Human nature, class, and ethnicity.* New York: Oxford University Press.

Gould, S. J. (1981). *The mismeasure of man*. New York: Norton.

Greeley, A. M. (1974). *Ethnicity in the United States*. New York: Wiley.

Guthrie, R. V. (1998). *Even the rat was white: A historical view of psychology* (2nd ed.). Boston: Allyn & Bacon.

Hall, C. C. I. (1997). Cultural malpractice: The growing obsolescence of psychology with the changing U.S. population. *American Psychologist, 52*(6), 642–651.

Hall, G. S. (1904). *Adolescence: Its psychology and its relations to physiology, anthropology, sociology, sex, crime, religion and education*. New York: Appleton.

Helms, J. (1994). The conceptualization of racial identity. In E. Trickett, R. Watts, & D. Birman (Eds.), *Human diversity: Perspectives on people in context* (pp. 285–311). San Francisco: Jossey-Bass.

Helms, J. E. (1996). Toward a methodology for measuring and assessing racial as distinguished from ethnic identity. In G. R. Sodowsky & J. C. Impara (Eds.), *Multicultural assessment in counseling and clinical psychology* (pp. 143–192). Lincoln: Buros Institute of Mental Measurements at the University of Nebraska.

Helms, J. E. (2001). An update of Helm's White and people of color racial identity models. In J. G. Ponterotto, J. M. Casas, L. A. Suzuki, & C. M. Alexander (Eds.), *Handbook of multicultural counseling* (pp. 181–198). London: Sage.

Helms, J. E., & Cook, D. A. (1999). *Using race and culture in counseling and psychotherapy: Theory and process*. Needham, MA: Allyn & Bacon.

Hogben, M., & Waterman, C. K. (1997). Are all of your students represented in their textbooks? A content analysis of coverage of diversity issues in introductory psychology textbooks. *Teaching of Psychology, 24*(2), 186–191.

Holliday, B., & Holmes, A. (2003). A tale of challenge and change: A history and chronology of ethnic minorities in psychology in the United States. In G. Bernal, J. Trimble, A. K. Burlew, & F. Leong (Eds.), *Handbook of racial and ethnic minority psychology* (pp. 15–64). Thousand Oaks, CA: Sage.

Honigmann, J. J. (1959). *The world of man*. New York: Harper & Row.

Irvine, S., & Carroll, W. (1980). Testing and assessment across cultures: Issues in methodology and theory. In H. Triandis & J. Berry (Eds.), *Handbook of cross-cultural psychology: Vol. 2. Methodology* (pp. 181–244). Boston: Allyn & Bacon.

Jones, J. M. (2003). Constructing race and deconstructing racism: A cultural psychology approach. In G. Bernal, J. E. Trimble, A. K. Burlew, & F. T. Leong (Eds.), *Handbook of racial and ethnic minority psychology* (pp. 276–290). London: Sage.

Kobben, A. (1970). Comparativists and non-comparativists in anthropology. In R. Naroll & R. Cohen (Eds.), *A handbook of method in cultural anthropology* (pp. 1282–1289). New York: Natural History Press.

Kowalski, R. M. (2000). Including gender, race, and ethnicity in psychology content courses. *Teaching of Psychology, 27*(1), 343–349.

Morgan, H. W. (1981). *Drugs in America*. Syracuse, NY: Syracuse University Press.

Patterson, O. (1977). *Ethnic chauvinism*. New York: Stein & Day.

Perlmann, J., & Waters, M. C. (Eds.). (2002). *The new race question: How the census counts multiracial individuals*. New York: Russell Sage Foundation.

Poortinga, Y. (1983). Psychometric approaches to intergroup comparison: The problem of equivalence. In S. Irvine & J. Berry (Eds.), *Human assessment and cultural factors* (pp. 237–257). New York: Plenum.

Prewitt, K. (2002). Race in the 2000 census: A turning point. In J. Perlmann & M. C. Waters (Eds.), *The new race question: How the census counts multiracial Individuals* (pp. 354–360). New York: Russell Sage Foundation.

Pullum, G. K. (1991). *The great Eskimo vocabulary hoax, and other irreverent essays on the study of language*. Chicago: University of Chicago Press.

Root, M. P. (1999). The biracial baby boom: Understanding ecological constructions of racial identity in the 21st century. In R. H. Sheets & E. R. Hollins (Eds.), *Racial and ethnic identity in school practices: Aspects of human development* (pp. 67–89). London: Lawrence Erlbaum Associates.

Root, M. P. (2000). Rethinking racial identity development. In P. Spickard & W. J. Burroughs (Eds.), *Narrative and multiplicity in constructing ethnic identity* (pp. 205–220). Philadelphia: Temple University Press.

Ross, D. (1972). *G. Stanley Hall: The psychologist as prophet.* Chicago: University of Chicago Press.

Rushton, J. P. (1984). Sociobiology: Toward a theory of individual and group differences in personality and social behavior. In J. R. Royce & L. P. Mos (Eds.), *Annals of theoretical psychology* (Vol. 2, pp. 1–8). New York: Plenum.

Schermmerhorn, R. A. (1969). *Comparative ethnic relations: A framework for theory and research.* New York: Random House.

Smith, E., & Sapp, W. (Eds.). (1997). *Plain talk about the Human Genome Project.* Tuskegee, AL: Tuskegee University Press.

Sollors, W. (Ed.). (1989). *The invention of ethnicity.* New York: Oxford University Press.

Sollors, W. (Ed.). (1996). *Theories of ethnicity: A classical reader.* New York: New York University Press.

Steinberg, S. (1981). *The ethnic myth: Race, ethnicity, and class in America.* New York: Atheneum.

Thompson, R. H. (1989). *Theories of ethnicity: A critical appraisal.* New York: Greenwood.

Tiger, L. (1969). *Men in groups.* New York: Random House.

Toomer, J. (1996). Race problems and modern society. In W. Sollors (Ed.), *Theories of ethnicity: A classical reader* (pp. 168–190). New York: New York University Press.

Trimble, J., Helms, J., & Root, M. (2002). Social and psychological perspectives on ethnic and racial identity. In G. Bernal, J. Trimble, K. Burlew, & F. Leong (Eds.), *Handbook of racial and ethnic minority psychology* (pp. 239–275). Thousand Oaks, CA: Sage.

Trimble, J., Stevenson, M., & Worell, J. (2004). (Eds.). *Toward an inclusive psychology: Infusing the introductory psychology textbook with diversity content.* Washington, DC: American Psychological Association.

U.S. Bureau of Census. (2000). *Overview of race and Hispanic origin* (C2KBR/01-1). Washington, DC: U.S. Department of Commerce, Economics and Statistical Administration.

U.S. Bureau of Census. (2001). *Projections of the total resident population by 5-year age groups, race, and Hispanic origin with special age categories: Middle series, 2050 to 2070.* Retrieved June 30, 2004, from www.census.gov/population/estimates/nation

Van de Vijver, F., & Leung, K. (1997). *Methods and data analysis for cross-cultural research.* Thousand Oaks, CA: Sage.

Van de Vijver, F., & Poortinga, Y. H. (1997). Towards an integrated analysis of bias in cross-cultural assessment. *European Journal of Psychological Assessment, 13,* 29–37.

van den Berghe, P. L. (1981). *The ethnic phenomenon.* New York: Elsevier North Holland.

Whitten, L. A. (1993). Infusing black psychology into the introductory psychology course. *Teaching of Psychology, 20,* 13–21.

Wilson, E. O. (1975). *Sociobiology.* Cambridge, MA: Harvard University Press.

Yee, A., Fairchild, H., Weizmann, F., & Wyatt, G. (1993). Addressing psychology's problems with race. *American Psychologist, 48*(11), 1132–1140.

Yinger, J. M. (1986). Intersecting strands in the theorisation of race and ethnic relations. In J. Rex & D. Mason (Eds.), *Theories of race and ethnic relations* (pp. 20–41). Cambridge, England: Cambridge University Press.

Young, L. W., Jr. (1999). Race. In J. S. Mio, J. E. Trimble, P. Arredondo, H. E. Cheatham, & D. Sue (Eds.), *Key words in multicultural interventions: A dictionary* (p. 219). Westport, CT: Greenwood Press.

Young, G. (2003). Dealing with difficult classroom dialogues. In P. Bronstein & K. Quina, (Eds.), *Teaching gender and multicultural awareness* (pp. 347–360). Washington, DC: American Psychological Association.

Chapter
9

Using Narratives, Literature, and Primary Sources to Teach Introductory Psychology: An Interdisciplinary Approach

Rebecca M. Stoddart
Saint Mary's College

Marcia J. McKinley
Mount St. Mary's University

In *The Man Who Mistook His Wife for a Hat*, Sacks (1985) wrote: "If we wish to know about a man, we ask 'what is his story—his real, inmost story?'—for each of us *is* a biography, a story. Each of us *is* a singular narrative, which is constructed, continually, unconsciously, by, through, and in us." (p. 110). Sacks' book presents a compelling rationale for psychologists to include narrative readings in their courses. Some psychology professors may balk at this suggestion; after all, psychology is a *science*. Those of us who teach this science are concerned (rightfully so) that we represent data-driven, probabilistic behavior of groups, rather than individual behavior. However, in emphasizing the methodology and results of our science, we may fail to help students to connect individual people's stories with the science of psychology. If we want to know about people, then we must ask, "What are their stories—their real, inmost stories?" Using literature as it is defined in other fields, such as novels or memoirs, can help us to examine these topics.

English literature, however, is not the sole source of stories or narratives. Narratives are at the heart of science; many psychologists (e.g., Sigmund Freud, William James, Jean Piaget, and B. F. Skinner) wrote personal accounts of their theories and discoveries in lectures, diaries, and books long before scholarly journals became the paradigm for scientific writing. In fact, narratives are even the basis of formal, scientific writing: First we describe why the question is interesting and important, then we talk about how we went about trying to answer the question and what we discovered, and, finally, we discuss what we think it all means. Further, many of us share our personal narratives with students at the outset of a course because we want them to know what excited us about psychology in the first place, and what we hoped to discover about people's behavior by acquiring the research tools of our trade (Green, 2004).

This chapter is about using stories about individual people's behavior and psychologists' narrative writing to teach introductory psychology. Both authors teach our courses using narrative readings, although we followed different paths to adopting this teaching style. At Saint Mary's College, Stoddart joined the writing-across-the-curriculum program and began offering her introductory psychology course within that program. Because students could not meet the writing expectations of the course using only a textbook, she began supplementing the textbook with original writing by psychologists (i.e., primary sources). Eventually, she began using only primary sources and then joined a tandem teaching program, still within the writing program, in which students were enrolled simultaneously in her introductory psychology course and either an English literature or humanistic studies course, and the courses in the two different disciplines were jointly planned (for further details on psychology—English literature tandems, see Stoddart & Loux, 1992).

At Mount St. Mary's University, McKinley began adding narrative materials to her developmental psychology courses. After student evaluations indicated that students preferred these narrative readings, she began adding narrative readings to her introductory psychology courses. She experimented with using only narratives, but currently uses an introductory psychology text (e.g., Kosslyn & Rosenberg, 2004) supplemented by narrative readings.

Although we have different approaches to using narratives, both of us share learning goals for our students beyond introducing them to the field of psychology. Several of these goals stem from teaching introductory psychology from an interdisciplinary perspective: the ability to read books closely and analyze them critically; writing skills for narrative, creative papers as well as more formal research papers; critical thinking and problem-solving abilities; verbal skills in oral presentations, discussion, and debate; and the ability to integrate psychological theory with diverse materials related to a common theme. To accomplish these larger goals, students need the opportunity to question, critique, synthesize, discuss, and experiment with a diversity of personal and theoretical perspectives through dialogue, debate, and writing. Reading and discussing narratives and primary sources engage students in all of these cognitive activities. Textbooks, on the other hand, invite students to join the process after their authors have done most of the work.

PEDAGOGICAL BENEFITS OF USING LITERATURE AND PRIMARY SOURCES

There are numerous advantages to students in teaching psychology via stories, narrative memoirs, and primary sources in psychology. For one, stories may be more likely to arouse emotion (Caine & Caine, 1994) and aid in memory retention (LeDoux, 1996). Neurologically speaking, emotional stimuli presented in stories arouse different neural pathways, such as the limbic system of the brain, as compared to nonemotional stimuli; this activation is one factor in focusing attention and memory (LeDoux, 1996). Presenting stories, in addition to the psychological research found in textbooks or primary sources, helps students to focus on and to connect different areas of knowledge. The combination of stories and related research may create richer, more elaborate neural networks and facilitate memory for the information (for a related discussion, see Abrahamson, chap. 17, this volume).

Research on attitude formation and persuasion consistently finds that people are influenced more by personal examples and emotional appeals than by statistics and logic (Aronson, Wilson, & Akert, 2001). Perhaps this is one reason why students who read memoirs written by victims of prejudice and discrimination are more open to examining their attitudes and discussing psychological research on stereotypes and prejudice. Several memoirs that work well are Jacobs' (2000) *Incidents in the Life of a Slave Girl* and Levi's (1996) *Survival in Auschwitz*. Reading and discussing these authors' personal stories encourages students to respond emotionally and empathically, reducing their defensiveness about the topic and increasing their willingness to discuss the research.

Students also apply the results of research on prejudice in a more sophisticated way to their own experiences after reading articles by others who have done so. For example, McIntosh (1993) described some of the privileges afforded her as a White person, and the fact that racism taught her not to see these privileges. When White students read the list of privileges that McIntosh and her students identified, they are more comfortable discussing and expanding the list of privileges as they experience them in their own lives, and Black and Latino students discuss how these are denied to them. Further, the class as a whole is able to apply McIntosh's approach when asked to generate a list of the privileges that are afforded and denied other groups in our society, such as heterosexuals and homosexuals.

Other significant pedagogical advantages to using narratives relate to college students' development as adult learners who probably are located more toward the "novice" than the "expert" ends of the dimension in the field of psychology (Bransford, Brown, & Cocking, 1999). For example, students have a great deal of experience with reading stories and literature. They have read them in their English classes throughout elementary and high school and, as a result, have developed a variety of skills for analyzing themes in literature and applying them to a variety of social issues. By using narratives and primary sources, we are building on these existing skills, allowing students to approach psychology using more sophisticated schematic structures than they would as novice learners reading psychology textbooks. When examined from the perspective of constructivist pedagogy (e.g., Jonassen, 1999; Steffe & Gale, 1995), the strategy of using narratives from English and psychology literature supports and validates students as capable learners and effective problem-solvers.

A second issue related to students' developmental stage as adult learners is their response to and reliance on authoritative knowledge. Introductory psychology students are often at the beginning of their college careers and function developmentally as dualistic thinkers (Perry, 1970) searching for absolute truths revealed by authorities (Baxter Magolda, 1992). By their nature, textbooks reinforce students' search for authoritative truths: They present distilled, homogenous summaries of research by experts from areas representing the diversity of psychological science. Even when a textbook is well-written, it still carries the imprimatur of a "they" that beginning psychology students find daunting to question and debate. Confronted by a psychology teacher and an encyclopedic textbook, students respond to open-ended questions in ways that are predictable yet frustrating to teachers trying to encourage independent thinking: "I can't find it in the book." Their plea is clear even if implicit: "What's the right answer? Just tell me!"

On the other hand, when teachers use narratives and primary source readings in psychology, students encounter an author with a strong voice and perspective, and teachers who lead class discussions of the readings rather than giving lectures (the province of an authority). Some students may be hesitant initially to move out of their comfort zone as novice learners, oriented to learning absolute truths from the authorities. However, the real opportunity to use skills that they already are good at—talking about books, debating with their classmates, and developing their own ideas in their papers—usually proves irresistible to most.

On the whole, given the advantages to them as learners, perhaps it is not surprising that students are more motivated to read the narratives and primary sources that we assign and to complete the readings before coming to class, as compared to textbook assignments. For example, Casteel (1999) found that approximately 40% of undergraduates skip entire chapters of their introductory psychology texts. In contrast, instructors who have included narrative readings (e.g., novels or case studies) to supplement or replace textbook readings in their psychology courses report that this technique significantly improves students' motivation to read, memory for the information studied, and critical thinking skills (Fernald, 1989; Gorman, 1984; Stoddart & Loux, 1992; Williams & Kolupke, 1986). Students' ratings of courses using narratives are also significantly higher than those using textbooks (Stoddart & Loux, 1992; Williams & Kolupke, 1986).

Fernald (1987, 1989) compared students' preferences for narrative versus textbook readings in college psychology. Specifically, Fernald prepared multiple versions of several chapters of an introductory psychology textbook. He found that not only do students prefer textbook chapters that emphasize the narrative approach (typically via vignettes) rather than the traditional expository textbook, but they also scored higher when tested on narrative readings than on traditional textbooks.

TECHNIQUES IN TEACHING WITH NARRATIVES AND PRIMARY SOURCES

There are a variety of ways to use narrative writings or primary source texts to teach introductory psychology. Johnson and Carton (chap. 7, this volume) describe how they use primary sources in psychology (e.g., Hock's, 2002, *Forty Studies that Changed Psychology* and Milgram's, 1974, *Obedience to Authority*) to teach students to think like psychologists by having them analyze experiments.

This section describes examples of two other approaches to using narratives. One of us (McKinley) uses fiction and case studies to supplement textbook readings in a more traditional survey of introductory psychology topics. The other (Stoddart) foregoes breadth for depth, using primary source materials written by psychologists who represent major theoretical perspectives and systems of thought in psychology. Both of us would characterize ourselves as developmental constructivists in our teaching philosophies and thus plan class assignments and activities that maximize social interactions. These activities include small group and class discussions, debates, mock trials, individual and small group presentations, and writing. Many of our teaching strategies, such as modeling, scaffolding of difficult materials, and writing assignments that ask students to imitate an author's writing style, derive from learning principles gleaned from the fields of developmental and cognitive psychology (for an excellent overview of this research as applied to college teaching, see D'Avanzo, 2003).

McKinley on Supplementing the Textbook With Narrative Writing

Each semester, I address approximately nine of the topics covered in a typical introductory psychology textbook. Students are responsible for reading the corresponding textbook chapters. In addition, I assign narrative readings to accompany each topic. During some semesters, I have required students to purchase compilations of narratives, such as *Psychology in Context: Voices and Perspectives* (Sattler & Shabatay, 2000). During other semesters, I have made excerpts of narratives available through the electronic reserve system at the school library, or have required students to buy entire books (rather than using excerpts).

As an example of how I use narratives in the classroom, during the sleep unit, students read excerpts from Dement's (1999) *The Promise of Sleep*, which contains numerous narratives about both the author's research on sleep and individuals with sleep disorders. Often, I provide reading questions to guide students during their reading and to help highlight the key points of the reading; these questions do not require critical thinking. Examples of reading questions they receive include: "How is sleep studied? What is sleep debt? What are symptoms of insomnia?" I also ask students to take at least one Internet sleep quiz (easily located through a simple Internet search) that "diagnoses" various sleep disorders. These assignments are followed by my lecture on sleep and sleep disorders; however, because students have been exposed to material in multiple ways prior to the lecture, these class sessions often become more discussion than lecture based.

Finally, students are assigned roles for a mock trial. In short, the facts of this case (which are roughly based on a true case) involve a husband who has murdered his wife by stabbing her multiple times in the torso during the night. The husband's defense is that he was sleepwalking at the time. Students work together in "prosecution" and "defense" teams to prepare for the trial. They are given portions of several class periods to prepare for the trial, although a significant amount of time outside of class is also required to prepare adequately for this activity. Conducting the trial generally lasts 2 to 3 hours. In order to discourage uneven workloads within the groups, students are asked to grade their own effort and performance, as well as that of their fellow team members. (More information on staging this and other trials is available through the Society for the Teaching of Psychology at: www.teachpsych.org)

I employ other narrative techniques when teaching other topics. For example, for each topic studied, students read excerpts from case studies or fiction (examples of which are provided in Table 9.1) or watch movies such as *Awakenings* (Marshall, 2000) for neuroscience or *At First Sight* (Winkler & Cowan, 1998) for sensation and perception. Again, they are usually provided with questions to assist them in identifying the main points of the book or movie. When readings are particularly long, providing character sketches appears to help students remember the details of the books for later discussions and writing assignments. The class following the reading or viewing is usually heavily discussion oriented.

At the end of a topical unit, students either take an exam or complete a short (3–4 page) paper that links research and the narrative readings using critical thinking skills. I have experimented with letting students choose their own topics for these papers versus providing topics. I have found that students prefer having topics provided. The quality of the papers also seems better when I do this. Assigning specific topics to help them link the psychology textbook and the narrative readings is especially important for the first paper assigned, because it models the type of thinking that I expect in these assignments.

For example, on the sleep topic, I might ask students to write a paper based on the classroom trial. The assignment would list the evidence found at the murder scene and include Mr. Smith's claim that although he killed his wife, he should not be found guilty because he was sleep walking at the time. Students would be asked to argue whether or not he should be found guilty, given what they had learned about sleep disorders. As another example, in the section on cognitive development, I have assigned the following paper topic: "In *The Diary of Adrian Mole, aged 13-3/4* (Townsend, 1982), in which Piagetian stage would you classify Adrian? Support your answers with examples from the textbook that illustrate findings of Piaget and his student, David Elkind."

TABLE 9.1
Topics in Introductory Psychology Texts and Related Narrative Readings

Topic	Readings
Types of psychology	Career Paths in Psychology (Sternberg, 1997)
History of psychology	The Story of Psychology (Hunt, 1993)
	Portraits of Pioneers in Psychology, Vol. 3 (Kimble & Wertheimer, 1998)
	Portraits of Pioneers in Psychology, Vol. 1 (Kimble, Wertheimer, & White, 1991)
Ethics	Ethics in Psychology: Professional Standards and Cases (Koocher & Keith-Spiegel, 1998)
	Ethics in Plain English: An Illustrative Casebook for Psychologists (Nagy, 2000)
Research methodology	The Last Blue Plate Special (Padgett, 2001)
Brain and neuroscience	The Shattered Mind: The Person After Brain Damage (Gardner, 1976)
	Phantoms in the Brain: Probing the Mysteries of the Human Mind (Ramachandran & Blakeslee, 1998)
	The Man Who Mistook His Wife for a Hat (Sacks, 1985)
Learning	The Story of My Life (Keller, 1990)
	Is It Utopia Yet? An Insider's View of Twin Oaks Community in Its 26th Year (Kinkade, 1994)
	Always Faithful: A Memoir of the Marine Dogs of WWII (Putney, 2001)
Memory	Witness for the Defense: The Accused, the Eyewitness, and the Expert Who Puts Memory on Trial (Loftus & Ketcham, 1991)
	Committed to Memory: How We Remember and Why We Forget (Rupp, 1998)
	Searching for Memory: The Brain, the Mind, and the Past (Schacter, 1996)
	The Seven Sins of Memory: How the Mind Forgets and Remembers (Schacter, 2002)
	Aging With Grace: What the Nun Study Teaches Us About Leading Longer, Healthier, and More Meaningful Lives (Snowdon, 2001)
Language	Genie: A Scientific Tragedy (Rymer, 1993)

(continued on next page)

TABLE 9.1 (continued)

Topic	Readings
	Kanzi: The Ape at the Brink of the Human Mind (Savage-Rumbaugh & Lewin, 1994)
Thinking and creativity	Creating Minds: An Anatomy of Creativity Seen Through the Lives of Freud, Einstein, Picasso, Stravinsky, Eliot, Graham, and Ghandi (Gardner, 1993)
	Retarded Isn't Stupid, Mom! (Kaufman, 1999)
	Flowers for Algernon (Keyes, 2004)
	Of Mice and Men (Steinbeck, 1993)
Personality	The Murder of Roger Ackroyd (Christie, 2000)
	A Woman of Independent Means (Hailey, 1998)
	Still Me (Reeve, 1998)
Development	Madeleine's World: A Child's Journey from Birth to Age Three (Hall, 2004)
	Old Friends (Kidder, 1994)
	A Child's Work: The Importance of Fantasy Play (Paley, 2004)
	Another Country: Navigating the Emotional Terrain of Our Elders (Pipher, 1999)
Sleep	Sleep Thieves (Coren, 1996)
	The Promise of Sleep (Dement, 1999)
Stress, health, & coping	Go Ask Alice (Anonymous, 1998)
	Is It Worth Dying for? A Self-Assessment Program to Make Stress Work for You, Not Against You (Eliot & Breo, 1991)
	Man's Search for Meaning (Frankl, 1985)
Psychological disorders	Kissing Doorknobs (Hesser, 1998)
	An Unquiet Mind (Jamison, 1995)
	The Voices of Robby Wilde (Kytle, 1995)
	Welcome, Silence: My Triumph Over Schizophrenia (North, 2003)
Therapy	Undercurrents: A Life Beneath the Surface (Manning, 1994)
	The Quiet Room: A Journey Out of the Torment of Madness (Schiller & Bennett, 1994)
	Prozac Nation: Young and Depressed in America (Wurtzel, 1995)

In a typical semester, participation in class activities (e.g., the sleep trial), homework assignments (e.g., the sleep quiz), and formal papers (e.g., those described in the previous paragraph) will account for approximately 50% of the final course grade. Exams will account for the remaining 50%. Exams are equally weighted between multiple-choice questions, which are derived from the textbook, and essay questions, which are briefer versions of the essay questions used in formal papers. However, no question is used both as the topic of a paper and as an essay question on a test. Thus, the ability to apply each narrative reading or movie is assessed through either a paper or an exam question, but not both.

Stoddart on Teaching Using Primary Sources

In teaching introductory psychology, I include writers and theorists who represent major theoretical perspectives in the field of psychology and work with students to examine in depth their perspectives and contributions to the field. The focus is on helping students to unearth and examine the assumptions that the theorists have made about the nature of human beings, the areas of human behavior that they address in their theory, the methods that they employ to examine behavior, and how these relate to their assumptions. Finally, I work with students to examine ways to apply the theory to the lives of people we read about in literature and memoirs (assigned by my tandem course partner), as well as to their own experiences and contemporary social issues. Given that my course is also a writing-intensive course, I select theorists who represent a variety of writing styles, from the more literary (Skinner's *Walden Two,* 1969) to the theoretical, argumentative/persuasive (Freud's *Introductory Lectures on Psychoanalysis,* 1966), and empirical (Milgram's *Obedience to Authority,* 1974).

I often begin the discussion of a book by focusing on the assumptions the theorist makes. Examining scientific assumptions is initially challenging for introductory psychology students, who usually have little experience with this critical thinking process. My approach assists students in asking how theories stem from the author's assumptions, and how their lives and experiences may have shaped these assumptions. With modeling and coaching, students learn to think more like a psychologist, to look at the people or characters in the literature we read through "the lens" or perspectives of different psychologists who make different kinds of assumptions about human nature and behavior. Teaching students to examine assumptions helps them to more quickly develop the ability to think "like an expert," that is, make fewer conceptual errors, and be able to shift back and forth between different theories and concepts.

For example, in the preface to his second edition of *Walden Two*, Skinner (1969) listed the assumptions or principles that Thoreau (1854, 1977) made in *Walden; or, Life in the Woods*, and added five more of his own principles that guided the writing of his book and theory. Skinner admitted, however, that 20 years worth of experiences subsequent to the book's first publication in 1948 led him to realize that he would need to change some of these principles. One principle, for example, is the assumption that people would be motivated to work for the common good without contingencies of reinforcement in place. Students are amazed that theorists can change their mind, and that core assumptions supporting scientific theory can change. This realization helps them to be more critical readers, particularly when asked to use theory to analyze characters in stories from other cultures.

Because theorists construct knowledge in ways consistent with their experiences, those gained by living and developing as people within a particular culture, I have students read short biographies about them. By introducing students to theorists first as people with particular histories, students are willing then to speculate about what influenced the choices the theorists made in developing their theories, what they saw as important, and what they left out. Introducing students to the theorist behind the theory also helps to undercut beginning psychology students' tendency to either unquestioningly accept or reject a theory, and to become frustrated when we move from one theory to the next.

Students are excited, for example, to read Elkind's (1970) article describing Erik Erikson's life. They are fascinated with how Erikson wandered throughout Europe working as an artist and a Montessori teacher before training as a psychoanalyst. They note his experiences as a therapist with emotionally disordered children, his fieldwork with several groups of Native American Indians, and with soldiers who were veterans of World War II. My students are eager to ask about and theorize how these experiences contributed to Erikson's views of people and the development of his psychosocial theory. Starting the course this way sets the stage for how students approach each theorist and theory that we read in the course. They carefully study the details of the theorists' lives and debate the relative influences of these events as well as the historical and cultural context on the assumptions they make and their theories.

My current tandem partner is a professor in humanistic studies (HUST), a department that examines literature and writers from a variety of cultures and historical time periods. In our most recently taught tandem, I assigned readings on cross-cultural psychology to introduce students to the major distinctions between individualist and collectivist societies (see Table 9.2 for a list of readings in both courses). Then we read and discussed Elkind's (1970) short biography of Erikson and his description of psychosocial stages, followed by excerpts from Erikson's (1980) chapter on the problem of ego identity. In the HUST part of the tandem, students read Chang's (1996) *Bound Feet and Western Dress*, a memoir about Chang's aunt, Yu-i, who was born and raised in China in the early 1900s and whose life straddled traditional Chinese cultural values of family and duty, and Western influences of education and individuality.

I initially focus class discussion on the key concepts and psychosocial stages in Erikson's theory. We look particularly at Erikson's stage of identity versus role diffusion, and the importance of family, community, and culture in both defining and supporting the development of individual's identity. We then apply Erikson's concepts to the characters in *Bound Feet and Western Dress*. For example, we ex-

TABLE 9.2

Reading Assignments in Introductory Psychology and Humanistic Studies Tandem Courses

Topic	Readings	
	Psychology	Humanistic studies
Culture and identity: Cross-cultural psychology and psychosocial theory	"Continuing Encounters With Hong Kong" (Bond, 1994)	
	"One Man in His Time Plays Many Psychosocial Parts" (Elkind, 1970)	
	Identity and the Life Cycle (Erikson, 1980)	
	"Children's Social Networks and Social Supports in Cultural Context" (Tietjen, 1994)	Bound Feet and Western Dress (Chang, 1996)
Social class and ethnicity	Savage Inequalities (Kozol, 1991)	
	"A Cross-Cultural Research Contribution to Unraveling the Nativist-Empiricist Controversy" (Segall, 1994)	House on Mango Street (Cisneros, 1991)
Confronting prejudice and oppression	"Prejudice and Guilt: The Internal Struggle to Overcome Prejudice" (Devine & Zuwerink, 1994)	
	"White Privilege: Unpacking the Invisible Knapsack" (McIntosh, 1993)	
	Obedience to Authority (Milgram, 1974)	Incidents in the Life of a Slave Girl, Written by Herself (Jacobs, 2000)
		Survival in Auschwitz (Levi, 1996)
Gender and sexuality	An American Childhood (Dillard, 1987)	
	Introductory Lectures on Psychoanalysis (Freud, 1966)	
	"Femininity," New Introductory Lectures on Psychoanalysis (Freud, 1965)	

(continued on next page)

TABLE 9.2 (continued)

| | Readings | |
Topic	Psychology	Humanistic studies
	The Longest War (Tavris & Wade, 1984)	The Road to Coorain (Conway, 1989)
		"Yentl, the Yeshiva Boy," The Collected Stories of Isaac Bashevis Singer (Singer, 1983)
		Rubyfruit Jungle (Brown, 1973)
Memory and truth	Witness for the Defense (Loftus & Ketchum, 1991)	The Wife of Martin Guerre (Lewis, 1980)
Behavior and society	Walden Two (Skinner, 1969)	Herland and Other Stories (Gilman, 1992)
Consciousness and dreams	Psychology of Consciousness (Ornstein, 1975)	Kitchen (Yoshimoto, 1994)

amine how Yu-i's family and community contributed to her development as a woman whose identity integrated parts of both collectivist and individualist cultures. Students enjoy learning about the psychological research on these cultures, as well as Erikson's theory about identity development, and they then apply this information to Yu-i's life. They analyze the influence of different family members on Yu-i's struggle to form an identity, and debate in class the extent to which her identity became more individualistic. Finally, we use Yu-i's story and the cross-cultural psychology research to challenge and debate the universality of Erikson's identity theory.

Throughout the semester, my tandem partner and I assign integrative assignments that allow students to work in small groups and present their projects to the class. For example, students conduct a mock trial in the cognitive-memory section of the class after reading Loftus and Ketcham's (1991) book concerning errors in eyewitness testimony, and Lewis' (1967) historical novel, *The Wife of Martin Guerre*. In Lewis' novel, a man returns to a village after many years of absence and claims to be Martin Guerre. His wife, Bertrande, initially believes that he is her husband, but later develops doubts when other villagers challenge his identity. The man claiming to be Martin Guerre is subsequently charged and tried as an impostor, and the testimony by both his supporters and detractors hinges on their memories of a man they knew years earlier.

The students' task is to conduct a contemporary trial where the question focuses on whether or not Bertrande knew all along that the man claiming to be her husband was an impostor. Both the prosecution and defense teams operate from a perspective grounded in knowledge of memory errors, particularly those identified by Loftus in her research on eyewitness testimony. The students who function as the jury in the class trial have the final say, and defend their verdict by detailing how they evaluated the memory evidence presented by the defense and prosecution teams.

Students become engrossed in this assignment, and spontaneously introduce theory and research they have read earlier in the semester to bolster their arguments, in addition to the research they read about on memory and eyewitness testimony. For example, some students argue from a psychoanalytic perspective that Bertrande's initial identification of the man as her husband was due to her use of various defense mechanisms. Others use learning theory, cross-cultural psychology, and gender role development to argue that Bertrande was reinforced by her family and neighbors, and pressured by gender roles and her collectivist cultural values, to accept him as her husband. Assignments such as the mock trial allow students the opportunity to integrate the information they have learned during the semester, and to shift back and forth from different theoretical perspectives in weighing evidence and developing their arguments.

We ask students to develop in their formal papers their insights about the connections between the psychological theory and literature they have read. My tandem partner and I provide general guidelines for the paper topics, which always require the integration of material from both classes (see Table 9.3 for a list of writing assignments).

We insist that students use "I" when writing their papers, especially in the first ones they write. Many assignments are based on more inductive writing processes. For example, students may complete a paper in two parts over several weeks, beginning with a narrative of an experience, or question of significance to them. The following week they do research on the topic that they use to expand and revise their paper. This writing assignment reinforces the focus throughout the semester on how personal experiences and stories inform and often lead to the study of groups of individuals' behavior, the collective "we" of scientific research. Thus, students join the process of making science as beginning psychologists—they participate in the cycle of questions, research, and then evaluate whether their questions have been answered. Given that our classes are writing intensive, students work through several drafts of their papers. In each of our classes, students' grades on papers account for approximately 50% of their final grade. Essay exams, small group projects, and oral presentations contribute to the other half of the grade.

Throughout class discussion and in teaching and responding to their writing, both my tandem partner and I focus on building students' sense of authorship and authority. We come to each class with several, hopefully provocative, discussion questions but willingly set them aside in favor of our students' more interesting ones. We have learned to resist the urge to drive home a point or connection that seemed important as we read the books on our own but now, given students' ideas and the turn in the discussion, is less pressing to make. We do address misconceptions that may arise in each other's classes when students are working at integrating theory with literature, and model and encourage students to approach

TABLE 9.3
Writing Assignments from the Psychology and Humanistic Studies Tandem

- Connect Erikson's theories on identity development and the role of cultural support during adolescents' shift, and literature on adolescent development in collectivist cultures (e.g., use one or two of Erikson's stages to describe one of the character's struggles with identity development in Chang's (1996) *Bound Feet and Western Dress*, or analyze the cultural support or response that the character received using Triandis', 1994, Bond's, 1994, or Tietjen's, 1994 descriptions of individualist vs. collectivist cultures).
- Connect Kozol's (1991) research on the inequalities in public schools with research on identity development, or with individualist vs. collectivist cultures (e.g., analyze the arguments made by students from the wealthier vs. poorer school districts using the perspective of collectivist [equality] vs. individualist [freedom] social values).
- Connect Milgram's (1974) research with the literature on slavery or the Holocaust (e.g., in either Jacobs' (2000) *Incidents in the Life of a Slave Girl* or Levi's (1996) *Survival in Auschwitz*, examine the effect on slave or master, concentration camp inmate or capo/guard. Analyze their responses using results of Milgram's experiments).
- Connect Milgram's (1974) research with your own life, beginning with a personal example. (Step 1: Write a narrative about either your response to authority or your conduct as such, e.g., an experience of becoming victimized in a relationship with a controlling partner, or being a bully, etc. Step 2: Research the topic that you are examining, and integrate this information into your paper, e.g., examine research and theories on partner's behavior, history, etc. and victims of dating violence or bullying, etc.)
- Connect Skinner's (1969) *Walden Two* with other utopias and contemporary society. (Compare and contrast a common theme or aspect of the Utopian societies in Skinner's *Walden Two* and Gilman's [1992] *Herland*, such as government/social organization, work and careers, education, culture, family/childrearing, gender roles, relationships and sexuality. As an alternative, you may also contrast one of the previous aspects of *Walden Two* with contemporary culture in the United States.)
- Connect Loftus' research on eyewitness testimony described in Loftus and Ketchum's (1991) *Witness for the Defense* with either Lewis' (1980) *Wife of Martin Guerre*, or the account of the trial of Martin Guerre described by Jean de Coras (1560). (Select two specific characteristics of memory, such as sharpening, construction and filling in, etc., and use them to explain the villagers' identification of the imposter as Martin.)
- Connect Freud's theories with a character in one of the books, or one of your dreams. (For example, use Freud's chapter on Femininity from the *New Introductory Lectures on Psychoanalysis* (1965) to analyze the character Yentl in Singer's (1983) "Yentl, the Yeshiva Boy," using Freud's voice and writing style.)

assignments and class discussion as though they were experts on the topic. For example, we frequently ask a few students to research a specific question that has come up in class and share what they have learned when we meet next for class. Teaching within an interdisciplinary context has challenged us to share the role of authority first with each other, then with our students as we shift back and forth between theory and literature to construct knowledge together.

Although some readers may wonder whether or not I threw out the baby (the field of psychology) with the bathwater (textbooks), let me assure you that I have not. After 25 years of teaching using primary sources and many healthy debates in our department, my colleagues who continue to teach introductory psychology using a textbook would agree that foregoing breadth in favor of depth and teaching psychology in an interdisciplinary perspective has many merits. We find that psychology students who encounter primary sources in their writing-intensive introductory psychology tandem classes are frequently the best-prepared students in upper-division psychology classes, and our strongest majors. In fact, a higher percentage of our psychology majors come from tandem classes (25%) than any of the other stand-alone, introductory psychology classes (< 10% from each section). These students are able to develop their arguments and insights during class discussions, are quick to ferret out logical or empirical inconsistencies in the texts or studies they read, and are some of our most autonomous thinkers and skilled writers. Their entrée to psychology via narrative readings and primary sources helped forge a connection to their years of past experiences as thinkers and learners, and quick-started their apprenticeship in thinking as psychologists.

CONCLUSIONS

We presented an approach to teaching introductory psychology that involves the use of narratives and primary source readings. We described the pedagogical advantages of this approach for students, and provided several examples of ways that we each use narrative and primary source readings to teach introductory psychology. We hope that the research and examples that we have presented will encourage all psychology teachers to experiment with moving beyond traditional textbooks for reading assignments in their courses.

We began this chapter by arguing that in teaching psychology, we need to connect students through narrative readings to the science of human behavior and to the stories of the lives of individuals who ultimately validate its usefulness as a science. Regardless of whether teachers share our interdisciplinary and constructivist perspectives, we believe that most psychology teachers want their students to engage thoughtfully and personally with the information taught in their classes, and to question, challenge, and apply the theory and research. Our experience has led us to conclude that in order to be effective teachers, we need to be storytellers as well as scientists, teachers who share the story of psychologists' questions and discoveries as well as the ways that people's lives, both fictional and real, exemplify them. Unless we do, the theories and research studies students read about in textbooks will remain as two-dimensional abstractions that they memorize for tests and then quickly forget, and our students' questions and lives will remain outside of the narrative of psychological discovery.

ACKNOWLEDGMENT

This chapter is based on presentations by the authors at the "Taking Off: Best Practices in Teaching Introductory Psychology" conference, September 26–27, 2003, Atlanta, GA.

REFERENCES

Anonymous (1998). *Go ask Alice*. New York: Aladdin Paperbacks.

Aronson, E., Wilson, T. D., & Akert, R. M. (2001). *Social psychology* (4th ed.). Upper Saddle River, NJ: Prentice-Hall.

Baxter Magolda, M. (1992). *Knowing and reasoning in college: Gender-related patterns in students' intellectual development*. San Francisco: Jossey-Bass.

Bond, M. H. (1994). Continuing encounters with Hong Kong. In W. J. Lonner & R. S. Malpass (Eds.), *Psychology and culture* (pp. 41–46). Boston: Allyn & Bacon.

Bransford, J. D., Brown, A. L., & Cocking, R. R. (1999). *How people learn: Brain, mind, experience and school*. Washington, DC: National Academy Press.

Brown, R. M. (1973). *Rubyfruit jungle*. New York: Bantam Books.

Caine, R. N., & Caine, G. (1994). *Making connections: Teaching and the human brain*. Menlo Park, CA: Addison-Wesley.

Casteel, M. A. (1999, June). *How much of the textbook do students actually read?* Paper presented at the 1999 conference of the American Psychology Society, Denver, CO.

Chang, P. N. (1996). *Bound feet and Western dress*. New York: Doubleday.

Christie, A. (2000). *The murder of Roger Ackroyd*. New York: Berkley Publishing Group.

Cisneros, S. (1991). *House on Mango Street*. New York: Vintage.

Conway, J. K. (1989). *The road from Coorain*. New York: Vintage.

Coren, S. (1996). *Sleep thieves: An eye-opening exploration into the science and mysteries of sleep*. New York: The Free Press.

D'Avanzo, C. (2003). Research on learning: Potential for improving college ecology teaching. *Frontiers in Ecological Environments, 1*(10), 533–540. Retrieved May 5, 2004, from http://helios.hampshire.edu/~cdNS/Frontiers_PDF.pdf

Dement, W. C. (1999). *The promise of sleep*. New York: Delacorte Press.

Devine, P. G., & Zuwerink, J. R. (1994). Prejudice and guilt: The internal struggle to overcome prejudice. In W. J. Lonner & R. S. Malpass (Eds.), *Psychology and culture* (pp. 203–207). Boston: Allyn & Bacon.

Dillard, A. (1987). *An American childhood*. New York: HarperPerennial.

Eliot, R. S., & Breo, D. L. (1991). *Is it worth dying for? A self-assessment program to make stress work for you, not against you*. New York: Bantam.

Elkind, D. (1970, April 5). One man in his time plays many psychosocial parts. *New York Times Magazine*, pp. 207–218.

Erikson, E. (1980). *Identity and the life cycle*. New York: Norton.

Fernald, L. D. (1987). Of windmills and rope dancing: The instructional value of narrative structures. *Teaching of Psychology, 14*, 214–216.

Fernald, L. D. (1989). Tales in a textbook: Learning in the traditional and narrative modes. *Teaching of Psychology, 16*, 121–124.

Frankl, V. E. (1985). *Man's search for meaning*. New York: Washington Square Press.

Freud, S. (1965). *New introductory lectures on psychoanalysis*. New York: Norton.

Freud, S. (1966). *Introductory lectures on psychoanalysis*. New York: Norton.

Gardner, H. (1976). *The shattered mind: The person after brain damage*. New York: Random House.

Gardner, H. (1993). *Creating minds: An anatomy of creativity seen through the lives of Freud, Einstein, Picasso, Stravinsky, Eliot, Graham, and Ghandi*. New York: Basic Books.

Gilman, C. P. (1992). *Herland & selected stories*. New York: Penguin.

Gorman, M. E. (1984). Using the *Eden Express* to teach introductory psychology. *Teaching of Psychology, 11*, 39–40.

Green, M. C. (2004, April). Storytelling in teaching. *APS Observer, 17*, 37–54.

Hailey, E. F. (1998). *A woman of independent means*. New York: Penguin.

Hall, B. (2004). *Madeleine's world: A child's journey from birth to age three.* New York: Penguin.

Hesser, T. S. (1998). *Kissing doorknobs.* New York: Bantam Doubleday Dell.

Hock, R. R. (Ed.). (2002). *Forty studies that changed psychology* (4th ed.). Upper Saddle River, NJ: Prentice-Hall.

Hunt, M. (1993). *The story of psychology.* New York: Doubleday.

Jacobs, H. (2000). *Incidents in the life of a slave girl, written by herself.* New York: Penguin.

Jamison, K. R. (1995). *An unquiet mind.* New York: Knopf.

Jonassen, D. H. (1999). *Constructivist learning environments on the web: Engaging students in meaningful learning.* Retrieved May 20, 2004, from http://www.moe.edu.sg/iteducation/edtech/papers/d1.pdf

Kaufman, S. Z. (1999). *Retarded isn't stupid, Mom!* Baltimore: Paul H. Brookes.

Keller, H. (1990). *The story of my life.* New York: Bantam.

Keyes, D. (2004). *Flowers for Algernon.* Orlando, FL: Harcourt Brace.

Kidder, T. (1994). *Old friends.* Boston: Houghton Mifflin.

Kimble, G. A., & Wertheimer, M. (Eds.). (1998). *Portraits of pioneers in psychology* (Vol. 3). Washington, DC: American Psychological Association.

Kimble, G. A., Wertheimer, M., & White, C. (Eds.). (1991). *Portraits of pioneers in psychology* (Vol. 1). Washington, DC: American Psychological Association.

Kinkade, K. (1994). *Is it utopia yet?: An insider's view of Twin Oaks Community in its twenty-sixth year.* Twin Oaks, VA: Twin Oaks Books.

Koocher, G. P., & Keith-Spiegel, P. (1998). *Ethics in psychology: Professional standards and cases.* New York: Oxford University Press.

Kosslyn, S. M., & Rosenberg, R. S. (2004). *Psychology: The brain, the person, the world* (2nd ed.). Boston: Pearson.

Kozol, J. (1991). *Savage inequalities.* New York: HarperPerennial.

Kytle, E. (1995). *The voices of Robby Wilde.* Athens, GA: University of Georgia Press.

LeDoux, J. E. (1996). *The emotional brain.* New York: Simon & Schuster.

Levi, P. (1996). *Survival in Auschwitz.* New York: Touchstone.

Lewis, J. (1967). *The wife of Martin Guerre.* Athens, OH: Swallow Press/University of Ohio.

Loftus, E., & Ketcham, K. (1991). *Witness for the defense: The accused, the eyewitness, and the expert who puts memory on trial.* New York: St. Martin's.

Manning, M. (1994). *Undercurrents: A life beneath the surface.* New York: HarperCollins.

Marshall, P. (Producer/Director). (2000). *Awakenings* [Motion picture]. United States: Columbia Pictures.

McIntosh, P. (1993). White privilege: Unpacking the invisible knapsack. In V. Cyrus (Ed.), *Experiencing race, class, and gender in the United States* (pp. 209–213). Mountain View, CA: Mayfield.

Milgram, S. (1974). *Obedience to authority.* New York: Harper Torchbooks.

Nagy, T. F. (2000). *Ethics in plain English: An illustrative casebook for psychologists.* Washington, DC: American Psychological Association.

North, C. (2003). *Welcome silence: My triumph over schizophrenia.* Lima, OH: Academic Renewal Press.

Ornstein, R. (1975). *The psychology of consciousness.* New York: Vintage/Ebury.

Padgett, A. (2001). *The last blue plate special.* New York: Mysterious Press.

Paley, V. G. (2004). *A child's work: The importance of fantasy play.* Chicago: University of Chicago Press.

Perry, W. G. (1970). *Forms of intellectual and ethical development in the college years: A scheme.* New York: Holt, Reinhart.

Pipher, M. (1999). *Another country: Navigating the emotional terrain of our elders.* New York: Riverhead Books.

Putney, W. W. (2001). *Always faithful: A memoir of the Marine dogs of WWII.* New York: The Free Press.

Ramachandran, V. S., & Blakeslee, S. (1998). *Phantoms in the brain: Probing the mysteries of the human mind.* New York: HarperCollins.

Reeve, C. (1998). *Still me.* New York: Random House.

Rupp, R. (1998). *Committed to memory: How we remember and why we forget.* New York: Crown.

Rymer, R. (1993). *Genie: A scientific tragedy.* New York: HarperCollins.

Sacks, O. (1985). *The man who mistook his wife for a hat and other clinical tales.* New York: Simon & Schuster.

Sattler, D., & Shabatay, V. (2000). *Psychology in context: Voices and perspectives* (2nd ed.). Boston: Houghton Mifflin.

Savage-Rumbaugh, S., & Lewin, R. (1994). *Kanzi: The ape at the brink of the human mind.* Hoboken, NJ: Wiley.

Schacter, D. L. (1996). *Searching for memory: The brain, the mind, and the past.* New York: Basic Books.

Schacter, D. L. (2002). *The seven sins of memory: How the mind forgets and remembers.* New York: Houghton Mifflin.

Schiller, L., & Bennett, A. (1994). *The quiet room: A journey out of the torment of madness.* New York: Warner Books.

Segall, M. H. (1994). A cross-cultural research contribution to unraveling the nativist-empiricist controversy. In W. J. Lonner & R. S. Malpass (Eds.), *Psychology and culture* (pp. 135–138). Boston: Allyn & Bacon.

Singer, I. B. (1983). Yentl, the Yeshiva boy. In *The collected stories of Isaac Bashevis Singer.* New York: Farrar Straus Giroux.

Skinner, B. F. (1969). *Walden two.* London: Macmillan.

Snowdon, D. (2001). *Aging with grace: What the Nun Study teaches us about leading longer, healthier, and more meaningful lives.* New York: Bantam.

Steffe, L. P., & Gale, J. (1995). *Constructivism in education.* Hillsdale, NJ: Lawrence Erlbaum Associates.

Steinbeck, J. (1993). *Of mice and men.* New York: Penguin.

Sternberg, R. (1997). *Career paths in psychology: Where your degree can take you.* Washington, DC: American Psychological Association.

Stoddart, R. M., & Loux, A. K. (1992). And, not but: Moving from monologue to dialogue in introductory psychology/English writing courses. *Teaching of Psychology, 19*(3), 145–149.

Tavris, C., & Wade, C. (1984). *The longest war: Sex differences in perspective.* New York: Harcourt Brace Jovanovich.

Thoreau, H. D. (1854, 1977). *Walden; or life in the woods* (9th ed.). New York: Collier Books.

Tietjen, A. M. (1994). Children's social networks and social supports in cultural context. In W. J. Lonner & R. S. Malpass (Eds.), *Psychology and culture* (pp. 101–106). Boston: Allyn & Bacon.

Townsend, S. (1982). *The secret diary of Adrian Mole, Aged 13-3/4.* New York: Avon Books.

Triandis, H. C. (1994). Culture and social behavior. In W. J. Lonner & R. S. Malpass (Eds.), *Psychology and culture* (pp. 169–173). Boston: Allyn & Bacon.

Williams, K. G., & Kolupke, J. (1986). Psychology and literature: An interdisciplinary approach to the liberal curriculum. *Teaching of Psychology, 13*(2), 59–61.

Winkler, I. (Producer/Director), & Cowan, R. (Producer). (1998). *At first sight* [Motion picture]. United States: MGM Home Entertainment.

Wurtzel, E. (1995). *Prozac nation: Young and depressed in America.* New York: Riverhead Books.

Yoshimoto, B. (1994). *Kitchen.* New York: Washington Square Press.

Chapter
10

Teaching Introductory Psychology Online: Active Learning Is Not an Oxymoron

Diane L. Finley
Prince George's Community College

Integrating technology effectively into education continues to be both challenging and promising as the complexity of technology increases. Technology has generated many improvements in teaching and learning. Computers allow me to easily update my lecture notes. Videos permit me to show original experiments in psychology. E-mails make it easy for me to communicate with students. At the same time, the use of technology has raised questions about its efficacy and value. Does it lead to higher student achievement? Is it all "flash" without any substance? Does it create more problems than it solves?

A prime example of this conundrum is online learning. Online learning holds the promise of revolutionizing education in terms of time and space. It holds the possibility of reaching new students, especially in introduction to psychology. It is not, however, a panacea for all of the problems of education. Teaching introduction to psychology effectively in the online environment presents a major educational challenge.

PROMISES OF TEACHING INTRODUCTION TO PSYCHOLOGY ONLINE

Online education holds many promises. It is an answer to the needs of large segments of the population who have not traditionally been able to take advantage of higher education. I have taught at least 80 online courses, over 18 semesters, for three different colleges and universities. The diversity of my students is one of the pleasures of teaching online. Among students in my online courses, I have single parents working two jobs, soldiers guarding an embassy in Asia, military spouses living in Africa, and physically challenged individuals coping with limited mobility. These students enrich the material with examples from their own lives and give me a new perspective on many topics such as memory and stress.

Alternative formats such as online courses allow us to extend education to those whose lives do not allow them to attend school at traditional class hours. These nontraditional students are often my best students; I wonder how much more they would shine if they had the chance to attend traditional classes and focus solely on their education.

Not everyone needs or wants a traditional residential college experience. As educators, it is important to meet students where they are in their lives and work with them in ways that take advantage of their available time and interests. That being said, the rigor of online courses should be the same as, not less than, that found in face-to-face courses. Academic integrity should be maintained regardless of the delivery method. To downgrade expectations is to cheapen the educational experience.

CHARACTERISTICS OF AND ISSUES IN ONLINE LEARNING

This chapter focuses on the benefits, challenges, and promises of teaching introduction to psychology online. It is helpful to first have an understanding of the characteristics of the online classroom and the implications of those characteristics for teaching introduction to psychology in this manner. Online classes usually take place within a course management system such as Blackboard or WebCT. The course management system is password protected so that only registered users have access to it. Most course management systems provide web space for the syllabus, lecture notes, and PowerPoint presentations. They offer discussion boards, chat rooms, and testing functions. The instructor can customize each of these features and can add additional individualized content.

Online classes are generally asynchronous; that is, they do not occur in real time. Students complete their work at any time of day or night. Flexibility in time is one of the strengths of the online environment. That flexibility is often cited by my students as the primary reason for choosing the online section over a face-to-face, on-campus section.

In online courses, some synchronous or real-time chats may take place, but it can be difficult to find a common time when everyone can meet online. Such chats can also be difficult to manage when 20 students are online at the same time. Research shows that student perceptions of real-time chats are negatively related to the use of these synchronous tools (Carswell & Venkatesh, 2002). Other studies confirm the value of using asynchronous communication in online courses (Eriksson, Goller, & Muchin, 2001). My students' attitudes mirror these findings. They seldom request live chats, even though I offer the option weekly. When I hold synchronous chats, typically only three or four students participate.

Although the asynchrony has its advantages, it is also a source of potential problems. It can take longer to identify conflict between students when discussions occur over 4 or 5 days. In order to forestall such conflict, the instructor must be vigilant and monitor discussion boards daily. For sensitive topics, I monitor the discussion three times a day.

One myth about online courses is that they are self-paced. My online courses are not self-paced, and students must work on the schedule I have established. Students must complete weekly assignments and online quizzes. There are deadlines for each and points are deducted for late submission. Students cannot work ahead because I can control which areas of the course they can access. The course lasts all term and is not intended to be a compressed alternative to semester long sections of the course.

Another concern in the online classroom is the limited information that I have about those enrolled. Information about students, other than their names, includes only what they choose to share with me. Often the gender and age of a student is unknown. This lack of information can be problematic in certain situations. For example, I once had a student request an all-female discussion group. I could not guarantee the gender make-up of the group because I was not certain of the gender of many of the students.

There is also great potential for misinterpreting even simple comments in the online classroom. Students are often unfamiliar with the rules of "netiquette" that unofficially govern online communication. They often write in capital letters, the online equivalent of shouting, or they use the abbreviations of instant messaging. These writing conventions can lead to misinterpretations of the student's meaning. Grammatical and spelling errors can further distort a writer's intent.

Online courses rely heavily on writing, so good writing skills are critical. Many students lack these skills. Identifying weak writers before they enroll so remediation can occur is essential. I include a diagnostic writing assignment early in the term so that I can send poor writers to campus resources for writing assistance.

Additionally, most online courses are visual and text-based. Students need to be effective readers. Auditory learners may miss the aural component of face-to-face classes.

The Instructor's Role in Teaching Introduction to Psychology Online

Teaching online requires a shift in paradigm, from being more didactic as an instructor to being more of a facilitator. Many introduction to psychology courses tend to be lecture oriented due to the volume of information. Even interesting lectures are hard to use in an online class. Moving the course online entails rethinking the roles of both the teacher and the student, as well as reworking the course structure.

The teacher relinquishes some of the power and authority in the online classroom. For example, I cannot immediately control the course of a discussion when it gets off topic. Whereas such detours can be beneficial when a discussion takes an interesting turn, such detours can also go in troublesome directions. The deviations can be merely off topic, or they can be inappropriate. It is more difficult to redirect the discussion online. I have found that giving up some of the power is disconcerting at times, but it is a good way to convince students to share in the educational process.

Many introduction to psychology students are new to the college environment and, as a result, they often do not possess the skills needed to succeed academically. I spend a great deal of time creating documents on study skills and on how to succeed in college. My college's Student Support Services offers such workshops on these topics, however, few online students can come to campus to take advantage of their offerings.

The Student's Role in Introduction to Psychology Online

Online students share much more in the process of learning. For example, when I teach consciousness in a traditional classroom, I do most of the work by lecturing and showing a video. In the online classroom, students read and hold a discussion that spans the entire week devoted to this chapter. I have yet to get fewer than 80 entries (in a class of 25 students) in this discussion.

Online students must be self-starters who are self-disciplined. They must stay on task to meet deadlines. They must be aware of what they do not understand, and they need to be assertive enough to ask for clarifications. Students must manage their time efficiently, and they must be able to manage multiple tasks.

COURSE STRUCTURE AND TESTING ISSUES

Course Structure

I organize my course into *learning units*. Most learning units cover one chapter. The first element in the unit is a list of learning objectives for that chapter. The second element is a "lecturette," which is a short, informal introduction to the chapter topic. Its purpose is to introduce the chapter material. The lecturette is a short essay that includes major concepts and applications to current events. It is about 250 words and I include graphics to make the lecturettes more interesting. I plan to use streaming video for small segments as our campus infrastructure improves. That sort of technology also places technical demands on users' systems so I am cautious about incorporating them. I sometimes embed direct links to relevant interactive online activities. These activities may include a tutorial or a self-scoring inventory. The lecturette ends with questions to guide study of the chapter.

A PowerPoint presentation that highlights important concepts in the chapter is the third element of the learning unit. I usually post the PowerPoint presentations that come from the publisher. Students use the presentation to guide their note taking of each chapter. Fourth are hyperlinks to eight or nine related Web sites that are connected to ideas in the chapter. The fifth element is the weekly discussion board assignment. The discussion board assignment requires students to answer a question or complete an activity related to the chapter. Students must respond to the assignment and to each other. Finally, as the sixth element of the learning unit, I provide a direct link to the weekly online chapter quiz.

In addition to these weekly requirements, students have term projects, which serve to develop information literacy, critical thinking, and writing skills. Students must use the campus library and writing center to complete these assignments.

Whereas all learning units are visible at the beginning of the course, I only give students access to one learning unit per week. At the end of the week, I close the learning unit so students can no longer enter (post) assignments or complete the quiz.

Testing Issues

Testing online is a major issue. Most course management systems allow the instructor to upload the publisher's test bank as well as to create personalized exam questions. I give weekly quizzes that are untimed and open book. It is also possible to make tests timed, to allow random selection of questions from the test bank for each student, to set dates of test availability, and to require a password for accessing the test.

The quizzes I use are self-graded, and students get immediate feedback on their performance. I randomize the questions and give students access to the answers. I use my quizzes more as a personalized system of instruction.

A major concern in the online environment is the identity of the person taking the test. There is no way to verify that the student enrolled is the person who completes the online test. To account for this possibility, I give a proctored final exam at which students must show photo identification in order to take the exam. The final exam accounts for 30% of the final grade. If someone other than the registered student has been completing weekly work, then a poor showing by the student on the exam will adversely affect the final grade.

Grades on the weekly quizzes and the final exam tend to be in the same range, however, so I have not had to worry about someone other than the student enrolled completing the tests. Also, test scores tend to correlate with the quality of the weekly work, which makes me fairly confident that the student enrolled is actually doing the work. Although identity verification remains a concern in online testing, it should also be a concern in the traditional classroom. I have never verified the identity of a face-to-face student by asking for photo identification. It is possible that someone other than the registered student is completing the classroom section.

While cheating remains a concern as it does in any classroom, I have not seen the inflation in grades that would indicate widespread cheating. I actually think that cheating is less likely to occur in the online classroom because students never see each other, and it is easier to resist a faceless e-mail plea to cheat. I have had students contact me about such requests to cheat. They are reluctant to share their hard work. Not having to face fellow students may make it easier to resist requests to cheat from other students.

BENEFITS OF TEACHING INTRODUCTION TO PSYCHOLOGY ONLINE

Instructor Benefits

There are many pleasures in the online classroom. In introduction to psychology, I see the progression in the students' level of thought from the first chapter to later chapters. Because each student completes weekly discussion activities, I can watch students move from the knowledge level of thinking to application to synthesis and evaluation. I observe as students get excited about the application of course material to their own lives.

A high percentage of students, including those that I suspect would be quiet in the face-to-face classroom, participate actively. I see more thoughtful answers from online students because they do not have to answer immediately and can really think about the questions. The postings indicate that they have spent time with the course material and care about learning.

A student in my fall 2003 introduction to psychology class said, "As a first time online student, I found the online discussions as stimulating and thought provoking as the discussion in the more traditional classroom settings. I felt my fellow students were intelligent, articulate and very respectful of others' opinions" (J. Davis, personal communication, December 2003).

Paradoxically, I have better relationships with more students in the online classroom, even though I seldom see any of them in person. I get to know more students better because I require weekly participation in discussions and activities. Within a few weeks, I can identify the writer of most responses.

When I write recommendations for students, I have much more information on which to base my comments because I have seen work habits, conscientiousness, writing skills, and interaction with other students. Although I have not seen their faces (and it is always a surprise when I meet them in person because they never look as I imagined), I have a better sense of the abilities of online students than I do with most students in face-to-face classes.

Record keeping is easier in the online classroom. The computer keeps track of assignments turned in. Everything is time stamped to the minute, which means no more arguments about late papers. I never worry about losing assignments because all work is saved in the online classroom.

Teaching online also allows me to work during my best time. Although it is necessary to check the online classroom frequently, I can read and respond to student postings and questions when I am at my best. Teaching online allows me to travel to professional conferences without worrying about something meaningful for students to complete while I am gone. I can conduct class anywhere there is an Internet connection (Waschull, 2001).

Student Benefits

Time flexibility is the major benefit for students. Students who work full-time can still complete courses. Those who must travel or have irregular work schedules can continue their educations. I have had Secret Service agents take class during a presidential election, a semester in which they are never sure where they will be on any given day. Taking an online class additionally eliminates commuting time. In the Washington, DC area, it can take over an hour to drive 15 miles during rush hour. Online courses save that time.

Accessibility is another benefit for students. Online courses make it possible for students with physical challenges to more easily attend class. I once had a student who was undergoing chemotherapy. She was unable to attend traditional classes due to potential exposure to germs. Online courses enabled her to continue her education. I have also had students who had difficultly attending traditional classes due to religious reasons. Online courses enable those students to continue their educations without violating religious restrictions.

CHALLENGES IN INTRODUCTION TO PSYCHOLOGY ONLINE

Instructor Challenges

Whereas there are many benefits to teaching online, there are also challenges with this course delivery method. Online teaching takes far more time than traditional, face-to-face classes. I estimate that I spend at least one third more time with my online students than with face-to-face students, often as much as 12–14 hours per course per week. This estimate does not include time spent grading papers. I spend even more time with introduction to psychology students because they are frequently new to college.

The initial conversion of a course to an online format is incredibly time intensive. Keeping links to Web sites updated each term also involves a good deal of time. Learning to navigate the course management system requires many hours. New versions of the course management system with new features to be mastered appear frequently.

There is far more reading for the instructor than in traditional classes because all responses are written. It is not necessary to respond to each posting by each student, but the posts still must be read. Learning to manage time effectively is an ongoing struggle.

Communication of expectations is another challenge. It is important to be very clear in directions. No matter how much I simplify the wording of the course requirements, there are still students who do not understand (or read) the directions.

Another challenge is managing the student expectation of access to the instructor 24 hours a day, 7 days a week. Online students have much easier access to an instructor than do traditional students. It can be hard to get students to understand that although I am just a mouse click away, I am not online and available 24 hours a day, 7 days a week.

An ongoing concern is identifying and reinforcing boundaries. The informality of the online environment sometimes encourages students to cross the lines of propriety in terms of how they interact with both professors and other students. Students sometimes address me as they would address an e-mail buddy. They fail to recognize that I am not a peer. Such boundary crossing can result in misunderstandings when students receive negative feedback or low grades. For example, I recently had a student who persisted in calling me "teach," and his e-mails were written as though I were his friend instead of his professor. He became incensed at a suggestion on a paper that he needed help with his writing. He became even more infuriated when he asked for specific feedback and I detailed the problems with his writing.

Finally, there are the technology issues that prove challenging. Computer glitches and lost connections are a fact of technological life. Flexibility and patience are a must. Students often do not have the minimal technological competencies needed to succeed online, yet they enroll in online classes. Although psychology instructors are not expected to teach computer skills, it is essential that they are able to recognize whether problems are due to technology or due to student error.

Student Challenges

Students often have incorrect perceptions about the ease of taking a course online. They have mistaken ideas about the time involved. They think an online course is a quick, once weekly, visit to the course Web site, and they forget about the offline work needed for success. At the beginning of last term, I asked students how many hours they thought would be needed for my course. Their answer was 1 to 2 hours per week.

Students routinely underestimate their work and family commitments. Single parents who are working 40 hours per week and raising two children have few extra hours. Many students enroll in three or four online courses at one time and are surprised when I tell them that course load equates to a second full-time job.

Some students also fail to recognize the self-discipline needed to succeed online. A student must complete weekly work on time without constant verbal reminders. Some online learners find that they need the physical presence of an instructor to stay on task, which can mean that online courses are not necessarily going to allow them to demonstrate their best academic work.

Undergraduates must be able to recognize when course material is unclear. They must be assertive enough to ask for clarification. Without the nonverbal cues in a traditional classroom, I assume students understand what they read. Sometimes my assumption is false, but I do not know that until students inform me about their struggles with the assigned reading.

Finally, students often overestimate their computer skills. If they do not have a basic understanding of their own computer systems, they can encounter problems with how web pages display. They may not be able to save documents or to upload files. This lack of skill can interfere with learning the course material.

ACTIVE LEARNING ONLINE IN INTRODUCTION TO PSYCHOLOGY

Active learning has a long history of use in education from Socrates' method of questioning to John Dewey and his reflective thinking of the 1930s to Jerome Bruner and his discovery learning theories of the 1960s (Newlin & Wang, 2002). Active learning refers to pedagogy that involves students in their own learning by writing, discussing, and problem solving. They engage in higher order thinking such as analysis, synthesis, and evaluation. Active learning includes instructional activities that require students to engage the material and to think about what they are doing.

Active learning encompasses a range of activities that can be done individually or in groups (Isbell, 1999). Such techniques make course material more interesting. Research has shown that many students learn better when techniques other than lecture are used (Bonwell & Eison, 1991).

Active learning online is not an oxymoron. A good online course is more than just a correspondence course delivered electronically rather than through the U.S. mail. An online course can truly be more active than a course in the traditional classroom. In the online classroom, active learning can involve class debates, case studies, simulations, group work, and individual exercises (Graham, 2001).

Implementing active learning techniques online requires some effort if such methods are to be effective, but their use can make the online environment more interesting and can increase student involvement in their own learning.

Discussions

Discussion is one of the easiest active learning techniques to use in an online class. An online discussion can involve all students if it is designed effectively. Facilitating a successful discussion online takes management skills and practice especially in an asynchronous environment. In other words, there is a learning curve for both the instructor and the students. Students often do not know how they are supposed to behave in an asynchronous online discussion, especially when responding to one another.

Discussions can involve the whole class or be conducted in smaller groups. Discussions work best when students must post responses throughout the week, and when a specific number of responses per student is required. I give very specific guidelines for posting responses, as well as reminders about netiquette to the students.

For example, I require that the student's initial contribution to a discussion be at least 100–150 words, refer to the concept under examination, and include an academic reference. I set deadlines for each of the subsequent required responses so that all postings are not done 10 minutes before the final deadline. I view these discussions not as free-for-all conversation, but as scholarly exchange. Students do not receive credit for merely giving affirmations to other students. They must make substantive contributions and keep the discussion going.

The instructor must monitor the discussion on a daily basis in order to forestall any problems. I generally stay out of the discussion unless students make patently incorrect statements or make inappropriate remarks.

Another way to run discussions is to put students in groups and have the discussions within the group discussion area provided by the course management system, a feature in all course management systems. This approach requires students to interact more and to work with a small group of peers more intensively. Using small groups does increase instructor time, however, because the instructor needs to monitor each group.

Putting the groups together can also be problematic. I try to avoid group assignments until the semester is at least 3 weeks old, so that I have some sense of who will be actively participating in the class. One suggestion for configuring groups is to survey students about what time of day they plan to be online during the semester. I then group students by time of access.

Another method of grouping, which is not always successful, is to let students choose their own groups. I initially group students in a somewhat random manner. I put students who have been working during the first 3 weeks into groups together. I also reconfigure groups after the first group assignment, particularly if there are students who do not participate. I reshuffle after each group assignment so that only students who are actively participating are in a group together. To assuage student concern about group work, grades are based primarily on individual contributions rather than group products.

There are other steps that I take to facilitate discussion. I provide lengthy guidelines to help online learners prepare on-topic responses. I give specific examples so students learn how to give feedback to other students. I reword the original questions when responses are going in the wrong direction. I also provide discussion summary every 2 or 3 days where I include points missed in the exchanges. I make available an alternative location within the online classroom for off-topic discussion should students want to continue with such interactions. I privately reprimand learners who submit off-topic comments. I provide suggestions for improving future postings. For the most egregious cases, I can block a student from the discussion using the course management system. I have only had to do this once.

I grade all discussions. Students receive full points if they post on time, if the answer meets the minimum word requirements, and if I judge that it is on point and relevant. I use these discussions as participation activities so the grading is fairly lenient.

Case Studies

Case studies are another way to introduce active learning techniques. One favorite site for cases is at the University of Buffalo's National Center for Case Study Teaching (http://ublib.buffalo.edu/libraries/projects/cases/case.html). There are many other public domain Web sites with cases already created. Advice columns in newspapers provide another source of case study material.

Students work in pairs to analyze a case study. They must integrate relevant theory into the analysis. Each pair "presents" their findings to the class in a class discussion board. I also use case studies as exam questions or as term projects.

Video Analyses

Students watch videos or weekly television shows and react to the content in terms of psychological theory. I find this activity also helps students learn to critically evaluate what they watch. A favorite video activity for either the developmental or social psychology chapters is assigning students to view Saturday morning or afterschool cartoons. Students keep count of the number of aggressive acts that they see in the cartoon. Then, they analyze their results, either in terms of the literature on child development or on aggression. Such an activity allows students to connect the knowledge from these two chapters to a real-world phenomenon. Additionally, this assignment gives parents in the class a chance to look at what their children are watching.

Exam Questions

Groups of students generate potential exam questions. Two or three students summarize the chapter in 400 words or less, and they generate a list of 10 critical terms from the chapter. They then must create at least three multiple-choice questions and one essay question. Finally, they must locate a Web site that is relevant to the chapter's content.

This assignment is graded and helps students create a final exam study guide. An informal correlation shows that students do better on the chapters they have summarized as compared to those they have merely read. Anecdotal evidence from students also supports this finding.

Interactive Activities

Interactive online activities are plentiful. Many publishers have Web sites in the public domain, and quite a few professors have created activities that are available on public access Web sites. Such activities require students to become more involved in the material by participating actively. Among my students' favorites are activities on stress, positive reinforcement, and problem solving using anagrams. These activities are particularly helpful for learners who are kinesthetic learners (Grant, 2004).

Adapted Activities

It is also possible to adapt activities used in face-to-face classes for the online class. One that works well in both environments involves card playing and identifying the function of various brain parts (Halonen & Gray, 2001). I give students a list of 15 brain parts such as the hypothalamus, the occipital lobe, and so on. Students play a game of cards such as "Go Fish." Working in groups, students then identify the role each brain part plays during the game of cards. For example, I expect them to say that the occipital lobe facilitates seeing the cards and the other players. I have online students complete this activity offline. They play cards with their friends or families instead of with classmates.

Students enjoy the opportunity to spend time with family while also completing their schoolwork. The descriptions of brain functions I get from online students tend to be longer and more in-depth than those I get from face-to-face students who complete the activity in class. Online students report that this activity helps them understand and remember what can be a difficult chapter.

Specific Activities for Introduction to Psychology Online

Table 10.1 shows some examples of specific online learning activities I use in my online introduction to psychology class. One problem with online sources is that web addresses often change. If a URL is no longer valid, then enter the subject into a search engine such as Google to try to find the site's new address or to substitute a comparable site.

WHY I TEACH INTRODUCTION TO PSYCHOLOGY ONLINE

Online teaching has truly been a life-changing experience for me. Although I enjoy the traditional, face-to-face classroom and do not want to abandon that format, teaching online has renewed my passion for the profession. Online delivery allows me to connect with students I would not have had the chance to "meet" in the traditional classroom. The online environment allows me to develop a genuinely constructivist classroom in which the learners are involved in constructing their knowledge. I, as the instructor, am a partner in the educational endeavor, rather than the person most responsible for learning.

Changing to an online teaching format is not the best choice for every teacher. Giving up some of the control of the classroom has been a scary adventure. I have to wait for students to post answers or begin a discussion. I have no nonverbal feedback, and sometimes no feedback at all, to help me see if students understand what I am teaching. I have no control over any campus server problems or over the course management system problems.

It can be hard, too, to convince students that they must share in the learning process. However, once that shift has been made, the educational endeavor becomes a shared enterprise, and I am able to focus on other aspects of the process.

Embracing online teaching can be a challenge, but such challenges are often the most fun part of teaching. In fact, as in my case, the move to online can be a truly energizing experience. That energy has extended to other areas of my job and brought new passion to my professional life.

TABLE 10.1

Interactive Activities for Online Introduction to Psychology

Research	Students go to http://www.psychologymatters.org and read one of the studies. They outline the research components and then find an article from the newspaper related to the research. Finally, they explain the connection between the two items.
History of psychology	Students work as individuals or in pairs to choose a historical figure. They find biographical information about the person including the biggest contribution to psychology, one primary source by the person, and one obscure fact that is interesting about the person.
Consciousness	Students discuss the topic and begin with the questions: "Are altered states of consciousness (ASC) necessarily bad? Why or why not? How does culture affect your opinion?" They must support their answers with an academic source and also respond to others at least twice.
Learning	Students review http://tip.psychology.org/bandura.html and http://library.louisville.edu/government/subjects/television/violencetv.html In groups, they develop a plan for parents to use to minimize the effects of violent television on children.
Sensation & perception	Students visit the M. C. Escher site at http://www.mcescher.com/. They select a piece of art and then discuss the Gestalt principles in the piece.
Cognitive psychology	Students complete the puzzle at http://www.greylabyrinth.com/Puzzles/puzzle151.htm They take note of their thinking processes as they solve the problem. They reread the section on problem solving and discuss how they might better solve problems. They revisit the Web site and try solving a different puzzle. They repeat the metacognitive analysis.
Memory	Students play the Concentration-like game at http://www.seussville.com/games/concentration/ and describe the principles of memory involved in the game.
Motivation/ emotion	Students conduct a simple study. They find eight people of various ethnicities and ask each participant to identify what emotion the participant associates with the following list of colors: blue, red, white, black, green, yellow. After their data is collected, students compare their data to the data at http://www2.psych.cornell.edu/psych342/colorchoiceweb.html
Personality	Students explore online personality tests at http://www.keirsey.com, http://www.outofservice.com/bigfive, and http://www.queendom.com/tests/personality/type_a_r_access.html They identify the perspective on which each test is based.
Social psychology	Students read two articles about Milgram's classic study at http://home.swbell.net/revscat/perilsOfObedience.htm and http://designweb.otago.ac.nz/grant/psyc/OBEDIANCE.HTML They evaluate their own potential for participation in the study.
Abnormal	Students read the case on depression taken from http://ublib.buffalo.edu/libraries/projects/cases/ They identify the treatment they would choose and explain why.

I have been teaching for a long time, and when I moved to the online environment, I saw it as just another classroom. I thought it would make life easier because I would not have to go to campus as many days a week. I thought, however, that the teaching experience would not really be any different from the traditional classroom. I have found instead an unexpectedly exciting place to teach that has been revitalizing and has really taught me what the word "education" means. I have been able to mentor students and to watch their intellectual growth. In doing so, I have found new purpose in teaching and an exhilarating adventure for the next stage of my career.

ACKNOWLEDGMENTS

The author would like to thank the members of her department, as well as Dana Dunn, Stephen Chew, and Sherry Kinslow for comments on early drafts of this chapter.

REFERENCES

Bonwell, C. C., & Eison, J. A. (1991). *Active learning: Creating excitement in the classroom.* Washington, DC: ERIC Clearinghouse on Higher Education (ED340272). Retrieved August 30, 2003, from http://www.ericfacility.net/ericdigests/ed340272.html

Carswell, A. D., & Venkatesh, V. (2002). Learner outcomes in an asynchronous distance education environment. *International Journal of Human–Computer Studies, 56*(5). Retrieved April 20, 2004, from http://portal.acm.org/citation.cfm?id=636099&dl=GUIDE&coll=GUIDE

Eriksson, T., Goller, A., & Muchin, S. (2001). *A comparison of online communication in distance education and in conventional education.* Paper presented at ASEE/IEEE Frontiers in Education Conference. Retrieved April 10, 2004, from http://fie.engrng.pitt.edu/fie2001/papers/1225.pdf

Graham, T. A. (2001). Teaching child development via the Internet: Opportunities and pitfalls. *Teaching of Psychology, 28*(1), 67–71.

Grant, L. K. (2004). Teaching positive reinforcement on the Internet. *Teaching of Psychology, 31*(1), 69–71.

Halonen, J., & Gray, C. (2001). *The critical thinking companion for introductory psychology* (2nd ed.). New York: Worth.

Isbell, K. (1999). An interview on active learning with Dr. James Eison. *The Language Teacher, 23*(5). Retrieved November 17, 2004 from http://www.jalt-publications.org/tlt/articles/1999/05/eison

Newlin, M. H., & Wang, A. Y. (2002) Integrating technology and pedagogy: Web instruction and seven principles of undergraduate education. *Teaching of Psychology, 29*(4), 325–330.

Waschull, S. B. (2001). The online delivery of psychology courses: Attrition, performance and evaluation. *Teaching of Psychology, 28*(2), 143–147.

Chapter
11

Multimedia and Computer-Based Learning in Introductory Psychology

Thomas E. Ludwig
Hope College

Charles W. Perdue
West Virginia State University

The content of an introductory psychology course (and the supporting textbooks) is constantly evolving in response to advances in research and theory. The instructional methods and tools used in the course have also evolved, reflecting shifts in both the preferred pedagogical approaches and in the technological infrastructure available to the instructor and the students. This chapter focuses on the technology of computer-enhanced instruction, but also addresses some of the pedagogical paradigms that have developed to guide the widespread adoption of computer-based learning. It begins with an overview of media use in the classroom, considers computer-based activities for student use outside class sessions, and then examines how distance education replaces class sessions with an entirely online learning environment. We close with a look at some lessons learned from the past two decades of research and classroom experience with instructional technology.

MULTIMEDIA IN THE PSYCHOLOGY CLASSROOM

The term *multimedia* has many meanings (Mayer, 2001), but for the purposes of this chapter, it is any computer-based environment that incorporates some combination of text, graphics, sound, animations, and video.

History of Media Use

In a sense, teaching has always been a "multimedia" enterprise: Instructors have typically spoken aloud to, drawn pictures for, and attempted demonstrations for the benefit of their students. What has changed has been the evolving technology available for combining and delivering that information. Instructors who began teaching in the 1960s or 1970s probably remember a time when the chalkboard was the main form of instructional media used in psychology classrooms, perhaps supplemented by mimeographed handouts and occasional glimpses of a sheep brain, an operant chamber, or a plastic model of an eyeball. These instructors may recall the enthusiasm with which students greeted the introduction of "new technologies," such as photocopied illustrations, slides depicting visual illusions, filmstrips with audio narration, and especially full-motion 16-millimeter films with reenactments of classic experiments.

As classroom technology continued to improve, the 1980s saw the introduction of overhead transparencies and videotapes, and the 1990s brought first videodiscs and then CD-ROMs, the World Wide Web, and eventually digital projectors with the mixed blessings of Microsoft PowerPoint (see Atkinson, 2004). Technological innovation has accelerated in the first decade of the new century, with digital projectors as standard features in most classrooms, and CD-ROMs or DVDs accompanying many textbooks. Most classrooms (and dorm rooms) have high-speed Internet connections that allow reasonable quality video streaming, and many students now bring wireless laptops, tablet computers, or handheld devices into the classroom setting.

Rationale for Multimedia Use

Why would any instructor want to use multimedia materials in the classroom? To a certain extent, psychology instructors have adopted these new types of media simply "because they could." As each improvement in technology became available (in many cases with the support of textbook publishers), instructors who saw themselves as "hip, cool, and hi-tech" quickly incorporated the new tools, correctly perceiving that slick multimedia presentations have a certain amount of entertainment value for students. However, this rationale misses the point. In fact, the use of multimedia materials has substantial grounding in cognitive theory and research, although, as is often the case, the research evidence followed the widespread use of these materials rather than preceded it.

Several dozen studies indicate that computer-based multimedia can improve learning and retention of material presented during a class session or individual study period, as compared to "traditional" lectures or study materials that do not use multimedia (see Bagui, 1998; Fletcher, 2003; Kozma, 1991; Mayer, 2001). According to Najjar (1996), this improvement can be attributed mainly to *dual coding* of the information presented in two different modalities—visual plus auditory, or text plus images (Clark & Paivio, 1991; Paivio, 1986)—leading to increased comprehension of the material during the class session, and improved retention of the material at later testing times (Mayer & Moreno, 1998). There is general agreement that multimedia presentations are most effective when the different types of media support one another rather than when superfluous sounds or images are presented for entertainment value—which may induce disorientation and *cognitive overload* that could interfere with, rather than enhance, learning (Mayer, Heiser, & Lonn, 2001).

Finally, some studies have suggested that student satisfaction and motivation is higher in courses that use multimedia materials (e.g., Astleitner & Wiesner, 2004; Yarbrough, 2001). Shuell and Farber (2001) examined the attitudes of over 700 college students toward the use of computer technology in 20 courses representing a wide range of academic disciplines. Students were generally very positive about the use of technology, although females rated the use of technology for learning and classroom instruction somewhat lower than did their male peers. (Gender differences are considered later in this chapter.)

However, not everyone is excited about the new technology. On the basis of negative anecdotes described on student evaluations and in discussions at professional conferences, we can conclude that some students and instructors have had bad experiences with multimedia in the classroom. In our opinion, these negative experiences often seem related to lack of experience with computer technology or to overly optimistic expectations about the media (or to underpowered projectors that necessitate dimming the room lights). Our own classroom experiences, combined with the research evidence, lead us to summarize the pedagogical value and rationale for using classroom media in these three points:

- *To raise interest level*—students appreciate (and often expect) a variety of media
- *To enhance understanding*—rich media materials boost student comprehension of complex topics, especially dynamic processes that unfold over time
- *To increase memorability*—rich media materials lead to better encoding and easier retrieval

Instructional Techniques for Integrating Media Use

What do you need to get started with multimedia in the classroom? The equipment is relatively straightforward, and already widely available in many classrooms (Eskicioglu & Kopec, 2003): a standard computer system equipped with a

CD/DVD drive, external speakers, and an Internet connection with the computer output displayed through a digital projector. A TV/VCR may also be required for instructors who have not yet made the transition to an all-digital format, or for the presentation of commercial videotapes that cannot be digitized legally.

Acquiring Multimedia Assets.   The equipment will not be of much use unless you have a good set of multimedia materials and a carefully developed plan for organizing the entire class session to incorporate the media effectively. In the past, obtaining good media materials was quite a challenge; early adopters of technology often spent many hours scanning images from textbooks and creating their own audio and video clips. Fortunately, many textbook publishers now provide libraries of images, animations, and video segments licensed for use in class (although instructors may still want to augment these collections with other materials).

The same computer technology that facilitates multimedia creation and distribution makes it temptingly easy to obtain materials from a wide variety of sources. Photos may be scanned from magazines, and images and animations may be captured from web pages. For example, web search sites such as Google allow a user to scan the Internet for a vast selection of images using a powerful keyword search engine. Audio and video clips may be digitized from videotape or captured from CD or DVD sources, or downloaded from the Internet.

Although the *fair use* provision introduced by the 1976 Copyright Act grants educators and students remarkable latitude in the use of materials for noncommercial, instructional purposes (U.S. Copyright Office, 2002; specifically see Section 107 at www.copyright.gov/title17), aspiring multimedia authors should be vigilant about the inclusion of copyrighted content in their work. If in doubt, it is always wise to seek permission from the copyright holder, or consult with a library media specialist. Some colleges or universities have adopted specific policies about the use of such supplementary materials, including limits on the number of images that may be obtained from a single source, the duration of video that may be sampled (e.g., 10% of a complete film, or 3 minutes of a television program), or the length of time that an instructor may make the content available to students (e.g., 9 presentations, 45 consecutive days, or a single semester).

Preparing a Class Plan.   The class plan is perhaps the most important resource for the successful use of multimedia materials, because it guides the selection of media and provides the context for each media element. Instructors who begin integrating multimedia into their classes often report that the media use forced them to improve the organization of their class sessions, which may be an added benefit to students. Many instructors use PowerPoint to organize and present their lecture outline and media, despite strong criticisms of the "cognitive style" that PowerPoint induces (Tufte, 2003). Other experts argue that we should blame the presenter, not the tool, for mind-numbing presentations (Atkinson, 2004). Although multimedia materials may have some value when merely added to a PowerPoint lecture outline, many instructors are exploring ways to incorporate these materials in collaborative learning activities involving case-based scenarios or problem-based exercises (Gueldenzoph & Chiarelott, 2002; Rogers, 2002; Savery & Duffy, 1996).

COMPUTER ACTIVITIES IN PSYCHOLOGY COURSES

Although computer-guided instructional activities can be used in the classroom or by teams of students outside class sessions, the main use of these activities is as individual homework assignments. As described later, the past few decades have seen an evolution and expansion of computer-based learning (see Goldman-Segall & Maxwell, 2003, for a more comprehensive discussion).

History of Computer Activities

The Hobbyist-Programmer Years.   Although a few instructional activities in psychology were developed for the time-sharing mainframe and minicomputer terminals of the 1960s and 1970s, these activities were limited to text only, and were not very interesting or useful. The arrival of microcomputers such as the Apple II in 1977 and the IBM-PC in 1981, with their crude but useable graphics capability, led to an explosion of interest in developing computer-based instructional materials. Unfortunately, useful development tools did not yet exist, so educators had to learn programming languages in order to produce even the simplest instructional materials.

The Creative Soloist Years.   The debut of the Macintosh in 1984 brought improved graphics capability to education, allowing a level of detail and clarity in illustrations that was, for the first time, truly useful in instruction. The release of Windows 3.1 in 1990 meant that the "IBM-compatible" computer systems that had begun to populate faculty offices and student computer labs were no longer limited to crude DOS-style graphics. The development tools were also becoming more powerful and easier to use by nonprogrammers. HyperCard for Macintosh (1987) and ToolBook for Windows (1991) handled the technical details of the user interface, allowing educators to focus on developing the instructional content. From the late 1980s through the mid-1990s, most computer activities were produced by individual faculty members working alone, turning a creative idea into a useable computer-based learning activity (see Ludwig, 1994, 2004b, for an extended example).

The Instructional Team Approach.   In the mid-1990s, instructional media expanded on two fronts: The quality of visual images improved again, as graphics hardware became capable of displaying full-color photographs (more than 16 million colors instead of the 256 colors of the previous generation of hardware) at higher resolutions. In addition, computer systems became capable of displaying motion video clips (first at postage stamp sizes, but gradually at larger sizes and higher frame rates, approaching the quality of broadcast television). The inclusion of these improved forms of media greatly increased the technical complexity of the instructional projects, as well as the storage requirements (necessitating a move from floppy disks to CD-ROM). This change made it difficult for an individual educator to produce an activity at an appropriate level of sophistication and quality, so projects began to be produced by groups of content experts teamed with multimedia developers and video editors (e.g., Hilton & Perdue, 2003). The cost of producing materials continued to escalate, so project teams began breaking the content of an activity into small chunks called *learning objects* that could be reused in different types of activities. As the century turned, the increasing use of video clips moved many projects to multiple CD-ROMs or even to DVDs.

Types of Computer Activities for Student Homework Assignments

There have been numerous attempts to create a typology or taxonomy of computer-mediated learning activities, based either on the objectives of the activity or on what students actually do in the activity (e.g., Rogers, 2002). Most of these typologies distinguish at least four categories of individual activities (although the names vary): (a) *demonstration*—a brief exercise to illustrate a single concept; usually highly interactive; (b) *tutorial*—a more extended guided instruction on a topic; usually less interactive, with higher density of content; (c) *quiz*—a structured assessment to help students test their knowledge and identify areas for review; wide variety of formats, with multiple-choice questions as the most common format; (d) *journal*—a nonstructured assessment, often a reflective writing assignment, to help students process the new information and integrate it with what they already know.

In addition, several categories of activities involve collaborative learning: (a) *discussion*—a nonstructured group exercise centered on a content topic or on reactions to a course experience (with or without guidance from the instructor as discussion moderator); (b) *project*—a goal-oriented group activity involving both shared learning and shared assessment, with the outcome being a product that meets a specified standard; often built around a case study or a problem-based real-world scenario.

In the 1990s, most computer-based homework assignments were stand-alone exercises, linked from the instructor's web page. Now it is more common for instructors to use a course management system (e.g., WebCT, BlackBoard, or Moodle) to provide "one-stop shopping" for students, with all activities tied to the course syllabus and scores from all assignments available in one place.

Pedagogical Value of Computer Activities

Do computer activities provide real benefits to the students? If so, are these benefits over and above the learning that takes place when students read the textbook or work through a printed study guide? Mayer (2001) reviewed a number of studies on the effectiveness of guided multimedia instruction outside the classroom. The results of these studies show consistent evidence for a *multimedia effect* in computer-based learning: Students who received coordinated presentation of explanations in verbal and visual format outperformed those who received verbal explanations alone, or who received verbal and visual explanations that were not coordinated. Interestingly, the value of computer activities was most evident for students with low prior knowledge about the topic. This result suggests that the best students (or those with the best prior preparation) may not need the extra value that multimedia activities can provide.

In addition to the multimedia effect, computer-based learning can provide benefits for students whose preferred *learning style* is not well suited to classroom lectures. The contemporary discussion of learning styles is based in part on Gardner's (1983) theory of multiple intelligences. From the point of view of this theory, different students have different profiles of skill on each type of intelligence. In a classroom setting, it is most efficient to treat all students alike—presenting a single type of experience that may be congruent with the learning styles of some students, but not particularly helpful to other students. But with well-designed computer activities, it is possible to do a better job of matching the format of the instruction with each student's preferred learning styles (Mayer, 2003; Wagner & McCombs, 1995).

Do all instructors acknowledge the benefits of computer activities? Some of the same instructors who avoid using multimedia in class often also object to the use of computer-based assignments. Once again, these negative attitudes often seem related to lack of experience with computer technology, or to some negative experiences with crashed systems or incompatible browsers. Admittedly, there have been legitimate concerns when adopting new instructional technologies before they are "mature" (i.e., dependable). For the most part, however, the technologies we are discussing are sufficiently reliable to become staples of instruction.

Our own experience with computer activities, combined with the research evidence, suggests that the pedagogical value of computer-based learning assignments is similar to the rationale for using multimedia:

To raise interest level—because students appreciate "hands-on" learning activities, especially if the activities apply psychological principles to real-life experiences.

To enhance understanding—through the use of self-paced, repeatable instructional guidance through complex topics.

To increase memorability—because "doing it" encodes at multiple levels that improve retrieval, as compared to merely "hearing about it" or "reading about it."

In the case of computer-based homework assignments, we would add an additional benefit:

To improve instruction—by providing in-depth coverage of topics not covered in class, or in formats not feasible in a large group session.

The value of actually "doing something" was demonstrated in a study by Morris, Joiner, and Scanlon (2002) in which students were given various types of instruction on the statistical concept of central tendency of a distribution of scores. The results indicated that students who actually manipulated the data in a computer-based activity showed a greater improvement in understanding.

On the other hand, it is important to note that merely having students use computers does not make an activity "interactive." Tuovinen (2000) pointed out that there are various levels of interactivity in multimedia assignments, ranging from passively paging through presentations, to selecting a pathway through the material in order to achieve a learning goal, to manipulating objects or data in order to solve a problem, all the way to engaging in an authentic task in a simulated environment.

The Special Role of Animations

One of the most important benefits of the computer as a tool of instruction is its capacity to show dynamic processes unfolding over time. The time frame of some processes may be usefully compressed; for example, an animation may "fast-forward" a depiction of genetic changes in the characteristics of a population that normally would occur over many thousands of years (see the "Natural Selection" activity in Hilton & Perdue, 2003). Similarly, a "slow motion" animation of neurotransmitter release and reuptake in the synapse may allow the student a more leisurely inspection of a complex but usually very rapid process (see the "Neural Messages" activity in Ludwig, 2004a).

Several studies suggest that animations are very useful in helping students visualize and comprehend complex processes (see Nix & Spiro, 1990; Schneiderman, 2003). How can animations be used most effectively to promote understanding of scientific concepts? Mayer and Moreno (2002) reviewed research on the role of animation in multimedia learning and derived seven principles to guide the use of animation.

The most basic of the seven principles are the *multimedia principle* (explain a concept in words accompanied by an animation rather than using words alone), the *modality principle* (a visual animation is complemented better by an audio narration than by visual text), and the *personalization principle* (present words in conversational rather than formal style). The positioning and timing of the components is also important: the *temporal contiguity principle* recommends presenting the animation and narration simultaneously rather than successively, and the *spatial contiguity principle* states that, when a visual animation is accompanied by visual on-screen text, the text should appear near the animation. The final two principles acknowledge that adding more and more different types of media does not always enhance learning—as demonstrated in experiments measuring cognitive overload (Leahy, Chandler, & Sweller, 2003; Mayer et al., 2001). Mayer and Moreno called these points the *coherence principle* (focus on a single message and exclude extraneous words, sounds, and video because they will distract the student) and the *redundancy principle* (a visual animation accompanied by auditory narration is sufficient; adding additional redundant visual text adds no value and may actually reduce comprehension).

Practical Issues in Designing Computer Activities

Although detailed methodologies have been developed to guide the production of multimedia activities (e.g., Isakowitz, Stohr, & Balasubramanian, 1995), the development of good activities remains somewhat of an art form (Beyon, Stone, & Woodroffe, 1997). Three of the best-known pioneers in the design of multimedia instructional activities, Norman (1988), Nielsen (2000), and Schneiderman (1998, 2003) focused their attention on the user interface, emphasizing the need for the interface to be simple, intuitive, and consistent.

The problem is that the interaction components for computer activities have traditionally been designed by software engineers and programmers, not by cognitive psychologists. The result has been a wide range of interfaces with different levels of quality and usability. The rich variety of multimedia formats raises additional difficulties for both instructional designers and for inexperienced student users. Finally, the need for prototyping and intensive testing with users is even more pronounced in multimedia courseware than with traditional software applications, because users' tolerance of errors is very low when grades are at stake. Best practices in this area require design features that not only bring quality appearance, but also provide for the following characteristics (Brooks, Nolan, & Gallagher, 2001): a comprehensible metaphor; appropriate organization of data, functions, and tasks; efficient navigation between tasks; and effective sequencing of interactions.

Other instructional designers have concentrated on the importance of matching the instructional goals with appropriate technology (Bonk & Cummings, 1998; Wagner & McCombs, 1995). Their efforts have increased the popularity of an approach to instruction based on a *learner-centered* view of computer activities, which provides rich environments in which learners can actually build their own knowledge in a "discovery learning" format. This approach, drawn especially from the work of Piaget (1952), was endorsed in the set of principles for educational reform prepared by the American Psychological Association (1997).

Best practices here involve careful analysis, both of the content to be communicated, and the characteristics and skills of the potential student users. Each activity should have a clear goal statement summarizing the purpose of the activity and what the student should expect to gain from it (Beyon et al., 1997). On this point, many instructional designers refer to the work of Gagné (1984), who described five types of *learning outcomes* that students are expected to show as a result of their learning (an intellectual skill, a cognitive strategy, verbal information, a motor skill, or an attitude). Gagné also proposed a hierarchy of instructional events that promote those learning outcomes: gain the learner's attention, state the learning objective, stimulate recall of prior knowledge about the topic, present the new information, provide guidance, elicit the desired performance, assess the performance, provide feedback, and enhance retention and transfer of learning. This sequence of events is widely used as a template for structuring computer activities.

Theoretical Principles in the Design of Computer Activities

According to Mayer (2003), a cognitive theory of multimedia learning must draw on dual coding theory (Paivio, 1986), cognitive load theory (Chandler & Sweller, 1991), and constructivist learning theory (Mayer, 1999; Wilson, 1996). As described earlier in the section on multimedia use, dual coding theory and cognitive load theory have been incorporated into the technical design of most modern computer activities, so there is no longer much debate about these issues. On the other hand, *constructivist theory* is gaining increasing attention as an overall approach to guide the development and use of learning activities (Mayer, 2003; Rogers, 2002). This approach is based in part on Piaget's belief that learners construct their own meaning and knowledge from their experiences (Piaget, 1954). The constructivist approach is also congruent with Vygotsky's claim that social interaction about ideas precedes and facilitates comprehension and internalization of those ideas (Vygotsky, 1978).

Constructivist theory is leading to a gradual paradigm shift in the design and use of computer activities. Although there is still a valuable role for content-based tutorial activities (especially for remedial learning), more attention is now being focused on designing case-based or project-based learning activities, situated within authentic contexts (Savery & Duffy, 1996). These activities generally involve collaborative learning (students working in teams) on meaningful tasks that span many content areas (similar to the tasks performed by professionals in the field). For example, consider the issue of designing a set of computer activities that would help introductory psychology students better understand research methods and statistics. An "individual tutorial" approach would break the content into manageable chunks and develop guided instructional modules for each content topic, with a quiz at the end of each module. In contrast, a constructivist approach might develop an extended computer-based scenario in which students play the role of junior researchers on a real-world research question, working together to decide what information they need to learn and what data they need to gather in order to answer the question (see Herrington, Reeves, Oliver, & Woo, 2004). Although this type of role-playing scenario is more complicated to produce than a standard computer-based tutorial, a number of educators are working on templates that would handle the user interface and the scenario logic, so that instructors could easily create new scenarios by merely plugging in different media elements (see Key & Mundell, 2004). For example, a scenario involving a clinical psychologist diagnosing an eating disorder could be changed into a scenario about emergency room personnel treating a stroke patient, simply by replacing the video clips and text description, with no programming necessary.

Herrington et al. (2004) described 10 design characteristics for authentic activities based on a constructivist model. Some of the key characteristics include providing a complex task with real-world relevance that is capable of engaging students over a sustained period of time, with opportunities to examine the task from multiple perspectives, opportunities to use a variety of resources similar to those used by professionals, opportunities for collaboration and for individual reflection, and a culminating project involving the creation of a polished, valuable product (e.g., a professional quality report or a Web site).

A FEW THOUGHTS ABOUT DISTANCE EDUCATION

Integrating Media and Computer Activities in a Complete Online Course

Distance education in the form of correspondence courses has been around for a long time, but in the past decade distance education has shifted almost entirely to the Internet (for a related discussion, see Finley, chap. 10, this volume). The web-based format of distance learning has brought together the use of multimedia materials and computer-based learning techniques into the single package of a complete online course. The market for online courses has expanded rapidly (although not as rapidly as predicted): According to the National Center for Education Statistics (2004), enrollments in distance education courses doubled between 1997 and 2001 to more than 3 million students.

Compared to traditional classroom-based courses, online courses have some advantages and some disadvantages (Khan, 1997; Oliver & Herrington, 2001). Typically, students in an online course can do their work at any time of the day or night, in any location around the world. They can work through the course materials at their own pace, repeating activities and exercises (and digital lecture materials) as often as they want. They can often get individual help from the instructor, teaching assistants, or other students. However, many students miss the face-to-face interactions in the classroom, and without the personal experience of the instructor's enthusiasm for the course material, the drop-out rate is much higher than in traditional classes. Recognition of the strengths and weaknesses of "pure" online courses has led to a dramatic increase in *hybrid courses* that combine face-to-face sessions with online instruction (Veronikas & Shaughnessy, 2004; Young, 2002).

Special Issues with the Delivery of Instructional Materials Over the Internet

Berge, Collins, and Dougherty (2000) discussed some specific design principles for Web-based materials (see also Beyon et al., 1997; Brooks et al., 2001; Spector, 2000). The need for a simple, intuitive, consistent user interface becomes even more important when the student is physically removed from the instructor. *Bandwidth* (the speed with which materials can be transferred across the Internet to the student's computer) is another important issue (Lau, 2000). Most students on traditional campuses have high bandwidth connections, but many distance education students are still accessing course materials over slow dial-up modems. So, for the next few years at least, best practices in online courses will require careful design of materials for low bandwidth connections. Because video clips are becoming increasingly common and important in computer-based learning, online courses will need to provide two versions of each video assignment, including a low quality version for slow connections.

Copyright issues are especially relevant to educators and institutions that provide multimedia for instruction over the Internet. Even materials licensed for classroom purposes, or that are believed to be covered by the *fair use* provisions of copyright law, may be problematic when they are in essence "re-published" and disseminated on the Internet. To protect themselves in these instances, instructors delivering multimedia course content over the Internet should consider a system that allows student access only via password or identification number, to limit distribution of the media to those students actually enrolled in the course.

A related issue for faculty members who create materials for use in online courses is the actual ownership of those presentations. Traditionally, scholarly works created by faculty members, including lectures, articles, books, art, and educational software, have been considered their intellectual property. With online courses, however, universities have been more aggressive in asserting claims of ownership. Some educational institutions have argued that they have a legal interest in maintaining control over, and access to, such course offerings. Faculty planning to develop online instructional materials should determine whether their institution considers them to be normal scholarly products, or a commissioned "work for hire," or a "joint work" with shared ownership. For illustrations of differing perspectives on the issue of ownership, see the statements issued by the American Association of University Professors (1999) and by the Association of American Universities (1999).

LESSONS LEARNED FROM RESEARCH AND CLASSROOM EXPERIENCE

Some General Principles

Najjar (1998) presented a concise and helpful summary of the lessons from the past few decades of research on computer-mediated learning. Some of these principles involve characteristics of the materials, such as using the medium that best communicates the information, using multimedia for educational rather than decorative purposes, presenting related multimedia elements synchronously, and packaging it all in an interactive user interface.

Other principles refer to the characteristics of the learner or the learning task: Multimedia can be effective in focusing the learner's attention on the important concepts, but the design of the task should encourage learners to process the information actively, integrating the new material with prior knowledge. Assessments are most useful when there is a clear relation between the type of information learned and the type of information tested. Finally, remember that naïve and lower aptitude learners generally gain more from multimedia.

Gender and Computer Use

Research suggests that gender issues need to be considered when using multimedia materials in class and computer-based homework assignments. Although the research on this topic contains some contradictory findings, the general consensus seems to be that gender differences do exist in attitudes toward computer technology and in the way that males and females actually use computers (Bimber, 2000; Blum, 1999; Jennings & Onwuegbuzie, 2001). For example, males tend to see the computer as a tool to perform a particular task, whereas females tend to see the computer as a communication device (Jackson, Ervin, Gardner, & Schmitt, 2001). Females do more spontaneous writing (e.g., journaling or e-mail) on a computer, whereas males spend more time playing computer games. However, there are some signs that the increasing use of computer and communication technology by both males and females may be reducing the gender gap in attitudes toward computer use and in performance on computer-based learning tasks (see Ono & Zavodny, 2003).

CONCLUSIONS

As we have watched each wave of improvements in hardware and software, as well as the evolving trends in educational pedagogy, it appears that the most important lesson is the necessity of keeping the focus on the instructional goal, not on the technology itself. The experience of the past few decades predicts that technological change will continue and probably accelerate. Any classroom exercise or homework assignment that is tied to a particular hardware platform or proprietary software development tool will cease functioning when the technology changes. On the other hand, projects that stay focused on developing rich content and interactive pedagogy will be able to survive and prosper through each wave of technological change.

REFERENCES

American Association of University Professors. (1999). *Statement on distance education.* Retrieved July 24, 2004, from http://www.aaup.org/statements/Redbook/StDistEd.HTM
American Psychological Association. (1997). *Learner-centered psychological principles: A framework for school redesign and reform.* Retrieved July 2, 2004, from http://www.apa.org/ed/lcp.html
Association of American Universities. (1999). *Intellectual property and new media technologies.* Retrieved July 24, 2004, from http://www.aau.edu/reports/IPReport.html
Astleitner, H., & Wiesner, C. (2004). An integrated model of multimedia learning and motivation. *Journal of Educational Multimedia and Hypermedia, 13,* 3–21.
Atkinson, C. (2004). *Five experts dispute Edward Tufte on PowerPoint.* Retrieved July 6, 2004, from http://www.sociablemedia.com/articles_dispute.htm

Bagui, S. (1998). Reasons for increased learning using multimedia. *Journal of Educational Multimedia and Hypermedia, 7,* 3–18.

Berge, Z. L., Collins, M., & Dougherty, K. (2000). Design guidelines for web-based courses. In B. Abbey (Ed.), *Instructional and cognitive impacts of web-based education* (pp. 32–41). Hershey, PA: Idea Group Publishing.

Beyon, D., Stone, D., & Woodroffe, M. (1997). Experience with developing multimedia courseware for the World Wide Web: The need for better tools and clear pedagogy. *International Journal of Human–Computer Studies, 47,* 197–218.

Bimber, B. (2000). Measuring the gender gap on the Internet. *Social Science Quarterly, 81,* 868–876.

Blum, K. D. (1999). Gender differences in asynchronous learning in higher education: Learning styles, participation barriers and communication patterns. *Journal of Asynchronous Learning Networks, 3,* 46–66.

Bonk, C. J., & Cummings, J. A. (1998). A dozen recommendations for placing the student at the centre of web-based learning. *Educational Media International, 35,* 82–89.

Brooks, D. W., Nolan, D. E., & Gallagher, S. M. (2001). *Web-teaching: A guide to designing interactive teaching for the World Wide Web* (2nd ed.). New York: Kluwer Academic.

Chandler, P., & Sweller, J. (1991). Cognitive load theory and the format of instruction. *Cognition and Instruction, 8,* 293–332.

Clark, J. M., & Paivio, A. (1991). Dual coding theory and education. *Educational Psychology Review, 3,* 149–170.

Eskicioglu, A. M., & Kopec, D. (2003). The ideal multimedia-enabled classroom: Perspectives from psychology, education, and information science. *Journal of Educational Multimedia and Hypermedia, 12,* 199–221.

Fletcher, J. D. (2003). Evidence for learning from technology-assisted instruction. In H. F. O'Neil, Jr. & R. S. Perez (Eds.), *Technology applications in education: A learning view* (pp. 79–99). Mahwah, NJ: Lawrence Erlbaum Associates.

Gagné, R. M. (1984). Learning outcomes and their effects: Useful categories of human performance. *American Psychologist, 39,* 377–385.

Gardner, H. (1983). *Frames of mind.* New York: Basic Books.

Goldman-Segall, R., & Maxwell, J. W. (2003). Computers, the Internet, and new media for learning. In W. M. Reynolds & G. E. Miller (Eds.), *The handbook of psychology: Educational psychology* (Vol. 7, pp. 393–427). New York: Wiley.

Gueldenzoph, L., & Chiarelott, L. (2002). Using educational technology to improve constructivist instruction in higher education. *Journal on Excellence in College Teaching, 13,* 43–56.

Herrington, J., Reeves, T. C., Oliver, R., & Woo, Y. (2004). Designing authentic activities in Web-based courses. *Journal of Computing in Higher Education, 16,* 3–29.

Hilton, J. L., & Perdue, C. W. (2003). *Allyn & Bacon MindMatters* (Version 2.0). New York: Allyn & Bacon.

Isakowitz, T., Stohr, E. A., & Balasubramanian, P. (1995). A methodology for hypermedia design. *Communications of the ACM, 38,* 34–44.

Jackson, L., Ervin, K., Gardner, P. D., & Schmitt, N. (2001). Gender and the Internet: Women communicating and men searching. *Sex Roles, 44,* 363–379.

Jennings, S. E., & Onwuegbuzie, A. J. (2001). Computer attitudes as a function of age, gender, math attitude, and developmental status. *Journal of Educational Computing Research, 25,* 367–384.

Key, C., & Mundell, R. (2004). *Creating online case studies using LOGIC (Learning Object Generator in Case Studies).* Retrieved July 2, 2004, from http://www.logicproject.ca/text/LOGIC_Whitepaper.pdf

Khan, B. (1997). *Web-based instruction.* Englewood Cliffs, NJ: Educational Technology Publications.

Kozma, R. (1991). Learning with media. *Review of Educational Research, 61,* 179–211.

Lau, L. (2000). *Distance learning technologies: Issues, trends, and opportunities.* Hershey, PA: Idea Group Publishing.

Leahy, W., Chandler, P., & Sweller, J. (2003). When auditory presentations should and should not be a component of multimedia instruction. *Applied Cognitive Psychology, 17,* 401–418.

Ludwig, T. E. (1994). PsychSim II. In P. Morris, S. Ehrmann, R. Goldsmith, M. Howat, & V. Kumar (Eds.), *Valuable viable software in education: Case studies and analysis* (pp. 61–67). New York: McGraw-Hill.

Ludwig, T. E. (2004a). *PsychSim 5: Interactive graphic simulation and demonstration activities for psychology.* New York: Worth.

Ludwig, T. E. (2004b). PsychSim 5: Twenty years of instructional activities for psychology. In *Proceedings of ED-MEDIA 2004* (pp. 1877–1878). Charlottesville, VA: AACE Press.

Mayer, R. E. (1999). Designing instruction for constructivist learning. In C. M. Reigeluth (Ed.), *Instructional-design theories and models: A new paradigm of instructional theory* (Vol. 2, pp. 141–159). Mahwah, NJ: Lawrence Erlbaum Associates.

Mayer, R. E. (2001). *Multimedia learning.* New York: Cambridge University Press.

Mayer, R. E. (2003). Theories of learning and their application to technology. In H. F. O'Neil, Jr. & R. S. Perez (Eds.), *Technology applications in education: A learning view* (pp. 127–157). Mahwah, NJ: Lawrence Erlbaum Associates.

Mayer, R. E., Heiser, J., & Lonn, S. (2001). Cognitive constraints on multimedia learning: When presenting more material results in less understanding. *Journal of Educational Psychology, 93,* 187–198.

Mayer, R. E., & Moreno, R. (1998). A split-attention effect in multimedia learning: Evidence for dual processing systems in working memory. *Journal of Educational Psychology, 90,* 312–320.

Mayer, R. E., & Moreno, R. (2002). Animation as an aid to multimedia learning. *Educational Psychology Review, 14,* 87–99.

Morris, E. J., Joiner, R., & Scanlon, E. (2002). The contribution of computer-based activities to understanding statistics. *Journal of Computer Assisted Learning, 18,* 114–124.

Najjar, L. J. (1996). Multimedia information and learning. *Journal of Multimedia and Hypermedia, 5,* 129–150.

Najjar, L. J. (1998). Principles of educational multimedia user interface design. *Human Factors, 40,* 311–323.

National Center for Education Statistics (2004). *Distance education at postsecondary institutions.* Retrieved July 6, 2004, from http://www.nces.ed.gov/programs/coe/2004/section5/indicator32.asp

Nielsen, J. (2000). *Designing web usability: The practice of simplicity.* Indianapolis: New Riders Publishing.

Nix, D., & Spiro, R. (Eds.). (1990). *Cognition, education and multimedia.* Hillsdale, NJ: Lawrence Erlbaum Associates.

Norman, D. (1988). *The design of everyday things.* New York: Doubleday.

Oliver, R., & Herrington, J. (2001). *Teaching and learning online: A beginner's guide to e-learning and e-teaching in higher education.* Perth, Western Australia: Edith Cowan University Press.

Ono, H., & Zavodny, M. (2003). Gender and the Internet. *Social Science Quarterly, 84,* 111–121.

Paivio, A. (1986). *Mental representations: A dual coding approach.* Oxford, England: Oxford University Press.

Piaget, J. (1952). *The origins of intelligence in children.* New York: International Universities Press.

Piaget, J. (1954). *The construction of reality in the child.* New York: Basic Books.

Rogers, P. L. (Ed.). (2002). *Designing instruction for technology-enhanced learning.* Hershey, PA: Idea Group Publishing.

Savery, J. R., & Duffy, T. M. (1996). Problem based learning: An instructional model and its constructivist framework. In B. G. Wilson (Ed.), *Constructivist learning environments: Case studies in instructional design* (pp. 135–148). Englewood Cliffs, NJ: Educational Technology Publications.

Schneiderman, B. (1998). *Designing the user interface: Strategies for effective human-computer interaction* (3rd ed.). Reading, MA: Addison-Wesley.

Schneiderman, B. (2003). *Leonardo's laptop: Human needs and the new computing technologies.* Cambridge, MA: MIT Press.

Shuell, T. J., & Farber, S. L. (2001). Students' perceptions of technology use in college courses. *Journal of Educational Computing Research, 24,* 119–138.

Spector, M. (2000). Designing technology enhanced learning environments. In B. Abbey (Ed.), *Instructional and cognitive impacts of Web-based education* (pp. 241–261). Hershey, PA: Idea Group Publishing.

Tufte, E. (2003, November 9). PowerPoint is evil. *Wired.* Retrieved July 2, 2004, from http://www.wired.com/wired/archive/11.09/ppt2.html

Tuovinen, J. E. (2000). Multimedia distance education interactions. *Educational Media International, 37,* 16–24.

U.S. Copyright Office. (2002). *Copyright law of the United States.* Retrieved July 24, 2004, from http://www.copyright.gov/title17/

Veronikas, S. W., & Shaughnessy, M. F. (2004, July/August). Teaching and learning in a hybrid world: An interview with Carol Twigg. *Educause Review, 39,* 51–62.

Vygotsky, L. (1978). *Mind in society: The development of higher mental processes.* Cambridge, MA: Harvard University Press.

Wagner, E. D., & McCombs, B. L. (1995). Learner-centered psychological principles in practice: Designs for distance education. *Educational Technology, 35,* 32–35.

Wilson, B. G. (Ed.). (1996). *Constructivist learning environments: Case studies in instructional design.* Englewood Cliffs, NJ: Educational Technology Publications.

Yarbrough, D. N. (2001). A comparative analysis of student satisfaction and learning in a computer-assisted environment versus a lecture environment. *Journal on Excellence in College Teaching, 12,* 129–147.

Young, J. R. (2002, March 22). "Hybrid" teaching seeks to end the divide between traditional and online instruction. *Chronicle of Higher Education.* Retrieved July 2, 2004, from http://chronicle.com/free/v48/i28/28a03301.htm

Chapter
12

Teaching Ethics in Introductory Psychology

Mitchell M. Handelsman
University of Colorado at Denver

There is good news and bad news about teaching ethics in introductory psychology courses. First, here's the bad news: There are no chapters devoted to ethics in introductory psychology textbooks. Thus, if we want to teach ethics, we have to improvise the coverage to a much greater extent than we need to with other topics. We must also develop our own notions of why ethics needs to be covered, what material should be involved, and how it is to be taught. But, then there is the good news: There are no chapters devoted to ethics in introductory psychology textbooks. Thus, we can improvise the coverage to a much larger extent than we can with many other topics. And we have much more flexibility to develop our own goals and material for teaching ethics, without feeling as hampered by the text.

One important note before we begin: When I talk about teaching, or covering, ethics, I am not talking about discussing ethics a few times during the semester when it comes up in class (although that is a good idea). Rather, what I am talking about is covering ethics via dedicated class time, lesson plans, learning objectives, test items, or paper topics, the same as we prepare class time on topics like perception and motivation.

The goals for this chapter are, first, to have you consider where you are regarding teaching ethics, and then to take the next step if you want to. For readers who have never considered teaching ethics, the first two sections of the chapter

("Why?" and "Who?") will be the most important. For readers who want to teach ethics but haven't yet, I want to inspire you to take the plunge and teach ethics in effective, rewarding, and personally meaningful ways. If you are a full-fledged member of the choir I am preaching to, and you have already covered ethics in introductory psychology, the first couple sections may serve only to reinforce the choices you have made. The "How?" and "What?" sections may be more useful and expand your repertoire a bit.

WHY?

One way to justify any of our choices and practices in teaching is to think of our goals. We need to ask ourselves how we want students to be different after having taken our course. I contend that teaching ethics can fulfill a variety of goals that we have for our students.

One goal is for students to know more content. Like development, perception, and learning theory, ethics is a topic that students should know about. For example, students can learn about ethical principles that psychologists follow, the ethical standards that psychology shares with other professions, and the research that has been done on ethics.

Another goal is to help students develop particular skills. We want students to be able to act and think like psychologists. Many instructors have sections on statistical reasoning or research design; likewise, it may be desirable to teach students how psychologists think through ethical issues and dilemmas. One advantage to teaching these skills is that although not all students will enter psychology, many will enter fields such as law, medicine, business, accounting, real estate, journalism, and even teaching, all of which have ethics codes and all of which entail the necessity for ethical reasoning. In fact, many authors have published ethical reasoning procedures that are easily adaptable to the introductory psychology classroom (e.g., Corey, Corey, & Callanan, 2003; Handelsman, 1998; Kitchener, 2000; Koocher & Keith-Spiegel, 1998).

We can conceptualize ethical reasoning as a type of critical thinking, which has received much recent attention as a valuable and appropriate skill to be taught in introductory psychology (Halpern, 2003; and see Appleby, chap. 5, this volume). Although most students will not become psychologists, a large percentage of them will become psychotherapy clients (U.S. Department of Health and Human Services, 1999) and/or research participants. Thus, it would be useful for them to know that ethical reasoning is a useful skill.

In addition, learning to think ethically and critically may help students develop the ability to be wise consumers of psychological and other professional services. Again, not all students will go into professions, but all students will encounter professionals in their lives. Giving students a primer on the ethics of psychology is analogous to giving them a primer on critical thinking or statistical reasoning so that they may assess claims made about human behavior by psychologists, journalists, advertisers, and others.

If one of our goals is to have students become better people, covering ethics may help. There is a growing awareness in the literature that college can and should have some impact on the moral development of students, and that classroom discussions and course materials are part of that impact (e.g., Mathiasen, 1998). Teaching ethics in the introductory course may contribute to students' moral sense. Whether they become professionals, or merely interact with professionals, the exposure to ethics in introductory psychology may augment what students receive in other courses.

Why Not?

At this point, consider some of the major arguments against teaching ethics. Of all the arguments I have heard for not teaching ethics in introductory psychology, the most common revolve around issues of time: There is simply too much content and not enough time to cover it. Although I have some sympathy for this position, I would encourage you not to reject ethics completely and forever. Let us not lose sight of the fact that we are constantly making choices and value judgments about what the introductory course is about and how we teach it. For example, only recently has cultural diversity surfaced in texts and introductory classes. What did it replace? Likewise, issues such as statistics, research methods, and brain function may be gaining coverage time, as well.

Another argument against teaching ethics is that it is not relevant enough in introductory psychology. Some might argue that although ethics relates to how we go about *doing* psychology, it is not psychology itself. However, most of us would probably agree that it is important for students to realize that psychologists take ethics seriously (APA, 2002). Ethics does run through all of what psychologists do, even more so than do statistics or research methods. For instance, questions about confidentiality occur in relation to research participants, clients, students, consultees, and even callers to radio shows.

Finally, some would say that the introductory course is not the time. They would argue that ethics should be taught when students are seniors, when they are more developed in their thinking about psychology. I would argue that we provide basic information and skills in the introductory class about statistics, research design, and other topics, and then augment that information with specific upper-division courses (and as part of additional courses). In a similar way, information about ethics can be introduced very well at the introductory level and then augmented in advanced classes.

We should not think of students interacting with professionals in the future tense: Students are already involved with a psychologist in the role of teacher, and many are involved in the introductory class as participants in research conducted by psychologists. This means that students already have an immediate stake in knowing and thinking about psychology's ethics. It also means that all instructors are participating in activities that relate to ethics.

To wind up this section, I invite you to try this little exercise. It will give you a sense of what is important to you, and also how you might feel about covering ethics. First, think about the introductory psychology topic that is closest to your heart, whether it be development, statistics, learning, perception, social, or whatever. Now, put that topic into the blanks and rate the extent of your agreement with each of these sentences. Then, go back and do the same with "ethics" in the blanks:

Teaching (and learning about) _____ is important because:

1. _____ is an integral part of psychology.
2. _____ is the subject of some very interesting research in psychology.
3. Knowing _____ is just part of being an educated person.
4. Studying _____ will help students in their other college courses.
5. _____ has lots of practical applications.
6. _____ has always been considered an important topic.
7. _____ can be very important in students' lives.
8. Studying _____ will help students be better students in general.
9. _____ will help students become critical thinkers.
10. Studying _____ will make students better people.
11. _____ (fill in your own).

This exercise should give you a sense of your initial justifications for teaching ethics, or anything else.

WHO?

Teaching introductory psychology is a difficult job under the best of circumstances. For most of us, the course means that we need to stretch the range of our expertise into areas that we have not studied intensely (see Dunn, Schmidt, & Zaremba, chap. 3, this volume). But I have good news: Given the ubiquity of ethical issues in psychology, I contend that the opportunities are great for all instructors to utilize their existing expertise and develop the competence to teach ethics at this level. For example, many experimental psychologists can talk knowledgeably about the care and use of animals, adequate training of research assistants, and other research issues. Social psychologists can talk about issues such as using deception or giving false feedback to research participants. Those with a clinical background can talk about issues in therapy such as confidentiality and informed consent. At the very least, instructors have the ability to talk with students about the ethical issues they (teachers *and* students) face every day.

WHEN?

The reason I have a separate section on When (other than the gestalt of the headings in this chapter) is to reiterate a critical point: When I talk about covering ethics in relation to other topics (e.g., research, social, development), I am not talking about spending the last few minutes of class—after watching the film—telling students about how Milgram's (1974) studies couldn't be done today. That is fine to do, and sprinkling bits of ethics into several units is great, but that is not what I consider covering ethics. I am talking about treating it like other topics that are given explicit and planned class time (although it may be part of another unit) and assessed on examinations or papers.

That said, and given that there are no chapters devoted to ethics in introductory books, the choice of exactly when to cover ethics during the introductory course is entirely up to us. As we shall see in the "What?" section, ethics can be covered in relation to many different topics. Thus, decisions about when to cover ethics are wholly based on our own backgrounds and expertise, our comfort level with the issues, and what we want to cover about ethics.

HOW?

Certainly, the techniques of teaching we use flow from the content we want to cover, and we will explore some specific examples shortly. For now, I want to share some ideas about techniques that apply to any ethics topic we cover.

If we want students to know ethics in more than an abstract way, it helps to have them use what they are learning. Thus, as with most topics, it is a good idea to augment whatever lecturing we do with active learning opportunities for students. In other words, we want students to be *engaged,* which includes becoming emotionally involved (Mosenthal, 1999) and interacting with other students (Guthrie & Anderson, 1999; Skinner & Belmont, 1993). One way to accomplish this is to make issues as experiential for students as possible. We need to help students relate the material to their own experience, discuss cases from the media or other sources, and create experiences in the classroom that confront students with ethical situations.

Ethical issues are particularly well-suited to collaborative learning methods, for two reasons. First, ethics is an inherently social enterprise because it involves the welfare and treatment of others. Thus, having students interact with each other is a way to help them learn and experience ethical concepts such as respectfulness, humility, and competence. Second, the research shows that collaborative strategies are successful not only in helping students learn but in improving the "quality of interactions with classmates" (Cooper & Mueck, 1990, p. 71). Johnson, Johnson, and Smith (1991), Millis and Cottell (1998), and Silberman (1996) all published very useful compendia of collaborative learning strategies.

A particularly appropriate strategy that can be adapted to many ethics discussions is *structured controversy* (also called academic controversy; Johnson & Johnson, 1997). As described by Millis and Cottell (1998), structured controversy is a way to "examine issues for which there are no 'right answers'" (p. 140). This technique occurs primarily in groups of four. All four students discuss the support for both sides of an issue, and then two students take each side. Each pair argues a side, and then the group discusses both sides of the "debate" with the intention of learning as much as possible about both viewpoints. Then the pairs switch sides and argue for the position they previously argued against. Then "the team works together to synthesize their findings and prepare a group report" (p. 142), which may or may not be presented to the entire class.

The topics for structured controversies can come from case studies (e.g., Should a therapist publish client information in a scholarly article? Is a researcher justified in using deception in a study on gossip?) or from more general topics (e.g., Should elder abuse be a reason to violate confidentiality? Should people have the right to commit suicide?; Szasz, 1999; Werth, 1999).

Another useful strategy is called *think–pair–share* (Millis & Cottell, 1998). The basic outline is very simple: Instructors present students with a question, dilemma, or other task to think about—and write about—for a few minutes on their own. Students then turn to a person next to them or behind them, share their answers with each other, and develop an answer that is better than either individual answer. Instructors then call on random pairs (or all pairs in smaller classes) and have them report on their answers. Think–pair–share has many advantages: It is quick to prepare and execute, it can be used easily in classes of any size, and it can incorporate short writing experiences as well as discussion.

WHAT?

Depending on the goals we have for incorporating ethics into the course, we can choose what to cover, at what time in the course, and how to get students engaged in the learning process. In this regard, I have more good news: Ethics can be defined and approached in a variety of different ways. This section explores four categories of ethics (although I am not suggesting that the lines between them are solid): everyday ethics, professional ethics, the ethics of teaching itself, and ethical issues specific to psychology.

Everyday Ethics

One way to teach ethics is to approach it as a set of principles that apply to decisions that people make in "everyday" (i.e., nonprofessional) relationships. Issues of power, honesty, and loyalty may be especially relevant to students, who are continuously working out these issues with parents, other family members, significant others, teachers, supervisors, coworkers, and fellow students. Class discussions might focus on questions such as the following: Should a worker lie to a boss to protect a coworker who is playing video games on the job? What should a student do who accidentally obtains a copy of last year's test questions? Do parents have a right to search their adolescent child's room? Students may be especially willing to talk about the ethics of the television industry's recent "reality" shows that are often based on lies told to unsuspecting people about important issues like money and marital status. These discussions can also integrate some course topics, including moral development, altruism, and social traps such as the prisoner's dilemma.

Resources for instructors abound. Some good books include those by Kidder (1995) and by Gardner, Csikszentmihalyi, and Damon (2001), who talked about integrating ethics into work. These books can help introduce some of the moral values and principles that guide both personal and professional behavior, such as telling the truth, loyalty, and justice. Also, a growing number of colleges and universities have recognized the importance of teaching ethics in a variety of courses, and they have started programs in Ethics Across the Curriculum (see http://www.rit.edu/~692awww/seac/). Instructors can find valuable information and resources from these programs and from a variety of ethics centers. A comprehensive list of such centers can be found at http://www.uvsc.edu/ethics/other.html. Case examples, including those about social, family, personal, and academic ethics, can be found at http://www.uvsc.edu/ethics/casestudies/ and http:// ethics. sandiego.edu/resources/cases/HomeOverview.asp.

Covering everyday ethics provides a good opportunity to introduce issues of academic dishonesty, such as cheating and plagiarism (Davis, Grover, Becker, & McGregor, 1992; Deikhoff, LaBeff, Clark, Williams, & Haines, 1996; Genereux & McLeod, 1995; Graham, Monday, O'Brien, & Steffen, 1994; Tang & Zwo, 1997). Discussions of these issues in the context of ethical principles may serve the dual purposes of facilitating learning of course content and helping make the academic dishonesty policies in the syllabus more relevant and meaningful to students. For example, we can have students discuss the characteristics of an academic community and the roles and obligations of its members. To increase engagement, we can have students develop, perhaps in small groups, academic dishonesty policies for the class itself.

Professional Ethics

Students are and will be consumers of many different professional services. If one of our goals is to create good consumers of professional services, then discussing professional ethics is a good opportunity to introduce concepts that are not only applicable to psychology but are generalizable to all professions. For example, when I was shopping for a house many years ago, I was shocked to learn that real estate agents *always* worked for sellers and represented their interests, not mine. This fact changed my feelings and my strategies in this important enterprise.

Perhaps the most well-formulated set of professional ethical principles are those from biomedical ethics, formulated by Beauchamp and Childress (2001) and also explored by psychologists (e.g., Kitchener, 2000). These general principles and rules include autonomy (respect clients' rights and ability to make decisions), nonmaleficence (do no harm), beneficence (provide good, prevent harm), justice (treat equals equally), fidelity (keep promises), and veracity (tell the truth). These principles can be applied to the professional relationships that students may already have with doctors, bosses, police officers, attorneys, academic counselors, businesspeople, and journalists (relationships with teachers are discussed in the next section). For example, students might discuss how they feel and react when they are called by a "survey firm" that is really trying to sell a product, or whether a doctor should tell an adolescent's parents if that adolescent has a sexually transmitted disease.

Ethical dilemmas often stem from conflicts between the principles of autonomy and beneficence. An interesting exercise would be to have students, perhaps in groups, identify such dilemmas across a range of professions, and weigh the two principles. For example, students could discuss the cases of a physician who acts paternalistically (i.e., overriding autonomy for beneficent ends) by providing treatment that a patient does not want, and a legislator who votes against the expressed wishes of her constituents because she believes she knows better what would be best for them. Involuntary hospitalization of mentally ill people represents the same kind of autonomy versus beneficence dilemma.

In contrast to ethics based on adherence to a set of external principles, psychologists and others have recently been talking about virtue-based ethics (Jordan & Meara, 1990; Kitchener, 1996). These authors maintain that people need to develop internal virtues, characteristics such as prudence, integrity, benevolence, and respectfulness (Meara, Schmidt, & Day, 1996). The parallels between the principle versus virtue ethics discussion in the literature and the person–situation controversy in psychology are striking and useful. We might ask students to discuss the extent to which professionals are ethical because of the situation they are in (the profession has principles and codes), and because they have and exhibit personality traits that would be called virtuous.

Ethics discussion ideas and examples from a variety of professions are very easy to come by. Unfortunately, it has become amazingly easy to gather cases from the news media. We can find stories about unethical behavior in various professions: journalists faking their stories, members of the clergy engaging in questionable behaviors, academics falsifying their vitae, and deceptive business practices such as falsifying profit statements or knowingly marketing dangerous products. Thus, we have ample material to present (or to have students present), and the similarities across professional categories of issues such as trust, fidelity, and exploitation of power can be highlighted. The Internet is also a good source of cases (see, e.g., http://www.chowan.edu/acadp/ethics/studies.htm, which lists cases from business, accounting, journalism, engineering, the military, the media, medicine, as well as some from research and psychology).

Role-plays may also work well in covering professional ethics. Students could role-play cases based on a structured controversy debate. They can also role-play multiple sides of the issues, or alternative solutions to ethical problems. Having students switch between role-playing clients and professionals can give them an experience of the different pressures and perspectives of various stakeholders. For example, research participants want to choose whether or not to complete particular questionnaires, but researchers want complete data.

The Ethics of Teaching

Bridging the space between general ethics and psychology ethics is the activity of teaching. Instructors can make ethics personally relevant to themselves as well as to students by discussing the ethics of their own teaching behaviors

(Keith-Spiegel, Wittig, Perkins, Balogh, & Whitley, 1993). Covering the ethics of teaching has the benefits of introducing students to a major area of psychology ethics, providing information to students so that they can be better partners with faculty in the academic enterprise, and being immediately relevant, experiential, and engaging. The opportunities for demonstrations (of ethical behavior) and experiences are wonderful.

Among the issues we can explore are the *four C's of professional ethics*: competence, consent, confidentiality, and conflicts of interest. For example, we can have students discuss, debate, role-play, and/or experience questions such as the following: Can our department ask us to teach a course that we are not qualified to teach? Does teaching involve competences beyond knowledge of the material and good intentions? Are teachers ethically obligated to update their teaching methods in addition to their content? Must students be informed about, and consent to, exercises that might cause some discomfort? Can we post students' grades in public? What information about our students can we share with other faculty in the lounge? Can students and professors engage in romantic relationships? Can professors sell their own books to students?

Ethical issues can be found in almost any academic interactions once we decide to look for them. For example, we can think back to the last time students accused us of giving tests that were "unfair." What a wonderful teaching opportunity to discuss the ethical principles that underlie two possible interpretations of the students' concerns. Students might mean "unfair" in the sense of violating the principle of justice, or treating students unequally on the basis of some irrelevant variable such as ink color or physical attractiveness. Thus, two students who performed equally well on the exam would get unequal grades. More likely, however, students are invoking the principle of competence by alleging that the questions are so bad that they are not an effective indicator of learning. (Sometimes, of course, "unfair" simply means "too difficult.")

Any time we do anything other than lecture, such as demonstrations or experiential exercises in class, we can also cover ethics by exploring the ethics of the exercise itself. For example, I once taught a unit on assertiveness by walking into class, sitting down, and not starting to teach until a student asked me to (Handelsman & Friedlander, 1984). Many students felt uncomfortable with this situation (four classes of students spent the hour-long period in silence). The next day we discussed what happened and what the exercise demonstrated about assertiveness and the choices that were available to them. Then the question arose, "Is it acceptable, ethical, for professors to put students into uncomfortable positions as a way to help them learn?" This question was a perfect segue to introducing concepts such as nonmaleficence, beneficence, cost–benefit analysis, and competence.

Another way to cover teaching issues is to look at the empirical psychological literature on ethics in teaching, thereby introducing ethics as an area of empirical investigation. For example, surveys exist on the ethics of various teaching behaviors as judged by both teachers (Tabachnick, Keith-Spiegel, & Pope, 1991) and students (Keith-Spiegel, Tabachnick, & Allen, 1993). These surveys show that students and teachers agree to a large extent on the ethics of many teaching behaviors, such as sexual comments or behaviors, teaching under the influence of drugs, and requiring student self-disclosure. When there was disagreement between teachers and students, the students were typically more lenient in their judgments. For example, faculty having a part-time job was judged more ethical by students, as was faculty requiring students to give electric shocks to rats (Keith-Spiegel et al., 1993).

As we move closer to the interface between teaching and other "psychology" behaviors, we can begin to show how psychologists as teachers, therapists, and researchers share some common ethical constraints and aspirations. For example, in one small class (which, in the interests of full disclosure, was not an introductory course) I had two visitors in class who were actually there to observe me for a teaching award (which I did not get). But I did not tell the students the visitors' agenda right away. Rather, I asked the students—with the visitors by my side—whether I was ethically obligated to inform the students of the purpose of the visit, and/or seek their consent to have the visitors in the class. During the discussion, we reviewed what students had read about the ethical doctrine of informed consent, and how that doctrine might be applied differently in therapist–client relationships versus teacher–student relationships. Students were very active in this discussion because they were living the situation as well as discussing it. And I was involved, too, because my students were telling me about my obligations and potentially unethical behavior in the presence of two respected colleagues.

Other useful parallels exist between the teaching relationship and other relationships in which psychologists engage. For example, the course syllabus can be seen as an informed consent document (Handelsman, Rosen, & Arguello, 1987). Policies on posting grades can be compared to the privacy of research data or the privacy of psychotherapeutic communications. Another interesting discussion can emerge from exploring how we develop and maintain technical competence as therapists, teachers, and researchers.

Ethics Specific to Psychology

Having explored the ethics of teaching, let us now examine some of the other tasks that psychologists have: research, therapy, consultation, administration. If you want to focus your coverage on psychology ethics, the American Psychological Association's (APA, 2002) Ethical Principles of Psychologists and Code of Conduct is a good place to start. Students need to know that the APA has a code of ethics (available online at http://www.apa.org/ethics). Books about the code are very good resources (e.g., Knapp & VandeCreek, 2003). Cases based on the code are readily available as well (e.g., G. Corey, M. S. Corey, & Callanan, 2003; Kitchener, 2000; Koocher & Keith-Spiegel, 1998; Nagy, 2000). Instructors who cover the history of psychology can explore the development of the APA code from its original form (APA, 1953). Other APA guidelines may be of interest on units about cultural diversity (APA, 1991) and divorce (APA, 1994).

One of the dangers in talking about ethics codes is that there is a tendency to talk about rules and about violations of the rules. It is exciting and interesting—but limiting—to talk about people who violate the rules in the most flagrant fashion or engage in the most striking examples of unethical behavior. For example, therapists who have sex with clients, or experimenters who take advantage of participants for their own selfish reasons (Bill Murray's character in the movie *Ghostbusters*—Reitman, 1984—is a great example). The outcome may be that students learn that ethics is merely a set of rules and constraints, and that unethical behaviors are rampant, extreme, and easily identifiable.

To counteract this tendency, we can take a more positive and comprehensive view of ethics, and look at more than how people break the rules (Handelsman, Knapp, & Gottlieb, 2002). We can explore aspirational principles, which are positive goals that we strive for rather than a list of proscriptions that will help us avoid litigation. The aspirational principles listed in the APA (2002) code include beneficence, integrity, and respect for the rights and dignity of people. As an example, let us say an instructor wants to decide between two equally effective grading policies, neither of which violates any ethical standards. Some would say that there is no ethical dimension to such a decision. However, we can still ask students to consider this question from the perspective of the instructor: Which grading policy is more respectful of students?

Some might argue that aspirational principles give students a view of psychology that is too positive, or that such concepts might be too advanced for students at the introductory level. In response, I draw an analogy with research, which is also a very complex topic. Students should have some idea of how research is done when it is at its best, even though in the real world we know that not all studies have pure experimental designs, equal *n*s, or interpretable interactions. Likewise, students can get a sense that ethics is something they can aspire to, and that adherence to ethical principles, like adherence to good research design, leads to better outcomes.

Several excellent ethics texts offer instructors good background information, cases for discussion, and other resources (Bersoff, 1999; Corey et al., 2003; Kitchener, 2000; Koocher & Keith-Spiegel, 1998; Nagy, 2000; Pope & Vasquez, 1998). For example, Corey et al. (2003) provided a series of self-exploration exercises that are very engaging for students. Bersoff (1999) brought together a wealth of published work in all aspects of the field, including forensic psychology and the business aspects of psychology.

Research Ethics.   Students read about research methods and findings throughout the entire semester. Perhaps the most common discussions of research ethics occur when the Milgram studies are covered in class and issues of deception arise (e.g., Baumrind, 1985). Other issues for discussion include confidentiality, informed consent, debriefing, working with culturally diverse populations of participants, and compensation for participants. Several excellent classroom exercises have been collected in APA's *Activities Handbook for the Teaching of Psychology* (Vol. 3; Makosky, Sileo, Whittemore, Landry, &

Skutley, 1990), including several dealing with issues around research with animals. (This book also includes a useful bibliography on ethical issues.) For example, Reese (1990) described an exercise in which students read APA's *Guidelines for Ethical Conduct in the Care and Use of Animals* (available at http://www.apa.org/science/anguide.html) and then analyzed animal research that is described in popular press articles.

Many students get a firsthand exposure to research ethics when they participate in research during the semester, either as volunteers in outside research or as part of a departmental research participation requirement. Any course that has a research participation requirement has a built-in ethics component that can be utilized. For example, Ruth Ault of Davidson College (personal communication, January 22, 2004) requires her students to write a paper about their participation in research that details their ethical treatment. This assignment has the dual benefit of helping students learn about what ethical treatment means, and sensitizing students to ethical issues while they are interacting with professionals.

Ault also uses a combination of strategies to teach research ethics: First, she has students read parts of ethics codes, then lectures on ethical issues in class. Second, she has students write about cases based on research studies. Third, she has groups of 8–10 students discuss what they have written. Finally, she has students discuss the cases in the larger class.

An example of an experiential and collaborative exercise is to have groups of students design a research participation policy for the psychology department (see Sieber & Saks, 1989). The discussions can incorporate the APA (2002) ethics code, general principles, the virtues necessary, or any other ethical content. An interesting twist is to have different groups, or different students within each group, take the roles of interested parties, such as students, researchers who would be using the participant pool, instructors, school officials, and/or others.

Again, if our goals include teaching about empirical research, we can cover the growing empirical literature on ethics in research. For example, researchers have explored the validity of consent to research among children, the cognitively impaired (Stanley, Sieber, & Melton, 1987), and persons with mental illnesses (Lidz et al., 1984). Researchers have also studied such issues as student reactions to research participation requirements (Nimmer & Handelsman, 1992) and how ethical practice is reported in journal articles (Sigmon, Boulard, & Whitcomb-Smith, 2002).

Therapy Ethics.   Here is my favorite case to introduce ethical issues in therapy:

> Dr. Newman is just getting started as a psychotherapist. He has just come from his new house (with a big mortgage) in his new car (with big payments) to his new office (with big rent due every month). One of his first appointments is with an attractive woman, Ms. Eldridge, who is deciding whether to come for therapy. She reports that she has been experiencing panic attacks ever since she inherited a large amount of money from a rich relative.

Dr. Newman has little experience with panic disorders and knows a colleague who could treat this client much better than he could. As he looks out the window at his big car from his expensive office, however, Dr. Newman decides not only to treat Ms. Eldridge, but to charge her twice his normal fee. Moreover, he assures the client that she needs two sessions a week. Ms. Eldridge does not know what psychologists usually charge, but she has heard that some clients need more than one session a week. She decides to enter treatment with Dr. Newman. (Handelsman, 1998, p. 80, Copyright © 1998 by Pearson Education. Reprinted by permission of the publisher.)

To get students to feel more involved, I will tell them not to put themselves in the place of the therapist, but to imagine that they are a close friend or relative of Ms. Eldridge. I ask students to comment about whether or not they see anything wrong with Dr. Newman's behavior, and then play the devil's advocate. For example, in response to arguments that Dr. Newman overcharged his client, I suggest that this is America and we have a free market system. When students protest that there is another therapist who is better, I challenge students: "Does that mean that only the best therapist, doctor, lawyer, *college professor*, is allowed to work? If so, I can leave now!"

This case has never failed to spur lively discussion, even in classes of well over 100 students. Eventually, the discussion gets to some of the fundamental differences between professional relationships and strictly business relationships, power differentials, the potential exploitation of clients, and the need for ethical guidelines. From this starting point, I feel very comfortable lecturing on, leading a discussion about, or splitting the class into small groups to work on cases regarding any number of other issues, including informed consent, confidentiality (especially with minors; Gustafson & McNamara, 1987), and competence.

The issue of sexual exploitation of clients always gets students' attention (Pope, 1988; Pope & Bouhoutsos, 1986), but this blatant issue often does not stimulate as much discussion as some more subtle dual relationships and conflicts of interest such as therapists entering into business relationships with clients or accepting friends as clients (Kitchener, 1988). Gottlieb (1993) published a great decision-making rubric to help therapists determine if adding another relationship onto a therapy relationship is acceptable. Using this rubric on a variety of cases may be a good exercise for small groups of students.

Ethical issues revolving around diversity can be covered in dealing with competence to do therapy with people of different cultures (APA, 1991; D. W. Sue & D. Sue, 1990; Vasquez, 1996). Cases can be easily adapted for this purpose. For example, we can identify Ms. Eldridge and Dr. Newman as members of diverse populations and provide information about their level of acculturation and other cultural variables.

Alan Tjeltveit of Muhlenberg College (personal communication, January 21, 2004) does an exercise that spans both everyday ethics and professional ethics by exploring the value of helping others, which is inherent not only in psychotherapy but in all of psychology. He calls this exercise, "Change to What Good Ends." He provides a case about a suicidal person and asks students to consider what his life would look like if he got better. Then, he ties in personal ethics and values by asking students to consider their *own* lives, and what the good life would look like for them personally. Students reflect on their own moral values and explore the application of those values to a helping relationship. This process also lays a wonderful foundation for studying the psychotherapy chapter more effectively.

Finally, a growing body of empirical research exists regarding therapy ethics. Researchers have investigated issues such as therapists' own judgments about the ethical dilemmas they face (Pope, Tabachnick, & Keith-Spiegel, 1987; Pope & Vetter, 1992), attitudes of clients toward managed mental health care (Pomerantz, 2000), and the readability and effects on potential clients of written informed consent forms (Sullivan, Martin, & Handelsman, 1993).

CONCLUSIONS

Ethics is not one of psychology's "big issues" (Myers, 2004, p. 9). But because you have made it through this chapter, let me suggest that it could be a theme that can be used to tie together various elements of a course. Ethics as a theme offers great opportunities to tie in issues of development, social psychology, personality, research, and therapy. Whether ethics is taught as a general theme running throughout the course, or simply as a subtopic in a unit on research or therapy, covering ethics gives students a clearer picture of psychology. My hope is that this chapter has convinced you of both the value and the fun of exposing introductory students to ethical issues.

ACKNOWLEDGMENT

The author gratefully acknowledges the expert editorial assistance of Margie Krest.

REFERENCES

American Psychological Association. (1953). *Ethical standards of psychologists.* Washington, DC: Author.

American Psychological Association. (1991). *Guidelines for providers of psychological services to ethnic, linguistic, and culturally diverse populations.* Washington, DC: Author.

American Psychological Association. (1994). Guidelines for child custody evaluations in divorce proceedings. *American Psychologist, 49,* 677–680.

American Psychological Association. (2002). Ethical principles of psychologists and code of conduct. *American Psychologist, 57,* 1060–1073.

Baumrind, D. (1985). Research using intentional deception: Ethical issues revisited. *American Psychologist, 40,* 165–174.

Beauchamp, T. L., & Childress, J. F. (2001). *Principles of biomedical ethics* (5th ed.). New York: Oxford University Press.

Bersoff, D. N. (1999). *Ethical conflicts in psychology* (2nd ed.). Washington, DC: American Psychological Association.

Cooper, J., & Mueck, R. (1990). Student involvement in learning: Cooperative learning and college instruction. *Journal of Excellence in College Teaching, 1,* 68–76.

Corey, G., Corey, M. S., & Callanan, P. (2003). *Issues and ethics in the helping professions* (6th ed.). Pacific Grove, CA: Brooks/Cole.

Davis, S. F., Grover, C. A., Becker, A. H., & McGregor, L. N. (1992). Academic dishonesty: Prevalence, determinants, techniques, and punishments. *Teaching of Psychology, 19,* 16–20.

Deikhoff, G. M., LaBeff, E. E., Clark, R. E., Williams, L. E., & Haines, V. J. (1996). College cheating: Ten years later. *Research in Higher Education, 37*(4), 487–502.

Gardner, H., Csikszentmihalyi, M., & Damon, W. (2001). *Good work: When excellence and ethics meet.* New York: Basic Books.

Genereux, R. L., & McLeod, B. A. (1995). Circumstances surrounding cheating: A questionnaire study of college students. *Research in Higher Education, 36*(6), 687–704.

Gottlieb, M. C. (1993). Avoiding exploitive dual relationships: A decision-making model. *Psychotherapy, 30,* 41–48.

Graham, M. A., Monday, J., O'Brien, K., & Steffen, S. (1994). Cheating at small colleges: An examination of student and faculty attitudes and behavior. *Journal of College Student Development, 35*(4), 255–260.

Gustafson, K. E., & McNamara, J. R. (1987). Confidentiality with minor clients: Issues and guidelines for therapists. *Professional Psychology: Research and Practice, 18,* 503–508.

Guthrie, J. T., & Anderson, E. (1999). Engagement in reading: Processes of motivated, strategic, knowledgeable, social readers. In J. T. Guthrie & D. E. Alvermann (Eds.), *Engaged reading: Processes, practices, and policy implications* (pp. 17–45). New York: Teacher's College Press.

Halpern, D. F. (2003). *Thought and knowledge: An introduction to critical thinking* (4th ed.). Mahwah, NJ: Lawrence Erlbaum Associates.

Handelsman, M. M. (1998). Ethics and ethical reasoning. In S. Cullari (Ed.), *Foundations of clinical psychology* (pp. 80–111). Needham Heights, MA: Allyn & Bacon.

Handelsman, M. M., & Friedlander, B. L. (1984). The use of an experiential exercise to teach about assertiveness. *Teaching of Psychology, 11,* 54–56.

Handelsman, M. M., Knapp, S., & Gottlieb, M. C. (2002). Positive ethics. In C. R. Snyder & S. J. Lopez (Eds.), *Handbook of positive psychology* (pp. 731–744). Oxford, England: Oxford University Press.

Handelsman, M. M., Rosen, J., & Arguello, A. (1987). Informed consent of students: How much information is enough? *Teaching of Psychology, 14,* 107–109.

Johnson, D. W., & Johnson, R. T. (1997). Academic controversy: Increase intellectual conflict and increase the quality of learning. In W. E. Campbell & K. A. Smith (Eds.), *New paradigms for college teaching* (pp. 211–241). Edina, MN: Interaction Book Company.

Johnson, D. W., Johnson, R. T., & Smith, K. A. (1991). *Active learning: Cooperation in the college classroom.* Edina, MN: Interaction Book Company.

Jordan, A. E., & Meara, N. M. (1990). Ethics and professional practice of psychologists: The role of virtues and principles. *Professional Psychology: Research and Practice, 21,* 107–114.

Keith-Spiegel, P. C., Tabachnick, B. G., & Allen, M. (1993). Ethics in academia: Students' views of professor's actions. *Ethics and Behavior, 3,* 149–162.

Keith-Spiegel, P., Wittig, A. F., Perkins, D. V., Balogh, D. W., & Whitley, B. E., Jr. (1993). *The ethics of teaching: A casebook.* Muncie, IN: Ball State University.

Kidder, R. M. (1995). *How good people make tough choices.* New York: William Morrow.

Kitchener, K. S. (1988). Dual role relationships: What makes them so problematic? *Journal of Counseling and Development, 67,* 217–221.

Kitchener, K. S. (1996). There is more to ethics than principles. *The Counseling Psychologist, 24,* 92–97.

Kitchener, K. S. (2000). *Foundations of ethical practice, research, and teaching in psychology*. Mahwah, NJ: Lawrence Erlbaum Associates.

Knapp, S., & VandeCreek, L. (2003). *A guide to the 2002 revision of the American Psychological Association's Ethics Code*. Sarasota, FL: Professional Resource Press.

Koocher, G. P., & Keith-Spiegel, P. (1998). *Ethics in psychology: Professional standards and cases* (2nd ed.). New York: Oxford University Press.

Lidz, C. W., Meisel, A., Zerubavel, E., Carter, M., Sestak, R., & Roth, L. H. (1984). *Informed consent: A study of decision making in psychiatry*. New York: Guilford.

Makosky, V. P., Sileo, C. C., Whittemore, L. G., Landry, C. P., & Skutley M. L. (Eds.). (1990). *Activities handbook for the teaching of psychology* (Vol. 3). Washington, DC: American Psychological Association.

Mathiasen, R. E. (1998). Moral education of college students: Faculty and staff perspectives. *College Student Journal, 32,* 374–377.

Meara, N. M., Schmidt, L. D., & Day, J. D. (1996). Principles and virtues: A foundation for ethical decisions, policies, and character. *The Counseling Psychologist, 24*(1), 4–77.

Milgram, S. (1974). *Obedience to authority*. New York: Harper & Row.

Millis, B. J., & Cottell, P. G., Jr. (1998). *Cooperative learning for higher education faculty*. Westport, CT: Oryx Press.

Mosenthal, P. B. (1999). Understanding engagement: Historical and political contexts. In J. T. Guthrie & D. E. Alvermann (Eds.), *Engaged reading: Processes, practices, and policy implications* (pp. 1–16). New York: Teacher's College Press.

Myers, D. G. (2004). *Psychology: Seventh edition in modules*. New York: Worth.

Nagy, T. F. (2000). *Ethics in plain English: An illustrative casebook for psychologists*. Washington, DC: American Psychological Association.

Nimmer, J. G., & Handelsman, M. M. (1992). Effects of subject pool policy on student attitudes toward psychology and psychological research. *Teaching of Psychology, 19,* 141–144.

Pomerantz, A. M. (2000). What if prospective clients knew how managed care impacts psychologists' practice and ethics? An exploratory study. *Ethics and Behavior, 10,* 159–171.

Pope, K. S. (1988). How clients are harmed by sexual contact with mental health professionals: The syndrome and its prevalence. *Journal of Counseling and Development, 67,* 222–226.

Pope, K. S., & Bouhoutsos, J. (1986). *Sexual intimacy between therapists and patients*. New York: Praeger.

Pope, K. S., Tabachnick, B. G., & Keith-Spiegel, P. (1987). Ethics of practice: The beliefs and behaviors of psychologists as therapists. *American Psychologist, 42,* 993–1006.

Pope, K. S., & Vasquez, M. J. T. (1998). *Ethics in psychotherapy and counseling* (2nd ed.). San Francisco: Jossey-Bass.

Pope, K. S., & Vetter, V. (1992). Ethical dilemmas encountered by members of the American Psychological Association. *American Psychologist, 47,* 397–411.

Reese, E. P. (1990). Analyzing the value and ethics of animal research that is reported in the popular press. In V. P. Makosky, C. C. Sileo, L. G. Whittemore, C. P. Landry, & M. L. Skutley (Eds.), *Activities handbook for the teaching of psychology* (Vol. 3, pp. 261–265). Washington, DC: American Psychological Association.

Reitman, I. (Producer/Director). (1984). *Ghostbusters* [Motion picture]. United States: Columbia Pictures.

Sieber, J. E., & Saks, M. J. (1989). A census of subject pool characteristics and policies. *American Psychologist, 44,* 1053–1061.

Sigmon, S. T., Boulard, N. E., & Whitcomb-Smith, S. (2002). Reporting ethical practices in journal articles. *Ethics & Behavior, 12,* 261–275.

Silberman, M. (1996). *Active learning: 101 strategies to teach any subject.* Boston: Allyn & Bacon.

Skinner, E. A., & Belmont, M. J. (1993). Motivation in the classroom: Reciprocal effects of teacher behavior and student engagement across the school year. *Journal of Educational Psychology, 85,* 571–581.

Stanley, B., Sieber, J. E., & Melton, G. B. (1987). Empirical studies of ethical issues in research: A research agenda. *American Psychologist, 42,* 735–741.

Sue, D. W., & Sue, D. (1990). *Counseling the culturally different: Theory and practice* (2nd ed.). New York: Wiley.

Sullivan, T., Martin, W. L., Jr., & Handelsman, M. M. (1993). Practical benefits of an informed consent procedure: An empirical investigation. *Professional Psychology: Research and Practice, 24,* 160–163.

Szasz, T. (1999). *Fatal freedom. The ethics and politics of suicide.* Westport, CT: Praeger.

Tang, S., & Zwo, J. (1997). Profile of college examination cheaters. *College Student Journal, 31*(3), 340–347.

Tabachnick, B. G., Keith-Spiegel, P., & Pope, K. S. (1991). Ethics of teaching: Beliefs and behaviors of psychologists as educators. *American Psychologist, 46,* 506–515.

U.S. Department of Health and Human Services. (1999). *Mental health: A report of the surgeon general—executive summary.* Rockville, MD: U.S. Department of Health and Human Services, Substance Abuse and Mental Health Services Administration, Center for Mental Health Services, National Institutes of Health, National Institute of Mental Health.

Vasquez, M. J. T. (1996). Will virtue ethics improve ethical conduct in multicultural settings and interactions? *The Counseling Psychologist, 24,* 98–104.

Werth, J. L., Jr. (Ed.). (1999). *Contemporary perspectives on rational suicide.* Philadelphia: Taylor & Francis.

III

Assessment

Chapter

13

Standards and Outcomes: Encouraging Best Practices in Teaching Introductory Psychology

Randolph A. Smith
Kennesaw State University

Amy C. Fineburg
Spain Park High School

The introductory psychology class is a dynamic monster. Psychology evolves and grows with each new discovery, each new technology, each new idea. The daunting task before each introductory psychology instructor is to keep up to date with these discoveries, technologies, and ideas so students not only get accurate information, but also a good picture of psychology as a discipline today. When psychology formally began in 1879, psychologists sought to discover what the mind was. Through the years, psychology progressed through just about every imaginable perspective—Freud's racy theories of the unconscious, Watson's bold behaviorist vision, Maslow's ideas of human potential—to settle into the bio–social–cultural–behavioral–cognitive milieu now taught in introductory psychology. Introductory psychology is in the unique position of presenting this rich history of psychology and the up-to-the-minute ideas that are transforming modern views of behavior.

Add students who have varied preconceived notions about what psychology is (e.g., see Chew, chap. 15, this volume), and the recipe for a great intellectual challenge is in place.

A CRITICAL NEED FOR STANDARDS

In the past, instructors had limited resources with which to plan lessons and lectures in introductory psychology, so they had to rely on their knowledge of the subject to determine the scope and sequence of what to teach. When psychology was not as diverse as it is today, instructors' expertise was more limited, and their knowledge of psychology was more focused. Today, psychology instructors can hold doctoral or master's degrees in a variety of psychological subfields or a bachelor's degree in psychology or social studies education. Psychology instructors teach at middle schools, high schools, community colleges, technical schools, and 4-year colleges and universities. The diversity of psychology instructors and instructional environments, combined with the discipline's vast and varied emphases, make it important for psychologists to address the question of the core canon of skills and knowledge. This core canon should address not only the issue of what to teach, but should also define where psychology has been and where it is going for future generations of psychologists, students, and the general public.

The underlying burden for the introductory psychology teacher should be the content. What to teach is the central issue, and the resources available to address this issue are more numerous today than ever before. Organizations exist for psychology educators at all levels that promote high-quality instructional practices and choices. Talented instructors have written books and compiled essays on what makes a good introductory psychology course. The Internet has made the communication of ideas and activities among psychology instructors easier. Most of the resources available, however, address pedagogy rather than content.

There has been little direction regarding the content of the college introductory psychology course. Graduate training is so specialized that it would leave out large sections covered in the introductory course. Thus, college faculty are faced with making choices and teaching about topics for which they have received no training (see Hackney, Korn, & Buskist, chap. 6, this volume). Likewise, as psychology grew to become a greater presence in high schools, it became evident that what should be taught in the high school psychology course was a debatable issue. Content-wise, high school psychology courses have historically focused more on personal development and growth rather than science. An early textbook for high school psychology (Woodworth & Sheehan, 1951) focused on the usual topics related to the behavioral and cognitive perspectives of the day (i.e., learning, forgetting, and emotions), but devoted more space than college texts to practical problems like vocational choice and reading proficiency, reflecting a notion that high school students were less interested in the science of psychology than the practical application of psychology. Liddy (1945, 1946) argued that teaching high school psychology should improve students' lives by helping them develop critical thinking skills, improve intellectual ability, and understand human nature. More recently, Ragland (1992) found that content was typically determined by the individual teacher's personal preference rather than any standardized course of study.

The problem with this personalized choice of topics on the high school level is that many high school psychology teachers lack the extensive formal training in psychology of collegiate instructors. A good number of high school psychology teachers base their curriculum on a variety of sources—state standards (if they exist); remembrances of a psychology course in the past; a day-, week-, or month-long conference in psychology; or what a colleague can tell them in a series of conversations, phone calls, or e-mails. In 1992, the College Board instituted an Advanced Placement high school psychology course, complete with its own course description. Until 1999, there was no set of standards for teaching non-AP high school psychology, leaving the door open for a variety of representations of what psychology to teach in the introductory psychology course.

The National Standards: A Benchmark for Best Practices

In 1999, the American Psychological Association formally adopted the *National Standards for the Teaching of High School Psychology* (http://www.apa.org/ed/natlstandards.html). The *Standards*, formulated in 1996 by an appointed task force committee of high school teachers and college professors, sought to define psychology content for the high school classroom. The content that comprises the *Standards* document focuses on themes and skills students should know after taking a high school level course, not specific facts, ideas, or theorists that every teacher should include. To make the *Standards* an all-encompassing document, the committee decided to structure the *Standards* into five overarching content domains, with each domain including standard areas that cover the breadth of introductory psychology. Each domain's standard areas include relevant unit topics commonly emphasized in introductory psychology textbooks. A breakdown of each domain and its respective standard areas appears in Table 13.1. By teaching at least one unit from each domain, students in high school psychology courses should receive a full picture of the current state of psychology.

The *Standards*, however, do not stop at suggesting which unit themes fall into which domain. Each standard area is subdivided into content standards, which further define the scope of coverage in each area. For instance, in the biopsychological domain under the standard area of biological bases of behavior, students should understand the following content standards after completing the unit:

1. Structure and function of the neuron
2. Organization of the nervous system
3. Hierarchical organization of the structure and function of the brain
4. Technologies and clinical methods for studying the brain
5. Specialized function of the brain's hemispheres
6. Structure and function of the endocrine system
7. How heredity interacts with the environment to influence behavior
8. How psychological mechanisms are influenced by evolution

TABLE 13.1

The Five Domains and Respective Standard Areas of the National Standards for the Teaching of High School Psychology (1999)

Domain	Standard area
Cognitive	Learning
	Memory
	Thinking and language
	States of consciousness
Sociocultural	Individual differences
	Personality and assessment
	Psychological disorders
	Treatment of psychological disorders
	Social and cultural dimensions of behavior
Developmental	Lifespan development
Biopsychological	Biological bases of behavior
	Sensation and perception
	Motivation and emotion
Methodological	History of psychology
	Research methodology

These content standards break down the larger standard area into more manageable topic areas, yet they are still broad in scope.

The performance standards make up the "meat" of the standards. The performance standards delineate what students will accomplish after learning the material. For instance, "Content Standard 1: Structure and function of the neuron" has three performance standards that students should demonstrate after this particular lesson:

1.1. Identify the neuron as the basis for neural communication.
1.2. Describe how information is transmitted and integrated in the nervous system.
1.3. Analyze how the process of neurotransmission can be modified by heredity and environment.

It is at this point in the *National Standards* that teachers can plan the day-to-day objectives for their students. Teachers can easily cover one or two of these performance standards in a day's lesson, focusing on what students will need to accomplish that day in an active way. These objectives not only help define what content teachers should cover, but also what assessments they might use to measure performance. Under each performance standard are performance indicators, which are suggestions for how students might demonstrate the knowledge outlined in the performance standard. These performance indicators are authentic assessment suggestions based on best practices shared by teachers throughout the United States. Some of the performance indicators are designed for hands-on learning (e.g., using diagrams, models, or computer programs to identify the structure and function of different parts of the neuron), auditory learning (e.g., discussing how internal and external stimuli initiate the communication process in the neuron), and higher order thinking (e.g., contrasting excitatory and inhibitory transmission). The performance indicators, however, are suggestions rather than mandates. Each set of performance indicators is prefaced by the words "may indicate," which gives individual teachers freedom to develop their own authentic and traditional assessments to measure student progress.

Using the National Standards to Develop a High School Psychology Course

Flexibility is the key to the intent and purpose of the *Standards*. The committee recognized that the situations in which high school psychology was taught varied significantly. Some teachers were able to teach only a semester course, whereas others enjoyed the benefits of teaching all year long. Additionally, teachers with varied educational experience in psychology might not feel comfortable teaching more challenging concepts. The committee suggested that each high school psychology course, regardless of the length of the course or expertise of the instructor, cover all five domains, determining which standard areas would work best for the instructor's ability and audience's needs. To demonstrate the flexibility of the standards, the standards contain several possible combinations of domains and standard areas to cover in courses of varying length. Some sample outlines appear in Tables 13.2 and 13.3. Although shorter duration courses (semester or trimester courses) would by necessity include fewer topics, a traditional yearlong course could include all domains and standard areas. But teachers in all types of high school psychology courses can feel free to pick and choose which standard areas to teach and to emphasize, depending on the time available and interests of both the teacher and the class.

Every high school psychology teacher should use the standards as the framework for curriculum and lesson planning. Before deciding what to teach on a daily basis, teachers should first decide what overall thematic standard areas to address. The fundamental consideration at this point of planning is to include all five domains at some point in the course. Leaving out one or two domains will neglect an area of study that is important not only to understanding human behavior but also understanding what psychology is. Suppose teachers do not feel comfortable teaching about the scientific method because their background is in history rather

TABLE 13.2

Sample Course Outline for a 5-Unit Semester,
With Roughly 2½ Weeks Devoted to Each Unit

Standard area	Domain addressed
Introduction and research methods	Methodology
Biological bases of behavior	Biopsychological
Memory	Cognitive
Lifespan development	Developmental
Psychological disorders	Sociocultural

TABLE 13.3

Sample Course Outline for a 7-Unit Semester,
With Roughly 2 Weeks Devoted to Each Unit

Standard area	Domain addressed
Introduction and research methods	Methodology
Lifespan development	Developmental
Biological bases of behavior	Biopsychological
Sensation and perception	Biopsychological
Memory	Cognitive
Psychological disorders	Sociocultural
Therapy	Sociocultural

than science. By leaving out how psychologists study, assess, and draw conclusions about human and animal behavior, students may be left with the impression that psychology is mainly driven by insight and opinion rather than systematic study. The opportunities for teaching each and every domain far outweigh the temptation to neglect any one of them. Not only does each domain address critical content in psychology, but they also include skills students need to be successful. Critical thinking skills (methodological), problem solving (cognitive), and understanding and tolerance for mental illness and people from other cultures (sociocultural) are only a few of the overarching, domain-level goals a teacher can plan into a high school psychology course.

As lesson planning works down from the domain level, the scope and sequence of the course becomes clear. It does not matter when an instructor teaches a domain or standard area, only that it is taught. A teacher may want to start off the year with an interest-grabbing standard area like social psychology or memory instead of the traditional history of psychology unit. A psychological disorders and therapy concentration may be planned around a scheduled trip to a mental health facility or a guest speaker on mental illness. Because the standards document has divided the content into logical and manageable units, teachers can mix and match what they teach when in order to maximize student interest. The standards do not dictate scope and sequence or even breadth and depth. What the standards offer is the ability to design a high school psychology course around the needs of the teacher and students. The only mandate is that teachers make the responsible choice to include all aspects of psychology with each group of students to give them the best picture of what psychology is as a scientifically based field of inquiry.

Introductory Psychology at the College Level

We have noted the importance of the *National Standards for the Teaching of High School Psychology* to the integrity of the introductory course at the secondary level. These standards exist partly to provide structure and coherence to psychology at the next level. They should ensure a high-quality experience for secondary students that will give them a firm foundation for a college-level introductory psychology course or, perhaps, allow college faculty to present an introductory course with more depth. We turn next to the college-level introductory psychology course.

College-level instructors have been slow to embrace standardization in the introductory psychology course, perhaps because they are used to being more autonomous in designing their courses or because of the belief that standards might somehow infringe on academic freedom. PsycINFO searches combining "introductory psychology" or "general psychology" with "standards," "guidelines," or "uniformity" turned up no matches that relate to providing a uniform experience in the introductory course. Although there have been major studies of the psychology curriculum in almost every decade since 1951 (Brewer et al., 1993; Perlman & McCann, 1999), these reports have focused on the set of courses a psychology major should take rather than on the content or organization of specific courses.

It seems that a great deal of standardization already exists in the college introductory psychology course. The majority of standardization in the college introductory psychology course seems to have occurred because of the textbooks used. There are many published studies of introductory psychology textbooks that have shown, at least on the surface, a high degree of similarity among the available texts (see Griggs, chap. 2, this volume). Although Griggs and Marek (2001) argued that such texts are more different than appearances might indicate, they also found that there was little difference in chapter topics, chapter organization, and extent of topical coverage. In fact, Griggs and Marek were able to develop a prototypical organizational scheme based on the 41 introductory texts available between 1997 and 2000 (see Table 13.4). Griggs and Marek did note that the texts showed considerable variation in key terms, pedagogical aids and data graphs, critical-thinking programs, reference citations, and levels of difficulty, but these features tended to affect instructors' treatment within broad topics rather than the topics them-

TABLE 13.4

Prototypical Introductory Psychology Text Organization

Introduction and research methods

Biological processes (biopsychology, sensation–perception, consciousness)

Developmental psychology

Learning and cognitive processes (learning, memory, thought–language, intelligence)

Emotion–motivation

Clinical and health psychology (personality, disorders, therapies, health)

Social psychology

Note: Organization from Griggs and Marek (2001, p. 254).

selves. Griggs (personal communication, February 15, 2004) also found that the prototypical organization of introductory psychology texts varies little even based on the difficulty level of the texts. Thus, if psychology instructors follow the typical organization of chapters in a text, then there may be standardization in terms of the order of topics covered.

It may be the case that demands for assessment will bring about greater pressure to provide a standardized experience in the introductory psychology course. Even if assessment does not drive standardization across the country, state, region, or system, it may provide the impetus for standardization at the departmental level. If a department is developing an assessment plan (and what department is not these days?; see Dunn, Mehrotra, & Halonen, 2004), then the assessment efforts can start in the introductory psychology course. The remainder of this chapter addresses that thesis: Assessment starts with introductory psychology. Obviously, there are many different approaches that a department could take to assessment, even in introductory psychology. The focus is on two approaches, both based on current guidelines or standards. The advantage of using existing documents, of course, is that it is not necessary to reinvent the wheel.

TEACHING INTRODUCTORY PSYCHOLOGY BASED ON THE NATIONAL STANDARDS

The first portion of the chapter gave a thorough introduction to the *National Standards for the Teaching of High School Psychology* from the perspective of the high school psychology course. Could a college department of psychology use these standards to organize its introductory psychology course? The answer, of course, is yes. The standards do mandate content coverage in the ideal introductory psychology course, but they do not dictate how deep or broad that coverage is. Thus, using the *National Standards* to organize, plan, and direct a college-level introductory psychology course makes a great deal of sense.

To showcase a specific department's incorporation of the *National Standards* into their introductory psychology curriculum, we will examine St. Olaf College's Department of Psychology. St. Olaf College (Northfield, MN) is a highly selective liberal arts college that was founded in 1874. According to their Web site, St. Olaf ranked fifth in the nation in the number of graduates who went on to earn doctorates (1991–2000). Students at St. Olaf averaged almost 1300 on the SAT. The department of psychology "is committed to maintaining a rigorous academic curriculum" (http://www.stolaf.edu/depts/psych/deptinfo.html) and provides students with many opportunities to engage in research. In recent years, St. Olaf psychology majors have presented research at many conferences, including meetings such as International Society for the Study of Behavioral Development, Jean Piaget Society, Midwestern Psychological Association, Minnesota Psychological Association, Minnesota Undergraduate Psychology Conference, Society for Computers in Psychology, Society for Research in Child Development, the International Conference on Human–Computer Interaction, and the National Leadership Conference. These data show that the St. Olaf psychology department is a high-quality program. If such a strong department has chosen to base its introductory course on the *National Standards*, then this approach could serve as a model for others.

The St. Olaf psychology faculty adopted a set of guidelines for their Principles of Psychology course in April 2002 (C. Huff, personal communication, September 15, 2003). The department had received a National Science Foundation grant to establish a laboratory requirement for their introductory course (C. Huff, personal communication, February 15, 2004). At the same time, the department had committed itself to develop a program to introduce high school students to scientific psychology. While developing the laboratory and the program for high school students, the St. Olaf psychology faculty found the *National Standards* to be quite helpful. Because there was no set of standards for the college introductory psychology course, they based their guidelines on the *National Standards*. The St. Olaf guidelines mandate that faculty teaching the Principles course cover 10 areas from the *National Standards* grouped in 5 areas (see Table 13.5).

Although St. Olaf's psychology department used the *National Standards* to frame their Principles of Psychology course, they put their personal stamp on the standards with some adaptations. One manner in which they personalized the standards was through making some modifications to the areas under each domain. As you can see by comparing Table 13.5 to Table 13.1, the St. Olaf psychology faculty dropped two areas from the Biopsychological domain ("Motivation and Emotion" and "Stress, Coping, and Health") and one area from the Cognitive domain ("States of Consciousness"). In addition, they renamed the "Sociocultural" domain from the *National Standards* into their "Socioemotional" domain, deleted one area from that domain ("Individual Differences"), and cut back on two areas (from "Personality and Assessment" to "Personality"; from "Social and Cultural Dimensions of Behavior" to "Social Psychology").

A second way in which the St. Olaf faculty adapted the *National Standards* was by giving faculty some flexibility in the topics they cover under each area. Table

TABLE 13.5
St. Olaf Principles of Psychology Content Guidelines

Methods domain

I. Introduction and research methods

Biopsychological domain

II. Biology and behavior

III. Sensation and perception

Developmental domain

IV. Lifespan development

Cognitive domain

V. Learning

VI. Memory

VII. Thinking and language

Socioemotional domain

VIII. Personality

IX. Psychological disorders and treatment

X. Social psychology

Optional (included in *National Standards*, but not required for St. Olaf)

States of consciousness

Individual differences

Motivation

Stress

13.6 shows the specific topics listed within the "Introduction and Research Methods" area within the Methods domain. The faculty decided that topics listed in Roman type are the most important and that everyone teaching the Principles course should cover them. The coverage of italicized topics, on the other hand, is optional and at the discretion of the faculty member. Covering additional topics within each area is also at each faculty member's discretion.

The final manner that St. Olaf's psychology department customized the standards for their purposes was by deciding that some areas covered in the *National Standards* are not mandatory in the Principles of Psychology class (see Table 13.5). Thus, a high school student who has taken an introductory course organized around the *National Standards* may have covered topics that a student at St. Olaf has not (e.g., consciousness, motivation, stress, individual differences). However,

TABLE 13.6

Topics Listed Within Introduction and Research Methods

1. Research strategies used by psychologists to explore behavior and mental processes
2. Purpose and basic concepts of statistics
3. Ethical issues in research with human and other animals that are important to psychologists
4. Contemporary theoretical perspectives used by psychologists to understand behavior and mental processes in context
5. *Major subfields and career opportunities that comprise psychology*
6. *Development of psychology as an empirical science*

Note: From the faculty of the Department of Psychology, St. Olaf College, Northfield, MN. Topics listed in Roman type must be covered; italicized topics are optional.

such a discrepancy is not surprising considering that high school classes tend to meet more frequently and for more total hours than college courses.

In summary, psychology departments at colleges around the country could choose to use the *National Standards* developed for high school psychology courses to help organize their course, choose the topics they will cover in their course, or standardize the course among various instructors. As our look at the St. Olaf department of psychology guideline has shown, there is nothing mandatory about covering all aspects of the *National Standards* exactly as they exist for high school psychology. However, basing a college course on the *National Standards* would allow departments to offer their students a more consistent introductory experience and, thus, simplify any assessment procedures that they might wish to institute.

TEACHING INTRODUCTORY PSYCHOLOGY BASED ON THE UNDERGRADUATE PSYCHOLOGY MAJOR LEARNING GOALS AND OUTCOMES

In 2001, the American Psychological Association's Board of Educational Affairs (BEA) appointed a Task Force on Undergraduate Psychology Major Competencies. The BEA charged the task force with developing a set of goals and outcomes for undergraduate psychology majors. The members of the task force surveyed the relevant existing literature, examined a similar proposal from the California State University system (Allen, Noel, Deegan, Halpern, & Crawford, 2000), sought input from departments around the country, and shared their ideas with an advisory panel of faculty from a variety of types of institutions as well as with organizations with interests in the teaching of psychology. In March 2002, the task force released their report (http://www.apa.org/ed/pcue/taskforcereport.pdf) in which they listed 10 learning goals and outcomes (see Table 13.7). Beyond simply listing the learning goals and outcomes, the task force report clearly indicated that departments could use the information to develop curriculum plans and to assess departmental outcomes.

This section looks at the goals and outcomes in a manner that the task force apparently did not anticipate. We believe that a department could begin its planning

TABLE 13.7
Undergraduate Psychology Learning Goals and Outcomes

Knowledge, Skills, and Values Consistent With the Science and Application of Psychology

Goal 1. Knowledge Base of Psychology

Students will demonstrate familiarity with the major concepts, theoretical perspectives, empirical findings, and historical trends in psychology.

Goal 2. Research Methods in Psychology

Students will understand and apply basic research methods in psychology, including research design, data analysis, and interpretation.

Goal 3. Critical Thinking Skills in Psychology

Students will respect and use critical and creative thinking, skeptical inquiry, and, when possible, the scientific approach to solve problems related to behavior and mental processes.

Goal 4. Application of Psychology

Students will understand and apply psychological principles to personal, social, and organizational issues.

Goal 5. Values in Psychology

Students will be able to weigh evidence, tolerate ambiguity, act ethically, and reflect other values that are the underpinnings of psychology as a discipline.

Knowledge, Skills, and Values Consistent With Liberal Arts Education That Are Further Developed in Psychology

Goal 6. Information and Technological Literacy

Students will demonstrate information competence and the ability to use computers and other technology for many purposes.

Goal 7. Communication Skills

Students will be able to communicate effectively in a variety of formats.

Goal 8. Sociocultural and International Awareness

Students will recognize, understand, and respect the complexity of sociocultural and international diversity.

Goal 9. Personal Development

Students will develop insight into their own and others' behavior and mental processes and apply effective strategies for self-management and self-improvement.

Goal 10. Career Planning and Development

Students will emerge from the major with realistic ideas about how to implement their psychological knowledge, skills, and values in occupational pursuits in a variety of settings.

and assessment with the learning goals and outcomes even in the introductory psychology course. We will examine the 10 goals and outcomes with the introductory course specifically in mind.

Knowledge Base of Psychology

Certainly building a knowledge base of the discipline is one of the primary goals of most introductory psychology courses. Providing a broad survey of the discipline is one of the prime reasons that faculty complain about having difficulty covering all the material in an introductory text in a semester's time. Although some departments use two semesters to present the introductory course, they are in the clear minority (Messer, Griggs, & Jackson, 1999). It is in the introductory class that students who will major in psychology begin to build their knowledge of the discipline. Thus, the course plays an important role in the knowledge that departments will eventually assess as students complete their majors.

Research Methods in Psychology

Research methods is a crucial topic in introductory psychology. By presenting the scientific approach favored by psychologists, faculty aim to overcome some of the stereotypes students bring to the class about what psychologists do. According to Griggs, Jackson, Christopher, and Marek (1999), over half of all full-length introductory psychology texts ($N = 37$) included a separate chapter on research methods; overall, the texts devoted 4% of their pages to methods, and only one text provided no coverage of the topic. Griggs and Koenig (2001) analyzed 13 brief introductory texts and found that they devoted 3% of their pages to methods. Thus, it is clear that introductory text authors see the topic as being an important one, which means that the vast majority of introductory psychology students will learn about the topic. This introduction, in turn, should serve as an important introduction to later coursework in the area.

Critical Thinking Skills in Psychology

It is likely that many instructors of introductory psychology would list increasing critical thinking as one of the goals of their course (see Appleby, chap. 5, this volume). Nummedal and Halpern (1995) argued that psychologists have a special claim to the teaching of critical thinking. Griggs, Jackson, Marek, and Christopher (1998) examined 37 full-length introductory psychology texts and found that 65% mentioned critical thinking as a goal in the preface; only 8% did not mention critical thinking. Thus, if departments choose to use the learning goals and outcomes, then the inculcation of critical thinking can begin in the introductory psychology course.

Application of Psychology

Although instructors of introductory psychology present an academic discipline to their students, the principles from that discipline have a great deal of relevance to students' everyday lives. Although it may not be universal, many faculty are interested in having their students learn lessons that they can apply in their lives. Further, having students learn the wide variety of problems with which psychologists work will help students learn about the applications of psychology. Again, departments can begin to work toward an application goal in the initial course.

Values in Psychology

At first glance, psychological values might not appear to be a typical topic in introductory psychology. However, looking at this entry in Table 13.7 shows specific examples of weighing evidence, tolerating ambiguity, and acting ethically (see Handelsman, chap. 12, this volume). A typical introductory course would at least acquaint students with these values as psychologists view them. Thus, although it might not be expected that students would change much in their behavior, they should gain knowledge about psychological values in introductory psychology. Thus, again the process of developing psychology students who will have specific knowledge, skills, and values about the discipline begins with the first course.

The remaining five learning goals and outcomes are those the task force found to be primarily liberal arts goals that psychology can further enhance. It seems that Goals 6–10 should be outcomes that departments would hope to influence in their majors by the time of graduation. Thus, we will not cover these goals one-by-one as we did the first five. However, a glance at the later goals reveals that these, too, have possibilities in the introductory course. If instructors have their students complete a library assignment or outside paper, then it is likely that students will gain in information and technological literacy. If students have oral or written presentations in their class, they will gain in communication skills. Faculty who deal with culture in introductory psychology will have an impact on their students' sociocultural and international awareness. Instructors who teach units on study skills, obesity and eating disorders, stress and coping, motivation and emotion, and many other topics may give their students lessons that will result in personal development. Finally, although it is unlikely that many instructors teach much about career planning and development, students do typically learn about the occupations of psychologists in their introductory course.

It is clear that even the introductory psychology course can contribute greatly toward the goals and outcomes that many departments wish to see in their majors. As departments develop or revise their assessment plans, it would be wise to determine how the beginning course helps them achieve their objectives.

CONCLUSIONS

This chapter has attempted to illustrate why it is important that the introductory psychology course has an organizational scheme. As noted earlier, college faculty, in particular, may chafe at receiving direction from the outside about how to structure their course. Interestingly, however, one of the common complaints from college instructors regarding high school psychology courses is their uncertainty regarding what a high school psychology course covers: Is it merely a self-help or adjustment course, or does it cover the full range of topics in a typical college-level text? Resisting any attempt at standardizing the college-level introductory course thus seems inconsistent. Following an organizational scheme does not force faculty to teach exactly the same information, in the same way, at the same time. We do believe, however, that an organizational scheme will result in better outcomes from the course and a more uniform experience across instructors, institutions, and even educational levels. In turn, these outcomes and experiences can form the basis of outcomes assessment for a department or unit. Such uniformity in the introductory course is necessary for building a coherent psychology curriculum. We urge faculty of introductory psychology courses at all levels to consider implementing some type of organizing framework for their courses.

ACKNOWLEDGMENT

We appreciate Chuck Huff's assistance with information regarding the St. Olaf Department of Psychology.

REFERENCES

Allen, M. J., Noel, R., Deegan, J., Halpern, D., & Crawford, C. (2000). *Goals and objectives for the undergraduate psychology major: Recommendations from a meeting of California State University psychology faculty.* Retrieved February 15, 2004, from the Office of Teaching Resources in Psychology Web site: http://www.lemoyne.edu/OTRP/otrpresources/otrp_outcomes.html

Brewer, C. L., Hopkins, J. R., Kimble, G. A., Matlin, M. W., McCann, L. I., McNeil, O. V., Nodine, B. F., Quinn, V. N., & Saundra. (1993). Curriculum. In T. V. McGovern (Ed.), *Handbook for enhancing undergraduate education in psychology* (pp. 161–182). Washington, DC: American Psychological Association.

Dunn, D. S., Mehrotra, C. M., & Halonen, J. S. (2004). *Measuring up: Educational assessment challenges and practices for psychology.* Washington, DC: American Psychological Association.

Griggs, R. A., Jackson, S. L., Christopher, A. N., & Marek, P. (1999). Introductory psychology textbooks: An objective analysis and update. *Teaching of Psychology, 26,* 182–189.

Griggs, R. A., Jackson, S. L., Marek, P., & Christopher, A. N. (1998). Critical thinking in introductory psychology texts and supplements. *Teaching of Psychology, 25,* 254–266.

Griggs, R. A., & Koenig, C. S. (2001). Brief introductory psychology textbooks: A current analysis. *Teaching of Psychology, 28,* 36–40.

Griggs, R. A., & Marek, P. (2001). Similarity of introductory psychology textbooks: Reality or illusion? *Teaching of Psychology, 28,* 254–256.

Liddy, R. B. (1945). Psychology for secondary schools. *School, 33,* 476–481.

Liddy, R. B. (1946). Can psychology be helpfully taught at the high school level? *Bulletin of the Canadian Psychological Association, 6,* 9–12.

Messer, W. S., Griggs, R. A., & Jackson, S. L. (1999). A national survey of undergraduate psychology degree options and requirements. *Teaching of Psychology, 26,* 164–171.

Nummedal, S. G., & Halpern, D. F. (1995). Introduction: Making the case for "Psychologists Teach Critical Thinking." *Teaching of Psychology, 22,* 4–5.

Perlman, B., & McCann, L. I. (1999). The structure of the psychology undergraduate curriculum. *Teaching of Psychology, 26,* 171–176.

Ragland, R. G. (1992). Teachers and teacher education in high school psychology: A national survey. *Teaching of Psychology, 19,* 73–78.

Woodworth, R. S., & Sheehan, M. R. (1951). *First course in psychology.* Oxford: Holt.

Chapter
14

Assessing General Education Outcomes in Introductory Psychology

Jane S. Halonen
University of West Florida

Charles M. Harris
Dena A. Pastor
Craig E. Abrahamson
Charles J. Huffman
James Madison University

Most American colleges and universities stipulate a general education component in the design of undergraduate education; however, there is no consensus on an ideal design for a general education curriculum (Astin, 1993). There is even less agreement on effective strategies to assess the quality of general education outcomes (Ratcliff, Johnson, La Nasa, & Gaff, 2001). Because of the importance of the foundation provided by general education courses, assessing the quality of such courses should be of paramount importance for all institutions. Strategies for assessing general education tend to reflect an institution's mission and conceptualization of the curriculum.

This chapter focuses on introductory psychology as we explore one institution's evolution in assessing general education. We provide a description of the historic role of general education as a prelude for describing collaborative assessment undertaken at James Madison University. We offer details on two strategies, a content-based approach and a competence-based approach, for assessing the contributions of psychology and other social sciences courses to general education. We conclude our discussion with an analysis of the challenges and value of a collaborative approach to assessing introductory psychology courses as components of a general education curriculum.

HISTORICAL CONTEXT

The concept of general education can be traced to the establishment of the Junior College at the University of Chicago in 1891. Believing that a complete education should be both broad and specialized, President William Harper divided the college curriculum into two parts (*Centennial Catalogues,* 2004). The Academic, or Junior College, comprised the first part. It was a 2-year program of instruction that would minimize disparities among students from vastly different secondary schools. After students' academic skills were refined, they would proceed to the University, or Senior College, for advanced instruction in specialized fields of study. In 1932, the University of Minnesota expanded the concept of general education when it established the General College. The egalitarian mission of the General College was to provide equal access for all students without regard to race, religion, gender, national origin, disability, or age (*General College: Kiosk,* 2002). The great impetus for general education came as a result of sociopolitical conditions associated with World War II. Concerned about how highly educated populations could acquiesce to charismatic and totalitarian leaders (Gaff & Ratcliff, 1996), the Harvard Committee on General Education (1945) formulated a rationale for general education as a social construct: "It is important to realize that the ideal of a free society involves a twofold value, the value of freedom and the value of society, that is, the ideal of interaction irrespective of agreement on ultimates, which is to say, belief in the worth and dignity of the human spirit" (p. 76).

Although the concept of general education as a social construct was widely praised, most institutions adopted curricular structures that distributed responsibilities for general education broadly across disciplines. Administrators delegated decisions about the content, delivery, and monitoring of the curriculum to the respective disciplines comprising a university. As late as the 1980s, over 90% of all general education programs used such a distribution system (Astin, 1993). This practice proliferated discipline-based courses as student populations increased. The richness of scholarship generated by discipline-based specialization was offset by the disintegration of the academic community and the fragmentation of learning experiences for students.

During the 1980s, over 80% of colleges and universities engaged in some kind of revision of their undergraduate curriculum and implemented some kind of assessment of student learning (El-Khawas, 1995). There is little evidence that programs used information derived from assessment to improve the coherence or the quality of general education programs (Steele & Lutz, 1995). In a recent national survey of general education, Ratcliff et al. (2001) reported on curriculum revision and assessment by 279 colleges and universities. Approximately 57% of the institutions reported that they were currently reviewing their general education programs. Only 31% of the institutions reported regular assessment of student performance in relation to general education goals. Performance goals tended to be oriented toward mastery of content. Only 15% of the 159 institutions engaged in curriculum review reported regular assessment of cognitive outcomes.

ASSESSMENT AT JAMES MADISON UNIVERSITY

James Madison University (JMU), a public institution within the Virginia higher education system, offers 47 majors and awards 8 baccalaureate degrees in 5 colleges. The current student enrollment is approximately 16,229 students, of whom approximately 14,991 are undergraduates. In the Carnegie system that has demonstrated an unusual receptivity for institutions that develop assessment strategies to document and improve curricular quality, JMU is classified as a comprehensive institution.

Progress toward systematic and rigorous assessment of general education at JMU started in 1986 with the hiring of a director to oversee university assessment activities. In 1988, the State Council for Higher Education in Virginia allocated permanent funding to James Madison University for establishment of an assessment center, known today as the Center for Assessment and Research Studies (CARS). CARS is currently staffed by eight faculty members, trained in assessment, measurement, and statistics, and includes an innovative doctor of philosophy degree program in assessment and measurement. CARS supports a wide array of assessment activities at JMU, including assessment in student affairs, in academic majors, and in general education.

TABLE 14.1

Clusters and Competencies Within General Education James Madison University

Cluster number and title	Competencies
1: Skills for the 21st Century	Oral and written communication, critical thinking, and uses of technology
2: The Arts and Humanities	Understanding the cultural and intellectual significance of the arts and humanities
3: The Natural World	Using analytic methods to evaluate evidence and develop scientific theories
4: Social and Cultural Processes	Making informed judgments about underlying dynamics of American and global experiences
5: Individuals in the Human Community	Understanding physical, cognitive, and socioemotional development for individuals and diverse communities

In 1987, assessment of general education at JMU included the use of the ACT COMP (American College Testing Composite) and the ETS Academic Profile. Students were offered incentives to participate in assessment activities. Later, in the 1980s, faculty developed instruments specifically designed for assessing general education at JMU, and university-wide assessment days were implemented. It became standard procedure for all incoming freshman to be tested during an August assessment day and all students with 45–70 credit hours to be tested during a February assessment day (see Stoloff, Apple, Barron, Reis-Bergan, & Sundre, 2004). Blocking course registration until participation is fulfilled provides the motivation for students to participate in assessment days.

In 1997, the university implemented General Education: The Human Community, a major program revision based on five broad areas of knowledge, each defined by clusters of interdisciplinary learning goals. The reconceptualized general education program promoted the cultivation of habits of the mind and heart that are essential to informed citizens in a democracy and world community (Reynolds et al., 1998). Specific goals of the general education program are listed on the Web site www.jmu.edu/gened. Program requirements included a minimum of 14 general education courses or 44 credits, 37% of minimum baccalaureate credits, for graduation with coursework from each of the 5 clusters. Table 14.1 presents the competencies emphasized within each of the 5 clusters.

Courses within each cluster were organized into "packages," or multidisciplinary groupings of courses charged with meeting a cluster-oriented set of interdisciplinary learning goals. Two packages in Cluster 5 included introductory psychology courses—Package A: Individual and Community Wellness and Package B: Individual Health and Wellness. The third package in Cluster 5, Package C: Individual and Community Perspectives, consisted of two interdisciplinary courses that provided an integrated exploration of human development, health,

TABLE 14.2

Content-Oriented Assessment for Introductory Psychology Courses

Goals	M	SD	Cronbach's alpha
Describe ways in which both heredity and environment influence human development and individual behavior (14 items)	9.94	2.67	.68
Describe theories of human development and behavior (16 items)	8.41	2.97	.65
Development subtest total (30 items)	18.35	4.94	.77

Note: See Table 14.5 for examples of goals, objectives, and items in the current assessment of cognitive outcomes for introductory psychology courses.

and wellness for individuals and communities. Packages A and B required completion of an introductory psychology or sociology course and a course in either individual or community health and wellness.

An interdisciplinary steering committee, whose members represented administrative and academic units within the university, generated the learning goals for Cluster 5. Staff members in student life, residence life, multicultural awareness, and student health represented the student affairs division. Academic representatives came from departments of psychology, sociology, health, and kinesiology. The committee developed 13 interdisciplinary learning goals and charged that each goal be a primary, secondary, or tertiary theme within all Cluster 5 courses. This reconceptualization of the curriculum produced the first formal assessment strategy based on traditional testing of relevant content. However, no strategy was implemented for incorporating into individual courses the multidisciplinary content associated with the 13 interdisciplinary learning goals. Additionally, only 2 of the 13 goals focused on measurable content within the social sciences. The remaining goals addressed idiosyncratic aspects of personal knowledge and development.

STRATEGY 1: ASSESSING MASTERY OF CONTENT

JMU annually conducts assessment of the general education program during the campus-wide assessment day in February. Beginning in 1998, assessment within Cluster 5 used an 80-item selected-response instrument that included a 30-item Development subtest and a 50-item Wellness subtest (Finney & Owens, 2002). This approach emphasized students' ability to recall basic information from the courses included in a package. As such, this strategy replicated the weaknesses inherent in the cafeteria approach of a distribution system. Although the respective faculty members designed the courses within a package to have some conceptual overlap, the test strategy relied on multiple-choice items that could easily be drawn from the test banks of texts chosen for the individual courses. Despite the expanded set of outcomes designated in the design of the packages, assessment results were obtained annually for only 5 of the Cluster's 13 learning goals (Pastor, Davis, Miller, Horst, & Jones, 2003). Using the 30-item Development subtest, assessment results for introductory psychology courses were obtained for only two content-oriented goals, as depicted in Table 14.2. The Wellness subtest assessed only three discipline related goals. The other eight goals were too broadly stated to be assessed or were not germane to departmental goals for Cluster 5 courses.

In addition, students could be tested on content that might not have been included in the course they completed to fulfill the Cluster 5 requirement. The results of the content-based approach proved disappointing.

Two problems became apparent from the results of the Development subtest. First, after 5 years experience with content-oriented assessment, performance scores represented, at best, only moderate levels of achievement on only 2 of the 13 goals. For one goal, students were to describe ways in which both heredity

TABLE 14.3

Courses in Integrated Areas Within Cluster 5

Sociocultural dimension area:

GPSYC 101	General Psychology
GPSYC 160	Lifespan Human Development
GSOCI 240	Individual in Society
GEIC 102	
GHTH 100	Personal Wellness
GKIN 100	Lifetime Fitness and Wellness
GEIC 101	Individuals in the Human Community: The Individual Perspective

Note: Students are required to complete one course in each area.

and environment influence human development and individual behavior. For the other goal, students were to describe theories of human development and behavior. In the absence of norm-referenced or criterion-referenced standards, interpretation of performance scores was limited to percent correct: 71% correct for the first goal, 53% correct for the second goal, and 61% correct for the total Development subtest. Second, coverage of only 2 goals was not consistent with the charge for each course within Cluster 5 to address each of the 13 goals as primary, secondary, or tertiary themes.

These circumstances were not unique to JMU. Beginning in the 1980s, high profile institutions such as the National Endowment for the Humanities (Bennett, 1984), the Association of American Colleges (1985), and the U.S. Department of Education (1994) issued calls for reform of general education. Concurrently, most state legislatures mandated assessment at all levels of education (El-Khawas, 1995). Despite such efforts, assessment within most general education programs remained commensurate with individual course assessment (Ratcliff et al., 2001). In response to poor achievement on the content-based assessment instrument and reinforced by the national call for improved assessment measures, the faculty in Cluster 5 reconceptualized its general education curriculum to examine common competencies promoted within the packages. We reoriented the focus of the general education curriculum from acquiring domains of knowledge to assessing competencies students should learn.

STRATEGY 2: ASSESSING COGNITIVE OUTCOMES

In 2002, an external evaluation team conducted an academic program review of General Education: The Human Community (Allain, 2002). Recommendations

TABLE 14.4

Cognitive Outcomes-Based Goals and Objectives for Cluster 5

Goal 1: Make plausible interpretations about behavior in social contexts.
  a. Infer meaning of behavior.
  b. Reject inappropriately simplistic judgments about causes of behavior.
  c. Discern multiple causes of behavior.
  d. Identify assumptions underlying a perspective or worldview.

Goal 2: Identify implications of taking action regarding social/behavioral issues.
  a. Discern essential features of social/behavioral issues.
  b. Predict probable consequences of a course of action.
  c. Recognize flaws in reasoning that make alternative positions less viable.

Goal 3: Use evidence to develop and evaluate positions regarding social/behavioral issues.
  a. Discriminate between reputable and nonreputable sources of information.
  b. Recognize the criteria that constitute reputable sources.
  c. Identify potential bias in sources of information.
  d. Recognize potential for personal bias to influence choice.

Goal 4: Discriminate between ethical and nonethical practices in the social/behavioral sciences.
  a. Recognize the researcher's obligation to provide a rationale for methods selected to address specific questions.
  b. Identify procedures for protection of participants' well-being.
  c. Discern populations/situations to which findings may be generalized.

Goal 5: Identify relevant contributions of sociocultural/psychological variables to a perspective or worldview.
  a. Recognize complexity of the nature–nurture argument.
  b. Interpret interaction concept appropriately.
  c. Identify factors that influence construction of identity.

for improvement included increased integration among courses in each package, and comprehensive assessment of all cluster goals. In response to the academic program review, the Cluster 5 steering committee initiated a review of structure and assessment within the cluster. Although the organization of courses in interdisciplinary packages was conceptually appealing, the packages in Cluster 5 never met expectations for consistency and coherence within or among packages. We began a process that included the following steps: restructuring the area, establishing common outcomes, designing an assessment strategy, developing an assessment instrument, pilot testing the instrument, and using the feedback to make curricular revisions.

Restructuring the Area

The Cluster 5 steering committee realigned cluster courses from three interdisciplinary packages into two integrated areas: Sociocultural Dimension Area and Wellness Area (Table 14.3). We required students to complete one course in each area during their first 2 years at the university. Restructuring cluster courses into integrated areas offered the possibility of achieving the recommended integration by exploring common competencies among area courses. Achieving the recommended comprehensive assessment of all cluster goals required a complete reconceptualization of assessment procedures and intended outcomes.

Establishing Common Outcomes

The next step involved developing common cognitive outcomes as alternatives to the original 13 multidisciplinary goals. Committee members identified common expectations for students completing the Sociocultural Area courses within Cluster 5. Upon completion of any course, students would have developed a social sciences perspective for making sense of the world. Table 14.4 displays five goals with specific objectives the committee chose as overall outcomes for students completing Sociocultural Area courses.

Designing an Assessment Strategy

We developed a strategy for authentic assessment of students' ability to use skills learned in social science courses. The strategy involved the construction of a sce-

TABLE 14.5
Items for Assessing Outcomes-Based Goals and Objectives in Cluster 5

Goal 2: Identify implications of taking action regarding social/behavioral issues.

Objective a: Discern essential features of social/behavioral issues.

What is the largest problem with how Marty asked about parental alcoholism?

a) She assumed all student participants had parents as their guardians.

b) She should have inquired whether one or both parents were alcoholics.

c) She failed to define what she meant by alcoholism.

d) She didn't ask whether or not parents had graduated from college.

Goal 3: Use evidence to develop and evaluate positions regarding social/behavioral issues.

Objective a: Discriminate between reputable and nonreputable sources of information.

Which Internet site would you predict will provide the most reputable support for Marty's research?

a) Mother's Against Drunk Driving (MADD) Web site

b) Online refereed alcohol research journal

c) Washington Post editorial page Web site

d) Online personal accounts of experiences of teenage alcoholics

Note: Correct items appear in boldface.

nario that would engage students by means of realistic characters, themes, and the social context of the scenario. In order to be applicable to all students, the scenario had to be independent of discipline-based content specific to any Sociocultural Area course. The scenario depicted one student's experience in developing a problematic research proposal. The proposal included sufficient logical and methodological errors to facilitate a general education student's ability to think critically about the functions and values of a social science approach (cf. Halonen, 1986). The context for the research proposal was familial alcohol abuse. We chose that context because of its potential to be personally involving. Also, the familial alcohol abuse context offered a conceptual link to courses in the wellness component required for completion of Cluster 5. On assessment day, the scenario cast general education students in the role of consultants to the student struggling to develop a sound research proposal (see Appendix).

Developing an Assessment Instrument

We constructed a multiple-choice examination to assess students' critical thinking and understanding of the scenario. The questions addressed general research principles that would be explored in all social sciences classes. We compared the details of the scenario to the potential for each test question to provide evidence for achievement of one of the outcomes in Table 14.4. The process was iterative in that construction of some test items led to discussions of refining the scenario to set the stage for items that would address specific methodological issues. Eventually, each of the five goals was represented by five or six items in the scenario-based instrument. Members of the committee and graduate students in an assessment class under the direction of one of the committee members wrote the test questions. Table 14.5 depicts multiple-choice test items that provide evidence for two goals as cognitive outcomes.

Pilot Testing the Instrument

We selected three samples for pilot testing the competence-based instrument: incoming freshmen, sophomores who had completed a general education course, and senior psychology majors. The incoming freshmen were tested during the August assessment day. We examined the results of students who had just completed a general education course, despite the fact that the course reforms dictated by the committee would not have occurred. In addition, we tested graduating seniors, in psychology, with the expectation that their ability to apply critical thinking in a sociocultural context should be substantially better than those students completing the general education course.

For the pilot test results to support the validity of the test scores, means of the respective groups should range from low to high, with incoming freshman having the lowest mean, sophomores having a higher mean, and seniors having the highest mean. Descriptive statistics for the three groups are displayed in Table 14.6.

TABLE 14.6
Pilot Test Results for Cluster 5 Assessment of Cognitive Outcomes

	Pre-freshman	Sophomores	Seniors
Sample size	526	82	11
Reliability	0.59	0.63	0.71
M	19.24	21.36	24.45
SD	3.70	3.59	3.50
Minimum score	7	10	16
Maximum score	28	28	27

The differences among the means were in the expected direction, thus supporting the validity of the test scores. A one-way analysis of variance (ANOVA) was used to determine if there were significant differences among the means using an $\alpha \leq$ .05. The ANOVA indicated significant differences among the three groups in mean test performance, $F(2, 615) = 21.62, p < .01$. As a measure of practical significance, omega-squared indicated a medium effect in that 6% of the variance in the test scores could be attributed to the class standing of the students ($\omega^2 = .06$). Tukey's test was used post hoc to explore if there were any significant pairwise comparisons. All pairwise comparisons were both statistically and practically significant. Additional support for the validity of the test scores was evidenced by the positive relation ($r = .25$) between scores for the sophomore sample on this test and their scores on the final test in the introductory psychology course.

Examination of results at the item level for the three groups in the pilot test provided information for improving the instrument. It was thought that because seniors should have the knowledge necessary for correct responses, items that were missed by the majority of seniors reflected items that were either ambiguous or too difficult. As a result of this process, 6 of the original 30 items were revised. In contrast, examination of pilot test data for the incoming freshman focused on items that were answered correctly by the majority of respondents. When it was decided that an item was too easy for incoming freshman or the item's objective was mastered by freshman before coming to college, the reasoning for the objective was reconsidered. When a majority of incoming freshman answered an item correctly because it seemed to be too easy, that item was revised to make it more difficult.

Pilot test results were also examined at the item level to determine if there were some items that had problematic distractors as incorrect response options. A distracter was deemed problematic when the average overall test score of students selecting the distracter was equal to or higher than the average test score of students selecting the right answer. Having attended to such problems, the next step in revising the instrument was to create more items for each objective in order to more accurately evaluate the objectives for each goal. Overall, the pilot test produced promising results for our scenario-based assessment of general education outcomes within an introductory psychology course.

Using Feedback to Make Curricular Revisions

The process of collaborating on the assessment instrument has already had a salutary effect on curriculum design for the social sciences classes. For example, the test designers committed to more explicit discussions of the potential for bias of sources. In particular, all faculty acknowledged that they should be more effective in conveying to students that refereed sources in the social sciences are valued over popular sources. Concurrent with the process of refining our scenario-based instrument, the committee plans to convene meetings of the instructors of the social sciences classes to assist them in syllabus revision as well as to explore how unique elements of social science can be taught in all Sociocultural Area courses.

THE VALUE OF AUTHENTIC ASSESSMENT

Administrators immediately heralded the new plan for assessment as a substantial improvement, suggesting that it could serve as a model for restructuring and assessment within other general education clusters. In summary, the process had the following dramatic effects on interdisciplinary collegiality, our expectations for student learning, and our strategies for teaching our courses:

1. *Mutual respect among the involved disciplines.* Psychology and sociology have not always collaborated effectively. In the beginning, we tended to lapse into turf protection issues rather than exploring more fertile common ground. Once we were able to identify our common interests, it became easier to appreciate the distinctive contributions made by both disciplines, and the process had a transforming effect on interdisciplinary collegiality. Additionally, our adoption of core cognitive outcomes will allow each social science course to maintain the distinctive hallmarks of its respective discipline.

2. *Clarity of expectations.* The process by which we arrived at common cognitive expectations facilitated greater clarity of goals for student learning. Students and teachers should benefit from the ongoing process of articulating how to construct and implement integrated learning experiences that lead to the agreed on cognitive outcomes. Clearly stated goals and articulated instructional strategies should increase student awareness of intended outcomes within all social science courses.

3. *Potential for progress.* Because of our concerted effort in developing the cognitive outcomes, faculty are more likely to be diligent about how effectively they are facilitating students' achievement of those goals. Commitment to common outcomes may encourage greater compliance with the infrastruc-

ture agreed on by the committee. Our authentic assessment model provided clear standards for course development, student outcomes, institutional assessment, and curricular revision. The five goals for cognitive outcomes were designed to function as the catalyst for course development leading to coherence and consistency among Sociocultural Area courses and across multiple sections of area courses. Establishing consistency across all sections of a course will result in a similar educational experience for students in all sections. Faculty will benefit as they engage in dialogue to formulate strategies for organizing content and selecting methods to consistently achieve the Sociocultural Area goals and objectives. Improving consistency across all sections will increase confidence in the validity of institutional assessment of student experiences within Sociocultural Area courses.

Briefly stated, our experience has resulted in an integrated group of social science courses, measurable goals and objectives for our students, a framework for course development, increased motivation among our faculty, a basis for interdisciplinary collaboration, development of a promising scenario-based instrument, and a structure for authentic assessment of student outcomes. For these reasons, we think the potential advantages of our outcomes-based assessment warrant recommending this process to others who are looking for meaningful ways to assess introductory psychology courses within a general education curriculum.

APPENDIX: SCENARIO AND MARTY'S RESEARCH PROPOSAL[1]

Scenario

Marty is a junior, majoring in the social sciences at James Madison University. She grew up in a home where her father missed a lot of work because of alcohol abuse. Marty has had some difficulties succeeding in her courses. She believes that her academic difficulties are directly linked to growing up in an alcohol-abusing home. Her father began abusing alcohol when he was a fraternity member in college. Marty made a commitment to an alcohol-free college experience and so far has been successful in staying alcohol free.

She has developed a strong interest in the consequences of alcohol use patterns and created the following research proposal for her social science methods course based on those interests. She has heard that you have some social science knowledge and asks for your help in reviewing the proposal that she will be submitting to the Institutional Review Board (IRB), the committee that reviews and approves all campus research projects. Read her proposal and answer the questions that follow.

Marty's Research Proposal

Purpose. To discourage college students from using alcohol recreationally.

Method. Marty plans to train a group of female volunteers to conduct her survey about alcohol patterns on the JMU campus. The interviewers will stand outside fraternity houses from 3–9 p.m. on Friday, Saturday, and Sunday during Homecoming weekend to gather Marty's data on the first 100 students who agree to participate. Marty will train her interviewers to avoid gathering identifying information about students to protect the students' identity. The interviewers will identify themselves a representatives of Student Affairs because Marty thinks the students will be more willing to participate if students believe that they are helping out the University rather than participating in an undergraduate study. At the conclusion of gathering data, the interviewers will provide a brochure that discusses the legal consequences of drunk driving.

Survey Items.

- Whether or not participants have an alcoholic parent.
- Sex, annual family income, ethnicity, and religious identification.
- Quantity of alcohol consumed during the prior week.
- Number of classes missed during the prior week.
- Self-report of current grade point average.

Marty's Hypotheses.

1. Students who report having an alcoholic parent will have *lower* grades.
2. Students with an alcoholic parent will drink less than their peers whose parents don't abuse alcohol.
3. Information about alcohol's dangerous effects can reduce students' alcohol use on campus.

REFERENCES

Allain, V. A. (2002). *Academic program review internal self-study report*. Unpublished manuscript, James Madison University.

Association of American Colleges. (1985). *Integrity in the college curriculum: A report to the academic community*. Washington, DC: Association of American Colleges.

Astin, A. W. (1993). *What matters in college? Four critical years revisited*. San Francisco: Jossey-Bass.

Bennett, W. (1984). *To reclaim a legacy*. Washington, DC: National Endowment for Humanities, Carnegie Foundation for the Advancement of Teaching.

Centennial Catalogues, The University of Chicago. (2004). William Rainey Harper, 1856–1906. Retrieved February 22, 2004, from www.lib.uchicago.edu/projects/centcat/centcats/pres/presch01_01.html

El-Khawas, E. (1995). *Campus trends* (Higher Education Panel Rep. No. 85). Washington, DC: American Council on Education.

Finney, S. J., & Owens, K. M. (2002). *Cluster five assessment report*. Unpublished manuscript, Center for Assessment and Research Studies, James Madison University.

Gaff, J. G., & Ratcliff, J. L. (Eds.). (1996). *Handbook of the undergraduate curriculum: A comprehensive guide to purposes, structures, practices, and change.* San Francisco: Jossey-Bass.

General College: Kiosk, University of Minnesota. (2002). Retrieved February 22, 2004, from http://www.gen.umn.edu/gc/images/kiosk_article.pdf

Halonen, J. S. (Ed.). (1986). *Teaching critical thinking in psychology.* Milwaukee, WI: Alverno Publications.

Harvard Committee on General Education. (1945). *General education in a free society.* Cambridge, MA: Harvard University Press.

Pastor, D. A., Davis, S., Miller, B. J., Horst, J., & Jones, C. (2003). *Cluster five assessment report.* Unpublished manuscript, Center for Assessment and Research Studies, James Madison University.

Ratcliff, J. L., Johnson, D. K., La Nasa, S. M., & Gaff, J. G. (2001). *The status of general education in the year 2000: Summary of a national survey.* Washington, DC: Association of American Colleges and Universities.

Reynolds, C. W., Allain, V. A., Erwin, T. D., Halpern, L. C., McNallie, R., & Ross, M. K. (1998). Looking backward: James Madison University's general education reform. *Journal of General Education, 47,* 149–165.

Steele, J. M., & Lutz, D. A. (1995). *Report of ACT's research on postsecondary assessment needs.* Iowa City, IA: American College Testing Program.

Stoloff, M. L., Apple, K. J., Barron, K. E., Reis-Bergan, M. J., & Sundre, D. L. (2004). Seven goals for effective program assessment. In D. S. Dunn, C. M. Mehrotra, & J. S. Halonen (Eds.), *Measuring up: Educational assessment challenges and practices for psychology* (pp. 29–46). Washington, DC: American Psychological Association.

U.S. Department of Education, Office of Educational Research and Improvement. (1994). *The national assessment of college students learning: Identification of the skills to be taught, learned, and assessed.* Washington, DC: U.S. Government Printing Office.

IV

Focus on Student Learning

Seldom in Doubt but Often Wrong: Addressing Tenacious Student Misconceptions

Stephen L. Chew
Samford University

A few years ago at my university, a student was working on a research project with a colleague that involved correlations. The student told my colleague that she had thought that correlations could only be a negative one or positive one, and did not know they could be values in between. This student's misunderstanding might not seem remarkable, except that she was a senior psychology major and a good student. By this time in her undergraduate career, she had probably had correlations explained in class no fewer than 10 times. She had passed (with good grades) two statistics courses, one in psychology and one in math, in which she learned to calculate, plot, and interpret correlations. Yet, after all this instruction and experience, here emerged a misconception about correlations.

Is the story of this student uncommon or extraordinary? In terms of having a misconception that is resistant to change, I will argue that the answer is *no*. Students bring many misconceptions and misunderstandings with them into psychology classes, and this is particularly true of introductory psychology. Teachers often underestimate the number, influence, and tenacity of these misconceptions. This chapter reviews where these misconceptions come from, how they influence learning, how resistant they can be to correction, and ways to try to address them.

SOURCES OF MISCONCEPTIONS

Anyone who has taught introductory psychology is aware that students possess misconceptions about what the field of psychology is about and, as a consequence, what the course will be like. These misconceptions come from a variety of sources. The popular media promulgate many. Most obvious are therapists (of widely varying integrity) who appear on talk shows, who usually serve to reinforce the popular stereotype that all psychologists are clinicians or counselors who dispense common sense or help people get in touch with their feelings. Further examples include the popular beliefs, portrayed in many a melodrama, that being hit on the head causes complete retrograde amnesia and that subliminal messages are powerfully persuasive. Self-help programs claim that we only use 10% of our brain or only the left hemisphere of our brain (or 10% of the left hemisphere). Even mainstream news reports about psychological research are often written in an incomplete or misleading way, and the research that is reported is chosen more for its sensational value rather than its merit. If such research is later discredited, that information rarely makes the news reports. The so-called Mozart Effect, where listening to Mozart raises a person's IQ, is a perfect example of how a single research report can garner huge media attention but the subsequent refutational work typically goes by unnoted (e.g., Nantais & Schellenberg, 1999; but see Schellenberg, 2004).

Some misconceptions result from "rules of thumb" built up through subjective experience and strengthened by confirmation bias (e.g., Gilovich, 1991). For example, most people believe they are good listeners, good judges of character, and generally, more capable than they really are (Nickerson, 1998). Stereotyped and prejudicial beliefs about certain groups of people also fall into this category (e.g., Greenwald & Banaji, 1995; Nisbett & Ross, 1980).

Mistaken beliefs can occur because they seem intuitively logical, fair, or just, such as the belief that blind people develop greater sensitivity in other senses, a baby and parents develop attachment at birth, and actions always flow from attitudes. These mistaken beliefs fit our mental model of how the world ought to work. Some simplistic misconceptions take hold because they are easier to grasp than more complicated, confusable, or counterintuitive concepts. Examples familiar to all introductory psychology instructors include students' difficulty distinguishing negative reinforcement from punishment, learning that genetics and environment interact and are not additive, believing that schizophrenia and multiple personality are the same thing, and understanding that negative correlations can be as strong as positive ones.

Unfortunately, another source of misconceptions is our academic colleagues, both from outside and within psychology. I have had colleagues from other disciplines tell me that they advised students to take introductory psychology because they are more of a "touchy-feely" kind of person. Colleagues have told me that a course they are teaching contains a significant psychology component because of an assigned reading by Freud. Within psychology, teaching the introductory course requires instructors to teach topics outside their area of specialization (see

Dunn, Schmidt, & Zaremba, chap. 3, this volume). When this happens, it increases the possibility of misinformation and misconceptions being taught. This problem is most acute among new instructors, but even seasoned teachers are not immune because they cannot keep up with the latest developments in all areas of psychology and lecture notes are often updated only sporadically. As a department chair, I make a point of visiting the classes of all new instructors. I typically find that there are some factual errors in the presentation, especially if instructors are teaching outside their area, but more than once I've discovered that my understanding of a topic I have been teaching for years, usually in an area outside my specialization, is either incomplete or contains a misconception.

Finally, some misconceptions are developed and entrenched because they are part of a person's self-image. A good example is social influence. When I teach about Milgram's (1974) obedience studies, many of my students are aghast that 65% of subjects would administer the highest level of shock, yet few of my students are willing to believe they might be among that 65% if they were put in that situation. Conformity, diffusion of responsibility, deindividuation, and group-think are things that happen to other people.

I have listed only a few, but many common misconceptions have been documented (e.g., Brown, 1983; Gutman, 1979; Lamal, 1979; Landau & Bavaria, 2003; Vaughan, 1977) and many more are familiar to psychology instructors. They range from global ideas (e.g., the belief that psychology is about getting in touch with one's feelings or is just common sense) to the highly specific (e.g., mind and body are separate and one can choose to ignore one's brain). Such misconceptions are not unique to psychology. They have also been studied extensively in physics and biology (for an overview, see Gardner, 1991). The problem is that such mistaken beliefs are probably even more pervasive in psychology due to its direct application to everyday experience, and this presents special teaching challenges.

TENACITY OF MISCONCEPTIONS

Not only are misconceptions common, they can be remarkably resistant to correction through instruction. Research on student learning indicates that the tenacity of misconceptions even in the face of contradictory evidence is a general phenomenon (Bransford, Brown, & Cocking, 1999), and psychology is no different (e.g., Cerbin, Pointer, Hatch, & Iiyoshi, 2000; Gutman, 1979; Landau & Bavaria, 2003). Consider the extramission theory of vision, the mistaken belief that people see by emitting rays from their eyes that reflect off objects. This seems like a relatively simple misconception that should be easily corrected by reading the sensation chapter of any introductory psychology textbook. Winer, Cottrell, Gregg, Fournier, and Bica (2002) summarized a series of studies that found this belief to be fairly common and hard to correct. To the naïve layperson, the idea that we see by emitting rays seems intuitively logical because it is phenomenologically true; we say we look at things rather than saying we move our eyes to gather the light reflected from an object. The extramission view is also reinforced through popular images (e.g., Superman's x-ray vision). Winer et al. reported that, depending on how one tests for it, more than one half the population may hold some version of this belief. Moreover, after reviewing a number of studies that tried to correct extramission beliefs, Winer et al. "found no evidence that traditional readings presented immediately before the test, formal classroom experiences, or the combination of both improved performance" (p. 421). They did find, however, that when college students were shown a highly simplified lecture on vision containing explicit refutational statements about extramission beliefs, there was a reduction in those beliefs. The improvement, however, was temporary and disappeared after 5 months. Thus, it may be that students leave our psychology courses with their misconceptions intact (Cerbin et al., 2000). Indeed, they may actually feel more confident in their mistaken beliefs because they have taken a psychology course (Landau & Bavaria, 2003)!

Within psychology, Benassi and Goldstein (chap. 16, this volume) demonstrate how beliefs in the paranormal can resist correction through course instruction. Anderson, Lepper, and Ross (1980) created false beliefs in subjects about the best personality traits for selecting firefighters. They found that once this belief was established, it was highly resistant to debriefing and dehoaxing. Vosniadou and Brewer (1992) provided an excellent example of the difficulty facing teachers in changing an entrenched misconception. They studied how children move from the intuitive belief that the earth is flat to the correct belief that the earth is a sphere. They found that internalizing the correct belief takes many years and involves many incorrect transitional beliefs. This finding underlines the challenge of changing misconceptions. Cerbin et al. (2000) conducted an extensive study of the change, or lack of change, in simplistic student preconceptions throughout an educational psychology course. They found that, even with extensive, active learning, student misconceptions were likely to triumph over course concepts when students are asked to apply their knowledge to new situations.

IMPLICATIONS OF MISCONCEPTIONS FOR TEACHING AND LEARNING

The finding that students have misconceptions and these misconceptions are resistant to change would matter little to teachers if such beliefs had no consequence for further learning. A large body of literature on schema and learning, however, indicates this is not the case. People's schema or belief system can have a major impact on what is noticed, what is learned, what is forgotten, and how memories may become distorted (e.g., Bower, Black, & Turner, 1979; Bransford & Johnson, 1972; Schacter, 1999).

If these misconceptions are prevalent and if they influence learning, then why are they not a more central issue in teaching? Some teachers mistakenly assume these mistaken beliefs are benign or weak. Many instructors believe that their primary responsibility in teaching is presenting information accurately and clearly. What the students bring to and take away from their teaching is not the instructor's responsibility. These teachers may not even be aware of the existence of misconceptions or, if they are aware, fail to address these misconceptions because they are not their responsibility. It is only when a teacher shifts the primary focus of teaching away from what is taught to what students are actually learning that misconceptions become a major concern.

ADDRESSING STUDENT MISCONCEPTIONS

Conceptual Change

The next question, then, is how to correct the tenacious misconceptions that affect whether and what students learn. This question addresses the fundamental issue of how systems of belief are changed or refined through experience (cf. Schnotz, Vosniadou, & Carretero, 1999). When a person experiences something that does not fit into prior beliefs, either the beliefs may change to fit the new information or their memory of the event may be distorted to fit the prior beliefs. Although many researchers have studied one or the other phenomenon, no one has yet specified the conditions under which one or the other, or both, will occur. Piaget, for example, distinguished between accommodation and assimilation, but he never specified under what conditions accommodation will occur and under what conditions assimilation will occur. Beliefs must be related to memory processes. In a review, Schacter (1999) discussed suggestibility, bias, and persistence as general principles of memory, but did not discuss when one or others, or some combination of the three, will occur. Schema theorists since Bartlett (1932) have known that sometimes a schema influences comprehension of new information and sometimes new information modifies a schema, but none have ever specified the conditions under which one or the other occurs.

As already discussed, some beliefs are highly resistant to change, but research on reconstructive recall indicate that, in some conditions, beliefs can be malleable and are easily changed such that people will believe events have occurred that did not occur at all (e.g., Loftus, 1997; Roediger & McDerrmott, 1995). Why is it that some beliefs are easily changed (e.g., the misinformation effect) and others are resistant (e.g., prejudice)?

Strategies for Changing Misconceptions

Even without a theoretical framework of conceptual change to guide research on changing beliefs, several researchers have developed methods of challenging misconceptions with some success. Winer et al. (2002) suggested a process they called "activation" to counter misconceptions. Activation involves alerting students to misconceptions before presenting the relevant, accurate information. One method of achieving activation is through the use of examples that are engaging, relevant, and make clear the shortcomings of a misconception. Although virtually all teachers use examples, relatively few actually select or design examples explicitly to meet these criteria (e.g., Ward & Sweller, 1990). Even when they do, however, using examples effectively is not straightforward (e.g., Lee & Hutchison, 1998).

Bransford et al. (1999) summarized two methods of changing misconceptions that have come out of physics education but should be applicable to the teaching of psychology. The first is the use of interactive lecture demonstrations (e.g., Thornton & Sokoloff, 1998), which is similar to the use of examples discussed earlier. Students are presented with a concrete demonstration of a counterintuitive principle of physics, but before the demonstration is performed, students first discuss the demonstration with classmates and record their prediction—which is usually wrong—of the outcome. The demonstration is then performed and students see that their predictions were incorrect. Giving students immediate feedback about the error of their predictions seems to be critical for correcting the misconception.

A second method for challenging misconceptions, discussed by Bransford et al. (1999), is called "bridging" (e.g., Clement, 1993). In bridging, the teacher begins with a correct belief on the part of the student and tries to create a bridge between that belief and a misconception through analogical reasoning. This technique might be used in teaching conformity, for example. After reviewing the research on conformity, students might generate examples of conformity in their own lives and compare it to the conditions under which conformity occurred in the research, and this might help students understand the role that conformity plays in their lives.

Cerbin et al. (2000) conducted an in-depth study on using problem-based learning (PBL) to challenge tenacious misconceptions in an educational psychology course. PBL involves organizing a course around authentic, open-ended, ill-structured problems. Students must gather and synthesize information to develop a solution to the problem. As students develop hypotheses about the problem, more information is revealed to give students feedback about the adequacy of their approach. In the course, Cerbin assigns problems that usually activate simplistic misconceptions among students. For example, he assigns a scenario, called the "Middle School Science Problem," in which a new teacher gives a test to her students and finds they do poorly. Cerbin's students must develop strategies to help the teacher improve student learning. This assignment occurs early in the course and most students resort to their own personal experience and simplistic suggestions, such as giving students a study outline. Cerbin then addresses why these solutions are superficial and will not lead to a deeper understanding, and the stage is then set for exploring basic principles of learning that students can then use to develop more effective teaching strategies to address the problem. Cerbin uses a variety of these kinds of problems to activate and challenge misconceptions. His analyses of student performance at the end of the course shows that PBL is effective in changing mistaken beliefs, but a large percentage of the class maintain or revert to these preconceptions in the face of new problems. These results mirror those found by Benassi and Goldstein (chap. 16, this volume) in trying to change student beliefs in the paranormal.

A method that I have used with success is the *ConcepTest*, which was developed by Mazur (1997) as part of a larger teaching method he called Peer Instruction. Mazur developed Peer Instruction to improve the teaching of introductory physics, and he documented the effectiveness of the technique. *ConcepTests* are at the core of Peer Instruction, and their use is easily adapted for teaching psychology (Chew, 2004). They provide an active and engaging way to make both teacher and students aware of the limits of student understanding. They can be used to highlight and help correct common yet tenacious student misconceptions. Furthermore, they are easy to prepare, take relatively little class time, and can be used in any size class.

A *ConcepTest* is a problem that requires understanding of a key concept to solve. A set of possible answers is given with the problem, one of which is correct while the other answers are intuitively appealing but wrong. Essentially, a *ConcepTest* is a good multiple-choice question that has a common misconception as a lure. Here is one I use for correlations:

> A marriage counselor studies four different tests designed to predict marital happiness to see which one is best. She administers the four tests to 80 couples who are about to get married. After 2 years, she measures the marital happiness of the couples and correlates it with each of the four tests with the following results:
>
> Test 1: $r = -.73$ Test 2: $r = .62$
>
> Test 3: $r = .25$ Test 4: $r = .10$
>
> If the therapist wanted to pick the single best test to use in her work, which one should she choose and why?

The correct answer is Test 1: $r = -.73$, because it is the strongest correlation and therefore the best predictor. Many students, however, have the misconception that positive correlations are better than negative ones, so they pick Test 2, the strongest positive correlation. Students who fail to distinguish between $r = .10$ and $r = 1.0$ pick Test 4.

The key to using *ConcepTests* effectively is how they are used in the classroom. I use the following procedure adapted from Mazur (1997). First I explain correlations to the class. Afterward, I present the *ConcepTest* in the following way:

1. I present the *ConcepTest* to the class on overhead or PowerPoint and give them time to think privately about which answer they believe is correct. This takes about 3 minutes.

2. On my signal, all students publicly indicate their answer by raising their hands with the number of fingers of their chosen alternative, one through four. The distribution of responses within the class is obvious to both students and teacher.

3. I have students pick a classmate, preferably with a different answer, to discuss their choices and try to come to a consensus. This takes a minimum of 2–3 minutes.

4. I repeat Step 2 to see how choices have changed, and if there is a class consensus.

5. Finally, I have students explain their choices and discuss the correct answer as a class. This final step typically takes a minimum of 2 minutes, but often an extended class discussion can ensue.

Notice how all students must publicly and simultaneously commit to an answer, justify the answer to a peer, and then commit again. Their misconception, or correct understanding, is activated, and they get immediate feedback about the accuracy of their choices and the correct reasoning. Thus, activation of the misconception and comparison to the correct concept is achieved. Students are actively engaged and are learning from each other as well as the teacher. The instructor also gets immediate feedback about how well the class understands a concept and whether or not more explanation is needed.

ConcepTests are no harder to develop than good multiple-choice questions. In fact, when I use them in class, I emphasize to my students that these *ConcepTests* are similar to the kinds of questions they will see on the exam, which increases their engagement. According to Mazur (1997), a good *ConcepTest* should focus on a single concept; require conceptual understanding to solve; have adequate response alternatives (ideally the incorrect answer choices should reflect the student's most common misconceptions); and be neither too easy nor too difficult, with about a 60%–80% initial correct response rate.

I tested the effectiveness of *ConcepTests* in correcting misconceptions about correlations using two different sections of introductory psychology with about 50 students each. In one section of introductory psychology, I gave my usual presentation on correlations and then administered the *ConcepTest* in the manner described earlier. In the next semester, I gave that section of introductory psychology just my usual presentation on correlations without the *ConcepTest*. I should note that my presentation on correlations is one I developed over 15 years of teaching introductory psychology and includes interactive examples of different strengths of correlations, including one that shows that a negative correlation can be stronger than a positive one.

In order to assess the impact of the *ConcepTest*, as part of the midterm exam, which occurred about 2 weeks after the presentation on correlations, I had three questions to test student understanding of correlations. The first question, shown in Table 15.1, was factual, simply asking which among four correlations was the strongest (with a negative correlation being the strongest). The second question, shown in Table 15.2, was more conceptual and applied in nature in that it asked which of four statements was a conclusion that could legitimately be drawn from a given correlation. Three of the statements were causal and one, the correct answer, was descriptive. This question tested the concept that correlations do not entail causality, which is another common misconception. These first two questions were given as part of the 60-question multiple-choice portion of the exam that all

TABLE 15.1

Results for the Factual Question

Question and alternatives	No ConcepTest % Response (N = 49)	ConcepTest % Response (N = 49)
Which of the following is the strongest correlation?		
a. r = .10	22.00	8.33
b. r = .57	16.00	0.00
c. r = −.63 (Correct Answer)	62.00	91.67
d. r = .25	0.00	0.00

TABLE 15.2

Results for the Conceptual Question

Question and alternatives	No ConcepTest % Response (N = 49)	ConcepTest % Response (N = 49)
A psychologist determines that the correlation between level of shyness and the strength of self-esteem is −.70. What can be concluded from this correlation coefficient?		
a. Being very shy causes people to have low self-esteem.	8.33	4.08
b. Because you don't like yourself, you want to avoid interacting with other people.	2.08	0.00
c. A third factor is controlling both shyness and self-esteem.	12.50	10.20
d. People who have low self-esteem tend to be very shy. (Correct Answer)	22.92	34.69
e. All of the above are reasonable conclusions.	54.17	51.02

students had to complete. The third question, shown in Table 15.3, was also an applied problem that required students to utilize their understanding of correlations. It was essentially another *ConcepTest* about correlations. This question was presented as an optional bonus question at the end of the exam. This question was most similar to the *ConcepTest* used in class, because it contained the same kinds of intuitive but incorrect answer alternatives. It also required students to supply a written justification for their answer as well as selecting the correct alternative. This allowed me to distinguish those who got the right answer merely through guessing from those who truly understood correlations. It also helped me identify students who selected the wrong answer, but through their explanation showed that they really understood the concept. I call this question an Understanding Probe because it gives me insight into students' true level of understanding of a concept, and these probes are very useful for assessment.

The results for the factual question are shown in Table 15.1. The majority of students selected the correct answer even without *ConcepTests*. Only a small proportion of students manifested the misconception that positive correlations are always better than negative ones when the question was so simply and directly stated. Even so, the use of *ConcepTests* led to a significant increase in the percentage of students who selected the correct answer, $\chi^2 [2] = 14.27, p < .05$.

Table 15.2 summarizes the results for the conceptual question. Correctly answering this challenging question requires students to both distinguish causal from descriptive conclusions and to apply the understanding that correlations do not imply causality. The *ConcepTest* used in class did not cover this aspect of correlations. Not surprisingly, the differences between the groups was not significant, $\chi^2 [4] = 3.12, ns$, although the *ConcepTest* group did had a higher percentage of correct responses as compared to the No *ConcepTest* group. The results showed that most students chose the incorrect alternative of "All of the Above," regardless of whether or not they had experienced the *ConcepTest*. The trend for a higher percentage of students who had the *ConcepTest* to answer the question correctly over the control group is intriguing. In future research, I plan to eliminate the "All of the Above" lure to examine the pattern of results when students are forced to choose among alternatives.

Table 15.3 shows the results from the Understanding Probe. In scoring this question, I required that the student both select the correct alternative and explain the choice correctly. Answers that did not have an explanation, were obvious guesses, or were ambiguous explanations were not counted as correct. The results show that the *ConcepTest* group had a higher percentage of correct responses than the No *ConcepTest* group. In fact, more students chose the correct response than chose Test B, the incorrect alternative that reflected the misconception that positive correlations are stronger than negative ones. The opposite was true with the No *ConcepTest* group. The highest percentage of students chose Test B, demonstrating the misconception. When comparing the response rates for the two groups for these two alternatives, the *ConcepTest* group showed significantly better performance, $\chi^2 [1] = 3.83, p = .05$.

These results show that *ConcepTests* can lead to significant increases in learning at both the factual and conceptual levels of understanding. Furthermore, they are an effective means of addressing common but mistaken student beliefs about psychology. Although *ConcepTests* do lead to significant improvement in understanding, student performance is far from perfect, indicating the difficulty of over-

TABLE 15.3

Results for the Understanding Probe

Question and alternatives	No ConcepTest % Response (N = 49)	ConcepTest % Response (N = 49)
Samford decides that the ACT and SAT are obsolete, and decides to find a new college entrance exam to use for admissions. They have incoming freshmen take four new entrance exams. After the end of the first year, the student's GPA is correlated with each of the four scores. Which exam should Samford adopt? Explain your answer.		
Test A: r = .10	18.18	8.51
Test B: r = −.64 (Correct Answer)	29.55	53.19
Test C: r = .55	50.00	36.17
Test D: r = −.50	2.27	2.13

coming entrenched misconceptions. Of course, this is not a true experiment because there was no random assignment to groups and the experimenter (me) was aware of the conditions. Even though it is imperfect, it is still evidence in an authentic context that *ConcepTests* are effective in improving student learning, especially in light of their success in other fields. Replication of these findings in future classes will reduce the uncertainty caused by the quasi-experimental design.

One interesting aspect of the results reported here is that the likelihood of a misconception manifesting itself in student thinking depends on the kind of question being asked. Many students answered the factual question correctly but reverted to their misconceptions in conceptual and applied questions. The key issue in misconceptions may not be whether or not students have them, but under what conditions they are likely to emerge and dominate student thinking.

CONCLUSIONS

In conclusion, I have tried to describe how students often possess misconceptions about psychology, especially in the introductory class, and how difficult they can be to correct. These misconceptions have a major impact on what students do and do not learn in a course. Many teachers choose to ignore their presence and impact, acting as if they are benign or irrelevant to teaching. Unfortunately, this in itself is a dangerous misconception. I have outlined several methods for challenging misconceptions reported in the literature. Furthermore, I reported research that I have done on the use of *ConcepTests*. The results provide evidence that *ConcepTests* are effective for overcoming mistaken beliefs in introductory psychology. Even though the teaching strategies outlined here are effective in addressing misconceptions, the evidence indicates that a significant percentage of students still cling to mistaken beliefs despite the strategies, that the mistaken beliefs can re-emerge under different conditions or at later times, and that even when students develop correct understandings, these understandings are often fragile and students are likely to revert to the mistaken beliefs. The greatest challenge facing psychology teachers may not be teaching students new information, but teaching them that what they already believe to be true about psychology is often wrong.

ACKNOWLEDGMENTS

A briefer version of this chapter appeared in: Chew, S. L. (2004, March). Student misconceptions in the psychology classroom. *E-xcellence in Teaching*, article posted to Psychteacher electronic mailing list (http://teachpsych.lemoyne.edu/teachpsych/div/psychteacher.html), archived at http://teachpsych.lemoyne.edu/teachpsych/eit/index.html. Any portions of that article that appear in this chapter are used with permission.

The author thanks Dana Dunn, Bryan Saville, and Tracy Zinn for their thoughtful comments on earlier versions of this work.

REFERENCES

Anderson C. A., Lepper, M. R., & Ross, L. (1980). Perseverance of social theories: The role of explanation the persistence of discredited information. *Journal of Personality and Social Psychology, 39,* 1037–1049.

Bartlett, F. (1932). *Remembering: A study in experimental and social psychology.* Cambridge, England: Cambridge University Press.

Bower, G. H., Black, J. B., & Turner, T. J. (1979). Scripts in memory for text. *Cognitive Psychology, 11,* 177–220.

Bransford J. D., Brown, A. L., & Cocking, R. R. (Eds.). (1999). *How people learn: Brain, mind, experience and school.* Washington, DC: National Academy Press.

Bransford, J. D., & Johnson, M. K. (1972). Contextual prerequisites for understanding. Some investigations of comprehension and recall. *Journal of Verbal Learning and Verbal Behavior, 11,* 717–726.

Brown, L. T. (1983). Some more misconceptions about psychology among introductory psychology students. *Teaching of Psychology, 10,* 207–210.

Cerbin, W., Pointer, D., Hatch, T., & Iiyoshi, T. (2000). *Problem-based learning in an educational psychology course.* Retrieved June 30, 2004, from Carnegie Foundation for the Advancement of Teaching Web site: http://gallery.carnegiefoundation.org/bcerbin/Course_Overview/course_overview.html

Chew, S. L. (2004). Using *ConcepTests* for formative assessment. *Psychology Teacher Network, 14,* 10–12.

Clement, J. (1993). Using bridging analogies and anchoring intuitions to deal with students' preconceptions in physics. *Journal of Research in Science Teaching, 30,* 1241–1257.

Gardner, H. (1991). *The unschooled mind: How children think and how schools should teach.* New York: Basic Books.

Gilovich, T. (1991). *How we know what isn't so: The fallibility of human reason in everyday life.* New York: The Free Press.

Greenwald, A. G., & Banaji, M. R. (1995). Implicit social cognition: Attitudes, self-esteem, and stereotypes. *Psychological Review, 102,* 4–27.

Gutman, A. (1979). Misconceptions of psychology and performance in the introductory course. *Teaching of Psychology, 6,* 159–161.

Lamal, P. A. (1979). College students' common beliefs about psychology. *Teaching of Psychology, 6,* 155–158.

Landau, J. D., & Bavaria, A. J. (2003). Does deliberate source monitoring reduce students' misconceptions about psychology? *Teaching of Psychology, 30,* 311–314.

Lee, A. Y., & Hutchison, L. (1998). Improving learning from examples through reflection. *Journal of Experimental Psychology: Applied, 4,* 187–210.

Loftus, E. F. (1997). Creating false memories. *Scientific American, 277,* 70–75.

Mazur, E. (1997). *Peer instruction: A user's manual.* Englewood Cliffs, NJ: Prentice-Hall.

Milgram, S. (1974). *Obedience to authority: An experimental view.* New York: Harper & Row.

Nantais, K. M., & Schellenberg, E. G. (1999). The Mozart effect: An artifact of preference. *Psychological Science, 10,* 370–373.

Nickerson, R. S. (1998). Confirmation bias: A ubiquitous phenomenon in many guises. *Review of General Psychology, 2,* 175–220.

Nisbett, R. E., & Ross, L. (1980). *Human inference: Strategies and shortcomings of social judgment.* Englewood Cliffs, NJ: Prentice-Hall.

Roediger, H. L., III, & McDermott, K. B. (1995). Creating false memories: Remembering words not presented in lists. *Journal of Experimental Psychology: Learning, Memory and Cognition, 21,* 803–814.

Schacter, D. L. (1999). The seven sins of memory: Insights from psychology and cognitive neuroscience. *American Psychologist, 54,* 182–203.

Schellenberg, E. G. (2004). Music lessons enhance IQ. *Psychological Science, 15,* 511–514.

Schnotz, W., Vosniadou, S., & Carretero, M. (Eds.). (1999). *New perspectives on conceptual change.* New York: Pergamon.

Thornton, R. K., & Sokoloff, D. R. (1998). Assessing student learning of Newton's laws: The force and motion conceptual evaluation and the evaluation of active learning laboratory and lecture curricula. *American Journal of Physics, 64,* 338–352.

Vaughan, E. D. (1977). Misconceptions about psychology among introductory psychology students. *Teaching of Psychology, 4,* 138–141.

Vosniadou, S., & Brewer, W. F. (1992). Mental models of the earth: A study of conceptual change in childhood. *Cognitive Psychology, 24,* 535–585.

Ward, M., & Sweller, J. (1990). Structuring effective worked examples. *Cognition and Instruction, 7,* 1–39.

Winer, G. A., Cottrell, J. E., Gregg, V., Fournier, J. S., & Bica, L. S. (2002) Fundamentally misunderstanding visual perception: Adults' belief in visual emissions. *American Psychologist, 57,* 417–424.

Students' Beliefs About Paranormal Claims: Implications for Teaching Introductory Psychology

Victor A. Benassi
University of New Hampshire

Gary S. Goldstein
University of New Hampshire at Manchester

Pat awoke early on Monday to get ready to attend an 8 AM introductory psychology class. After referring to his personal biorhythm chart to check up on his physical, emotional, and intellectual well-being, he finished reading an advertisement for a firewalking workshop that he planned to attend and read his daily horoscope on the Internet. As he left his dorm room, he smiled and thought to himself, "It's going to be a great day!"

The beliefs and conceptual frameworks that guide students' thinking are often inconsistent with or contradictory to what we know from study of the physical, biological, and social sciences. Students may also hold "naïve theories" about the nature of reality that are often formed during childhood (Resnick, 1983). As a result, many students enter college with a wide variety of beliefs about putative paranormal and other "extraordinary" phenomena. (In this chapter, when such phrases as "paranormal phenomenon" are used, this means putative paranormal phenomenon.) They also believe that they "know things" about these phenomena, often based on personal experiences and what they are exposed to in public media. The introductory psychology course is an ideal forum to address paranormal claims and students' beliefs and understanding of them, because these phenomena are fundamentally psychological in nature (cf. Zusne & Jones, 1989).

In addressing students' beliefs about the paranormal, teachers of introductory psychology may want to consider college students' cognitive development, their naïve theories about human behavior and the physical world, and the cognitive heuristics and biases that shape their beliefs and influence their judgments. Further, general principles of psychology may assist students in learning about the normal bases of these so-called paranormal phenomena (Zusne & Jones, 1989). This chapter first describes some representative beliefs of introductory psychology college students about putative paranormal phenomena. Next, it discusses theories and research that may help introductory psychology teachers understand their students' belief systems. Finally, it offers some suggestions about what introductory psychology teachers can do to assist their students in developing alternative constructions of paranormal phenomena.

PARANORMAL BELIEF AND COLLEGE STUDENTS

Paranormal phenomena represent a class of phenomena that seem to violate physical laws. The term *paranormal* is applied broadly to many types of phenomena: extrasensory perception (ESP), psychokinesis (PK), ghosts, astrology, miraculous healing, psychic surgery, firewalking, numerology, unidentified flying objects (UFOs), homeopathy, reincarnation, witchcraft, and so forth. The scientific study of belief in such phenomena addresses issues related to the extent, causes, and correlates of such beliefs. Parapsychology is the scientific study of putative paranormal phenomena.

A recent National Science Foundation biennial report (2002) indicated that a majority of high school and college students in the United States believe in the reality of such alleged phenomena as ESP and magnetic therapy. Sizeable minorities believe that UFOs are vehicles of beings from other parts of the universe and in the reality of the claims of astrology. Additional studies have documented widespread paranormal belief among the general American population (e.g., Gallup & Newport, 1991; Newport & Strausberg, 2001).

Introductory psychology teachers who aim to present the discipline of psychology in the context of modern experimental science face an uphill challenge because of the extent and intransigence of paranormal beliefs. An understanding of cognitive processes and belief systems of college students is a good, and we believe necessary, starting point if teachers want their students to develop more informed and critical perspectives about paranormal claims. In addition, based on what we know about the intractability of paranormal beliefs, simple exposure to theories and data that support normal accounts of supposed paranormal phenomena will likely have little effect on promoting conceptual change in students.

PERSISTENCE OF BELIEF

One of us (VAB) taught a psychology course that provided analyses of alleged paranormal phenomena and covered theories and research that addressed the question of why belief in the paranormal seemed to be so strong and pervasive. Students analyzed various claims that ostensibly supported the existence of paranormal phenomena and found most of it wanting. In addition, there was ample discussion of psychological, sociological, and anthropological theories and research that could help students understand paranormal belief systems.

At the beginning of the last class of the semester, a student said that she had brought a friend to class who claimed to have psychic abilities. She asked if he could demonstrate his alleged feats. Permission was denied. Predictably, class members became upset. "Let the man perform. What are you afraid of!" Unknown to the students, the "psychic" was a confederate and, after some hemming and hawing by the professor, was allowed to perform. The confederate successfully completed three amateur tricks—bending a brass rod, teleporting cigarette ashes from one location to another, and finger reading (reading written material with his fingers while blind folded).

After a semester of review and investigation of a range of alleged paranormal claims, the expectation was that students would challenge the psychic with questions, provide numerous nonpsychic alternative explanations for what the confederate had done, and propose that he repeat his performance, this time with stringent controls. After all, most students had indicated on a questionnaire administered a short time before that their belief in psychic phenomena was lower than it was at the beginning of the semester. Furthermore, throughout the semester, most of the students demonstrated on examinations that they understood how to evaluate paranormal claims and to propose nonpsychic accounts of them. At the same time, on an anonymous feedback sheet to be given to the confederate, most students wrote comments indicating that they had witnessed a genuine psychic performance. (For a description of a study that examined this type of phenomenon with students enrolled in introductory psychology courses in an experimental context, see Benassi, Singer, and Reynolds, 1980.) During a question and answer period, many students were clearly in awe of the psychic. The results of this classroom demonstration illustrate that instruction can have apparent effects on belief change, only to be reversed when students are confronted by a relatively powerful personal experience. We suspect the students' thinking about paranormal claims did not undergo meaningful conceptual change during the course of the semester, a point we return to later in this chapter.

Lest the reader erroneously conclude that this type of belief persistence only applies to the paranormal, we need to emphasize that students' views in other areas may be colored by their informally acquired beliefs. For example, Brumby (1984) found that a majority of first-year students at an Australian medical school started their training as essentially "Lamarckians." At the beginning of their studies, "students seem to be extrapolating from changes seen within the lifetime of an individual to account for changes seen in populations selected over many generations. In their reasoning, insects become more immune, rather than more insects become immune" (p. 499). Did a year of medical school improve students' understanding of evolutionary theory? Brumby found that only a minority of students demonstrated their ability to recognize and apply principles of natural selection on a follow-up assessment of their understanding of evolutionary principles in applied contexts (cf. Singer & Benassi, 1981). Like many introductory psychology students who learn the skills of good test-taking, and like the students described earlier, the medical students in Brumby's study did well in learning factual information about evolutionary principles and then demonstrated that knowledge on exams. Still, when given the opportunity, many of them failed to apply that knowledge to actual contexts. In both of the previously described courses and in Brumby's study, exposure to relevant academic material did not seem to penetrate students' core beliefs.

In a different domain of science, McCloskey, Caramazza, and Green (1980) tested college students' understanding of the principle that objects move in a straight line when no external force operates on them. Even many students with training in physics did not properly answer simple questions concerning the motion of objects. For example, in one study, students were provided with a picture of a curved metal tube. They were asked to draw the path of a metal ball that is first inserted into one end of the tube and then is "shot out" of the other end. The students were instructed to ignore air resistance and any spin the ball might have when considering the path they drew. For this problem, 51% of the students indicated in their drawings that the ball would follow a curved path after it left the tube. Students who had taken a college physics course were less likely to make this error than students who had never taken a physics course. However, the type of errors made was the same in the two groups.

During postexperimental interviews, McCloskey et al. asked their subjects about the source of their beliefs about motion. These students seemed to hold "naïve beliefs" similar to the impetus theory of motion popular during the middle ages. McCloskey et al. suggested that "educators in the sciences should not treat students as merely lacking in the correct information. Instead, educators should take into account the fact that many students have strong preconceptions and misconceptions and problem-solving strategies that are different from those used by experts. When a student's naive beliefs are not addressed, instruction may only serve to provide the student ... with new terminology for expressing his erroneous beliefs" (p. 1141).

One implication of McCloskey et al.'s and Brumby's work is that it is not sufficient to simply offer a course on physics or biology, respectively, to successfully address students' naïve, inaccurate, and persistent views of certain phenomena. The same point applies to students' understanding of phenomena they believe may have a paranormal basis—namely, that an introductory psychology course that focuses on content may be insufficient in affecting students' understanding of and belief in paranormal claims. As we develop later in this chapter, introductory psychology teachers will likely need to employ specific teaching strategies if they hope to promote conceptual change in their students.

Pseudoscience and the Persistence of Belief

Students' beliefs about firewalking (walking over hot coals or similar substances) illustrate the persistence of belief as well as a tendency for them to, at times, rely on pseudoscience to support their view. For some students, pseudoscience is science and therefore provides a ready-made justification for the persistence of their beliefs. For example, some of our students believe with the proper training and the right "state of mind," people can walk across hot surfaces such as burning coals. Burkan (2004), the self-proclaimed leader of the firewalking movement, offered this advice:

> Knowing the secret behind firewalking can improve your life! Even if you never do it yourself, knowing how it works can bring you better health and increased personal power. Why? Because firewalking demonstrates how your thoughts impact everything else in your life. Thoughts change brain chemistry, and that results in an alteration of body chemistry as well. This is immediately apparent when you entertain a sexual fantasy. Firewalkers are instructed to pay close attention to their thoughts, since those very thoughts are the way in which we create our own realities. Positive thinkers literally live in a different chemical environment than negative thinkers. They impose less stress on their immune systems, and the result of that should be obvious. (Over Two Million Westerners Have Firewalked section, ¶ 1)

If students find Burkan's ideas about firewalking enticing, then it may be because he incorporates language that links mental state with physiological functioning. Introductory psychology students are also likely to have some knowledge related to the topic as well, although theirs is likely to be fairly nonspecific, for example, "The mind can influence the body." In both cases, the pseudoscientific approach manages to borrow enough scientific terminology to seduce people to consider its central theme. As teachers of introductory psychology, we would be well advised to recognize that pseudoscience can be quite convincing to our students and provide them with justification for maintaining their beliefs. When addressing pseudoscience with our students, it is important that we resist simply persuading them to adopt a scientific perspective. After all, that is what the proponents of pseudoscience do. Our challenge is to help students develop and refine a skeptical, critical, and balanced perspective based on the scientific approach.

Firewalking can be understood in simple physical terms if one appreciates the distinction between the concepts of temperature and heat (Leikind & McCarthy, 1985). A review of research has documented, however, that most children and college students do not distinguish between these concepts (Eylon & Linn, 1988). Burkan (2004) confused the issue when he asserted that the "conductivity" theory of how firewalking safely takes place does not explain successful firewalking.

Rather, he invoked the power of the mind over the body: "Because of my extensive research, I now counsel prospective firewalkers to avoid walking on the embers unless their bodies are relaxed. The body itself is an excellent reflection of mental state.... Thus, firewalking becomes an exercise in examining the mind/body connection" (Mind in Matter section, ¶ 11).

Our experience is that students can easily learn the physics of firewalking and they understand how these basic principles may be applied to account for successful firewalking. These same students may persevere, however, in the view that such physical explanations are inadequate. In their view, real firewalkers are not burned because of their mind's ability to prevent flesh from burning. Some invoke "auras" (a New Age metaphysical concept that refers to "energy fields" or "life forces") or other pseudoscientific accounts. We have even had our students tell us that they did not "buy" physicists' explanations of firewalking and that they find Burkan's account more "valid." They persist in their original views even though they have been provided a conceptual structure to understand a phenomenon in physical terms.

Confirmation Bias and the Persistence of Belief

Consider what, nearly 400 years ago, Bacon (1620) explained in *Novum Organum*:

> The human understanding, when any proposition has been laid down ... forces everything else to add fresh support and confirmation; and although most cogent and abundant instances may exist to the contrary, yet either does not observe or despises them ... rather than sacrifice the authority of its first conclusions.... It is the peculiar and perpetual error of the human understanding to be more moved and excited by affirmatives than negatives, whereas it ought duly and regularly to be impartial; nay, in establishing any true axiom, the negative instance is the most powerful. (Aphorisms section, ¶ 46)

Contemporary writers on this topic have echoed Bacon's proposition. The confirmatory bias has been documented in the psychological literature (e.g., Nickerson, 1998). It should not be surprising that this ubiquitous phenomenon has been demonstrated with introductory psychology students. For example, many introductory psychology teachers are familiar with Forer's (1949) classic demonstration of the fallacy of personal validation (the propensity of people to accept general and vague personality descriptions as accurately fitting them), which has been applied to belief in astrology (e.g., Munro & Munro, 2000; Ward & Grasha, 1986).

Russell and Jones (1980) examined a different aspect of the confirmation bias as it relates to paranormal belief. They assigned college students to either a high belief or low belief group based on their score on a measure of paranormal belief. Half of the students in each group read an abstract of a fictitious research study of

ESP in which the results of the study confirmed the hypothesis that ESP would be found. The other half of the students in each group read the same abstract, except the results of the study did not confirm the ESP hypothesis. Students then completed a 15-item recall task pertaining to the content of the abstract. The percentage of students who correctly recalled the outcome of the study described in the two forms of the abstract was similar for the low paranormal belief group (ESP occurred = 88%; ESP did not occur = 91%). The students in the high paranormal belief group also showed excellent recall when they read the abstract in which ESP was confirmed (100%). Strikingly, only 39% of the students in the high paranormal belief group who read the abstract in which ESP was not confirmed correctly recalled that finding. Jones and Russell's students' prior belief influenced their memory for belief inconsistent information. The implication of these findings for the introductory psychology teachers is straightforward. Students' prior beliefs about paranormal phenomena are likely to influence their processing and retrieval of belief inconsistent information. Some approaches that may ameliorate this problem are discussed later.

We may gain a better appreciation of the persistence of college students' beliefs in paranormal phenomena by examining confirmation bias among another group, practicing scientists. In *The Structures of Scientific Revolutions,* Kuhn (1970) argued that scientists do not reject scientific theories simply because of nonsupporting evidence. He observed, for example, that Newton's second law of motion "behaves for those committed to Newton's theory very much like a purely logical statement that no amount of observation could refute" (p. 780). Summing up the point nicely, Kuhn observed that "like artists, creative scientists must occasionally live in a world out of joint" (p. 79). Once a theory has reached the status of a paradigm, it is rejected only if a new theory is ready to replace it.

Mitroff (1974) conducted a series of interviews between 1969 and 1972 with a group of NASA geologists who studied moon rocks that were collected during the Apollo missions. Some scientists had publicly stated their beliefs about what the rocks would uncover concerning the origin of the moon. Did the most committed scientists among them change their beliefs with disconfirming evidence? As one scientist put it, "X is so committed to the idea that the moon is Q that you could literally take the moon apart piece by piece, ship it back to Earth, reassemble it in X's backyard and shove the whole thing … and X would still continue to believe that the moon is Q. X's belief in Q is unshakable. He refuses to listen to reason or to evidence. He's so hopped up on the idea of Q that I think he's unbalanced" (p. 586).

If scientists are sometimes reluctant to change their beliefs, then it should be no surprise that students in introductory psychology courses see confirmation of their beliefs when provided belief inconsistent data. People hold a variety of naive beliefs about the world, some of which fly in the face of accepted scientific knowledge but that are supported by personal experience and by the culture in which we live. Try to convince individuals who had a profound "psychic" experience that "came true"—for example, a premonition that a parent was about to unexpectedly die—that laws of probability predict that most of us can be expected to have such experiences from time to time; or tell them that an understanding of concepts such as cause, correlation, or confirming cases might make such an unsettling and inexplicable experience more understandable. Our experience is that such efforts will often only galvanize their original belief.

Cognitive Biases, Heuristics, and Belief

Numerous researchers have documented that college students and others frequently base their beliefs and judgments on a few relatively simple cognitive heuristics (e.g., Gilovich, Griffin, & Kahneman, 2002). One general type of cognitive heuristic relates to people's tendency to perceive associations, including causal ones, between certain events. Alcock's (1995) metaphor of the brain as a belief engine helps clarify this issue as well as account for the acquisition and persistence of beliefs including paranormal beliefs. One component of this belief engine is characterized by "magical thinking," which is the tendency for people to form an association between events that occur closely in time or space. For example, if a professional baseball player makes the sign of a cross as he comes to the plate in a crucial spot in a game and then proceeds to bat in the winning run of the game, he may associate the act with the fortunate outcome. Had he struck out, he may think, "Oh well" and then move on. To paraphrase Bacon (1620), who well understood magical thinking, superstitions are formed because people notice when things "hit" and not when they "miss" and they remember the former but not the latter.

Research related to the illusion of control illustrates the tendency of people to infer causal connections even when they are absent. Langer (1975) proposed a "skill" theory of control to account for the exaggerated estimates of personal control that people often make in situations in which they have no control. Although skill and chance factors are often closely associated in everyday life, people frequently fail to distinguish between controllable and uncontrollable events. Research has shown that people often perceive more control than they actually have, notice associations between events where none exists, and report inordinately high levels of prediction ability (e.g., Ayeroff & Abelson, 1976; Benassi, Sweeney, & Drevno, 1979; Langer, 1975). Thus, coincidence may be confused with prophecy, sampling error with ESP ability, and so on.

An experiment by Ayeroff and Abelson (1976) provides a clear demonstration of this type of confusion using a telepathy task in which a participant attempted to mentally send symbols to a "receiver" located in a different location. They proposed that people's belief in personal success on the task might be influenced by the introduction of skill-related but irrelevant variables into the situation. Although choice and practice are relevant factors in affecting performance in situations where skill is relevant, their introduction in this task was irrelevant because choice and practice had no effect on participants' performance on the telepathy task. Ayeroff and Abelson found that participants who chose the symbols to be transmitted in a mental telepathy task or who completed some practice trials reported greater belief in their success on a test task than participants not afforded these opportunities.

When introductory psychology teachers address cognitive biases and heuristics in their course, they have ample opportunity to demonstrate how paranormal beliefs may be established and maintained, in part, by these factors. (Later sections of this chapter explore teaching approaches that may be used in these contexts.)

Perry's (1970) Model of Cognitive Development

What do we know about the modes of thinking that guide young adults' understanding of the topics, issues, and approaches examined in the typical introductory psychology course? How do their prior beliefs support and conflict with their intellectual development? Although there are several useful frameworks in which these questions may be addressed (e.g., King & Kitchener, 1994), the focus here is on the classic model proposed by Perry (1970) because it is widely known, has generated considerable research, and applies directly to the issues discussed in this chapter. The four phases of development described in Perry's model are dualism, multiplicity, relativism, and commitment in relativism.

In his model of cognitive development, Perry (1970) proposed that, upon entering college, most young adults have a dualistic approach to knowledge (see also Knefelkamp, 2003). They tend toward absolutist belief systems and have difficulty appreciating gray areas in intellectual discourse. They rely on recognized authorities to transfer knowledge and to provide the "correct" answers to them. Students in the multiplistic phase of development acknowledge that there may be uncertainty in some areas of knowledge, but they are not troubled by this uncertainty. They expect that "experts" will eventually remove this ambiguity, but until they do, "anything goes." Students' intellectual values dramatically shift and become markedly less absolutist during the phase of relativism. Students rely much less on authority figures to be the owners of "truth" and recognize the contextual nature of knowledge. These contexts may be empirical, philosophical, historical, and so forth. Debates on issues can now be deconstructed and doubt becomes an element of intellectual growth. The rough seas of disequilibrium associated with relativism are calmed as the student passes into commitment in relativism, a phase characterized by a commitment to a set of ideas and values. But unlike the rigidity of dualism, these ideas and values are flexible and remain open to change based on reflection, new data, and alternate points of view.

How does Perry's model help us understand students in our introductory psychology courses and their beliefs about paranormal phenomena? Although students enter the introductory course with naïve theories or misconceptions about psychology, there are many topics about which they have limited background that relate to the subject matter of the course (e.g., opponent process theory of color vision, the principles of extinction and spontaneous recovery, deep structure theories in linguistics). In such cases, they act like prototypical dualists and turn to their teacher (i.e., the authority figure) to provide them with the "truth" because there are "answers" and the teacher is the expert. On the other hand, when it comes to the paranormal, students look a lot more like people in Perry's multiplistic phase. Not only do college students have considerable prior experiences with so-called paranormal phenomena, they are likely to hold affirmative beliefs about at least some of them. They also often believe that they have expertise about these phenomena, gained from personal experience and exposure to public media (which are strongly biased toward paranormal claims).

Consider a class, for example, in which the concept of therapeutic touch is introduced. One student claims that the underlying mechanism for the treatment is a bioenergetic field. When asked by the teacher to elaborate on this field, the student says, "It's like our aura." When further probed about the nature of this aura, the student says in an exasperated tone, "It's the life force that surrounds us all." The teacher then asks how we might measure this force. At this point another student exclaims, "Why can't we believe what we want? Who knows what truth is anyway? Your truth may not be mine." We have had many students in our introductory courses who think like this hypothetical student. Students' reliance on multiplistic thinking may provide the frame for paranormal beliefs. More important, multiplistic thinking provides students with what they need to see that their beliefs are confirmed. Therefore, we suggest that students in this phase of cognitive development may be particularly vulnerable to forming, maintaining, and strengthening paranormal beliefs.

BELIEF CHANGE AND INSTRUCTIONAL INTERVENTIONS

Before offering suggestions for addressing students' paranormal beliefs in the context of the introductory psychology course, we take a brief look at prior attempts to teach students about alleged paranormal phenomena. Research dating back to the first part of the 20th century suggested that a course in introductory psychology could promote paranormal belief reduction (e.g., Lehman & Fenton, 1929). More recently, Messer and Griggs (1989) found that both male and female students enrolled in an introductory psychology course who scored higher on exams had also scored lower on a paranormal belief measure administered at the beginning of the course. When students' SAT scores were controlled statistically, there was some indication that the relation between exam and belief scores was reduced or eliminated. Thus, the relation between students' paranormal beliefs and their examination performances was, at least in part, due to their mutual association with their academic ability as measured by SAT scores.

In addition to courses that have examined paranormal beliefs within the context of introductory psychology courses, many researchers have examined belief change in courses that focused on paranormal topics. For example, Banzinger (1983), Gray (1985), Jones and Zusne (1981), Tobacyk (1983), and Woods (1984) measured paranormal belief prior to and at the conclusion of such a course. Each study reported significant increases in overall skepticism following course completion. In contrast, Irwin (1990) and Clarke (1991), who were sympathetic to paranormal claims, did not find widespread belief change following their courses.

Assuming that belief change, in fact, occurred in the courses in which such change was reported, we still need to address two matters. First, the occurrence of belief change does not mean that either students' knowledge or understanding of paranormal topics *increased* as a result of a *decrease* in their beliefs. In fact, to the extent an instructor focuses on *debunking* paranormal claims rather than on increasing conceptual understanding of issues and on promoting conceptual change, belief change may be little more than a consequence of persuasion effects (cf. Seckel, 1989). Second, as suggested, belief may be reduced during a course only to reemerge later when a student is confronted with a firsthand paranormal experience. Our goal as teachers should be on directly addressing students' thinking related to paranormal topics and not on trying to persuade them that belief in putative paranormal phenomena is silly and not worthy of an educated person.

IMPLICATIONS FOR INSTRUCTION AND CHALLENGING STUDENTS

Students' paranormal beliefs are easily formed and resistant to change. What might introductory psychology teachers do to address this issue? Unfortunately, teachers can expect students to give lip service to scientific views on paranormal topics covered during the semester and respond thoughtfully during class discussion, only to return after the course ends to reading their horoscope and being impressed by a TV psychic. Recall our earlier comments on students who perform well on exams but who show little evidence of critical thinking when confronted with real-world examples of so-called paranormal phenomena (cf. Brumby, 1984).

Many standard introductory psychology textbooks include at least some coverage of parapsychology topics (mostly ESP and PK). McClenon, Roig, Smith, and Ferrier (2003) reported that over 50% of introductory psychology textbooks included coverage of parapsychology. This finding held up for samples of books from the 1980s, 1990s, and 2002. Most of the coverage was brief and negative toward the field of parapsychology. Be that as it may, our assessment of current introductory psychology texts is that the material contained in them will have little impact on students' beliefs about paranormal topics or, more important, on the way they think about these topics. Instead, the *pedagogy* used by course instructors will play the key role in determining whether these dimensions (belief and critical thinking) are impacted.

In the early 1980s, Singer and Benassi (1981) noted that "far from being a 'fad,' preoccupation with the [paranormal] now forms a pervasive part of out culture" (p. 49). More than two decades later, American popular culture remains imbued with paranormal beliefs that may be associated with problems in reasoning in other domains (cf. Halpern, 1998). Fascination with reports that appear in tabloid publications, Elvis sightings at the mall, and new age health cures have underlying them similar problems in thinking and reasoning that we see in the paranormal belief systems of our students. Thus, we address possible pedagogical approaches with a certain degree of caution. On the basis of what we have discussed to this point, we are fairly sure that introductory psychology teachers can reduce at least certain paranormal beliefs among their students, as assessed by paranormal belief scales. Still, there are important remaining questions about what this belief reduction actually represents and whether instructional efforts affect what students know about paranormal claims. There is also the issue of whether or not these efforts influence students' conceptual understanding of putative paranormal phenomena.

Halpern's Four-Component Model of Critical Thinking

Halpern (1998) provided a useful framework in which to understand paranormal beliefs and to address them in the introductory psychology course. She proposed a four-part model to help teachers improve thinking skills across knowledge domains. The first part is the *dispositional,* or *attitudinal,* component and emphasizes a point made in this chapter—namely, that students often enter the introductory psychology course with well-developed beliefs and attitudes about paranormal claims and they rarely engage these topics in an "effortful" manner (p. 452). Additionally, Halpern suggested there is a distinction between the willingness as opposed to the ability to think critically, and that "good instructional programs help learners decide when to make the necessary mental investment in critical thinking and when a problem or argument is not worth the effort" (p. 452).

The second component of the model describes the importance of educating students about specific thinking skills and providing them with the opportunity to practice them. The third component stresses the importance of transfer of training. What good are critical thinking skills if they cannot be applied in novel situations? As Halpern put it, "The critical component in an ecologically valid critical-thinking process is recognizing or noticing that a particular thinking skill may be needed" (p. 453). The key challenge is to prepare students so that, although the particular details may differ, they can detect the similarity of the structure of a new situation to one in which they were trained. For example, we teach our students about the probability of rare events so that they do not jump to the conclusion that a rare event (e.g., a "prophetic" dream) requires a paranormal explanation. Do they, when confronted with their own so-called prophetic dreams, appropriately reflect on the probability and psychology of rare events and consider that no paranormal explanation is required? This is the challenge for the introductory psychology teacher.

The final component in Halpern's model is metacognitive monitoring. She offered that this "term is usually defined as 'what we know about what we know' and the ability to use this knowledge to direct and improve the thinking and learning process" (p. 454). In terms of paranormal belief, effective metacognitive monitoring may focus students' attention to, for example, rival hypotheses that may explain why some people seem to feel better after having been "treated" by a therapeutic touch therapist. Naïve students will often accept the claim that therapeutic touch works because therapists are able to "realign energy fields." With proper education and critical thinking training, students may begin to evaluate such claims and understand them in terms of normal psychological processes. Unless they are able to monitor their thinking skills in everyday situations, they will likely fail to see the applicability of these skills to paranormal claims.

Halpern's (1998) assertions may be integrated into what often frames the introductory psychology course, the methods of experimental psychology. Discussions about such topics as rival hypotheses, confounded variables, and making causal inferences from correlational data could be presented using examples of so-called paranormal phenomena.

The remainder of this chapter discusses several general teaching approaches that may be implemented in the context of the introductory psychology course. How and the extent to which teachers employ these approaches will depend, of course, on instructors' course goals. Some useful ideas may be gleaned from Zusne and Jones' (1989) *Anomalistic Psychology: A Study of Magical Thinking.* The book is organized around many of the topics covered in standard introductory psychology textbooks. Chapter titles include: "Psychophysiology," "Perception," "Memory," "Cognitive Processes," "Personality," "Beliefs," and "Psychopathology." It is important to make clear that, even under the most favorable circumstances, students' understanding of and thinking about putative paranormal phenomena will most likely only be improved to some degree. Acquiring and transferring critical thinking skills takes time and practice and occurs as individuals develop cognitively.

A "Nudge": Sequential Assignments

Helping students to move from dualistic and multiplistic thinking to more advanced modes of thought (relativism and commitment in relativism) presents a major challenge to the introductory psychology teacher, especially when dealing with paranormal topics. Kloss (1994) reminded us of Perry's caveat that students' advancement through the stages of intellectual development may be slowed or even stalled by a tendency to retreat to less sophisticated modes of thought. Challenging existing belief systems and ways of knowing the world can be threatening to students. Therefore, Kloss suggested that "nudging" students is better than "shoving" them when formulating instructional strategies.

One strategy involves a developmental sequence of assignments. For example, early in the semester, students may be asked to explore how a particular paranormal topic is *described* in the popular media. They are not given much in the way of further direction and they are not explicitly asked to *evaluate* how the topic is treated (which is mostly superficial, uncritical, and pro-paranormal). In a follow-up assignment given later in the course, students' thinking is "nudged" by asking them to explore scientific perspectives on the same topic. The emphasis of these scientific perspectives will be skeptical of the claim, critical of the research done on the topic, and often concerned about fraud, deception, and human gullibility. Students are not only asked to describe the scientific focus on the topic, but they are also asked to *contrast* it with how the topic is generally treated in popular media. Finally, in a third iteration of this assignment, students are nudged even further. At this point, they are asked to develop a *critical analysis* of the strengths and weaknesses of the scientific viewpoint on the topic. In addition, they are asked to provide their own considered *critical commentary* on the quality of the scientific perspective. Some readers may recognize in this sequential strategy a hint of Bloom's (1956) taxonomy, which has much in common with Perry's (1970) perspective. Both these perspectives inform the introductory psychology teacher's pedagogy for facilitating a shift to more analytical, synthetic, and evaluative modes of thought about paranormal topics, as well as other areas that are covered in the introductory psychology course.

Classroom Assessment Techniques

Classroom assessment techniques (CATS) are useful tools for the introductory psychology teacher (e.g., Angelo & Cross, 1993). CATs are formative instruments that instructors use to facilitate students' learning of class material. They are particularly useful in the current context because they often require students to reflect on their thinking and reasoning process. These techniques could be very helpful in addressing the metacognitive component of Halpern's (1998) model.

The Background Knowledge Probe (BKP; Angelo & Cross, 1993, pp. 121–125) is a useful tool to assess students' beliefs about paranormal claims upon entering the introductory course. Instructors may develop their own questions that tap the topics in which they are interested or they may adapt any of the many paranormal belief scales that are available. With some minor additions, teachers may include questions that ask students to describe the bases for their beliefs (e.g., personal experience, popular media influences) and/or to offer their explanation for various paranormal claims. Information from the BKP will provide teachers with a baseline of the extent of their students' paranormal beliefs. Detailed examination of the BKPs can offer teachers a glimpse of students' naïve theories about these phenomena. Given that several researchers have suggested that naïve theories must be confronted directly in educational contexts (Halpern, 1998; Resnick, 1983), BKP data will assist teachers as they plan for interventions. Like the BKP, the Misconception/Preconception Check (Angelo & Cross, 1993, pp. 132–137) also assesses students' prior knowledge, but with a twist. Its focus is on uncovering prior knowledge or beliefs that may hinder or block further learning.

A useful follow up to BKPs is to ask students to offer personal examples that relate to their beliefs reported in the BKP (cf. Angelo & Cross, 1993, pp. 281–284, Focused Autobiographical Sketch). It may be useful to ask students to describe anonymously their personal experiences with so-called paranormal phenomena and, with students' permission, to read these descriptions to the class. Students may then be asked to offer rival accounts for such phenomena in normal, rather than paranormal, terms. If possible, the teacher can make an explicit link between students' expressed naïve theories and information the teacher gleaned from the BKPs.

Instruction About Belief Persistence Processes

Students' ability to critically evaluate specific paranormal claims or experience may benefit from direct instruction on belief persistence processes. This instruction may be needed throughout the introductory psychology course. Discussion of belief persistence processes fits in quite well when the topics of research methods, social psychology, personality psychology, and cognition are covered in the introductory course.

Ample experimental research has demonstrated that people persist in their beliefs and naïve theories under a wide variety of circumstances (e.g., Anderson & Lindsay, 1998). An instructional effort to address such belief persistence involves explaining the persistence process and the steps that might be taken to ensure that students are vigilant when their belief systems are challenged. To that end, students need to strengthen their metacognitive monitoring skills (Halpern, 1998). Consider an example in which students observe a "psychic" bend a metal rod by "psychokinesis." Following the demonstration, the psychic is exposed as a magician and the manner in which he performed his trick is described. Furthermore, the instructor describes the long history of psychics who, on closer examination, were unmasked as frauds. All's well so far. As described in the example provided earlier, these same students might be amazed by the "psychic" abilities of someone they observe at a later date. Instead of asking how the person managed to bend a spoon without them seeing how it was done, they resort to making a psychic attribution.

The task for teachers is to challenge students so that when they are in a situation similar to that described earlier, they recognize their tendency to rely on well-established and persistent personal beliefs. Hopefully, instead, the internal dialogue of the student might sound something like this:

> This seems very convincing and I'm finding myself believing this guy because it is consistent with some prior beliefs of mine. But I need to remember that people's tendency is to hold on to certain beliefs even if there isn't much evidence to support them. Like what I learned about the confirmation bias. And I need to remember that I previously saw somebody do something similar and my teacher showed me the trick. Also my teacher told us about the long history of fraud among so-called psychics. I wonder what this guy would do if I asked him to bend a spoon under more controlled conditions and with a trained magician present.

Direct Challenges to Paranormal Beliefs

The goal of all of the instructional activities we have addressed so far is conceptual change (Guzzetti, 2000). Several writers in the area of science education have suggested that students' nonscientific naïve theories must be challenged directly if the goal of conceptual change is to be realized (e.g., Resnick, 1983). Once students enter college, they already have a number of relatively fixed beliefs about putative paranormal phenomena that include naïve theories about how these phenomena "work." These beliefs and theories need to be directly confronted if conceptual change is to be achieved.

Researchers have examined the effects of various instructional methods on students' nonscientific beliefs and theories. Although not specifically focused on paranormal belief or on the introductory psychology course, this research provides insights that may be of value to the introductory psychology teacher. Guzzetti (2000) reported studies have shown that instructional approaches seeking to instigate cognitive conflict are effective means by which to affect students' naïve theories. The refutational text provides an example ("text structure that states a common misconception and *directly refutes it* [emphasis added] while providing the scientifically acceptable idea;" Guzzetti, 2000, p. 90). This approach could be easily adapted in the introductory psychology course. For example, exploration of the topic of "near death experiences," which is often couched in paranormal terms such as "crossing over and coming back," fits in nicely with the unit on the biological bases of behavior normally covered in the introductory psychology course. A text could be developed that presents the prototypical paranormal description and explanation of so-called near death experiences. Following this, a text representing accounts of these experiences in terms of normal biological processes could be presented (e.g., Jansen, 1990). If the general research findings hold true, then we might expect that this approach will lead to conceptual change in some, but not all, students. Guzzetti suggested that teacher-directed follow-up discussion may be needed for some students, particularly those whose reading skills are low.

We recommend a multimethod approach. For example, students read a pro-paranormal account of a phenomenon, followed by a written work that provides the best available theory and data in favor of a "normal" account of it. We have found that it is not easy for students to grasp that not all sources are of equal evidentiary value, so it may be important to discuss the "evidence" in class. Finally, where feasible, demonstrations of phenomena may be helpful. We have done this, for example, with demonstrations of "psychokinesis" (bending a nail) and smashing a cinder block on someone's chest while the person is lying on a "bed of nails." If these demonstrations are not feasible, then the teacher may consider using one of many available video demonstrations of so-called paranormal feats (e.g., Larsen, 2002). On the basis of our earlier discussion, it is critically important to include a discussion of the belief persistence process. Trocco (1998) provided some interesting examples of teaching approaches that are consistent with those described here, and Halpern (1998) described an approach to teach students about horoscopes and other paranormal topics that incorporates the elements of her four-part model.

CONCLUSIONS

Regarding students' beliefs about a variety of putative paranormal phenomena, we suggest that belief persistence is more common than belief change under a wide range of circumstances. Moreover, coming into belief is often more easily accomplished than leaving it. We are fairly sure that the introductory psychology teacher can get students to report that their beliefs are lower following belief-related instruction in the course. Whether or not this reduction represents conceptual change on the part of students, and whether or not observed changes will be maintained after students leave the course, is another matter. We suggest that real conceptual change, not just superficial belief change, is a desirable goal and one worth striving toward. We believe our earlier pedagogical suggestions may help students make this important transition and perhaps goad them into considering the kind of skeptical view illustrated in Skinner's (1987, p. 12) brief meditation on religion: "Science, not religion, has taught me my most useful values, among them intellectual honesty. It is better to go without answers than to accept those that merely resolve puzzlement."

Is there a strong case for addressing students' beliefs in the paranormal in the introductory psychology course? We offer three justifications for doing so. First, much psychological research and theory can help explain putative paranormal experiences. Students will sometimes say that science cannot explain this or that phenomenon when, in fact, the phenomenon can be easily accounted for by psychological principles (e.g., Zusne & Jones, 1989). Second, there has been a documented increase in Americans' belief from 1990 to 2001 in psychic healing, extrasensory perception, haunted houses, ghosts, extraterrestrial beings that have visited earth, communication with the dead, and astrology (National Science Foundation, 2002). At the same time, belief in alternative medicines is widespread and, in fact, many colleges and universities have offered courses on "therapeutic touch" and other "therapies" (National Science Foundation, 2002). Third, promoting critical thinking is a goal of introductory psychology courses (see Appleby, chap. 5, this volume) and the manner in which students approach and consider putative paranormal phenomena at the conclusion of their course may serve as an important barometer of whether or not this goal has been achieved.

There appears to be a need for promoting better thinking about science. Introductory psychology is an ideal course in which to do so and an examination of alleged paranormal phenomena provides the opportunity to apply psychological science to matters of considerable interest to our students. By taking into consideration the instructional methods and contemporary research on cognitive processes and development of college students that have been addressed here, introductory psychology teachers will have some tools to challenge students to consider the value of scientific thinking, not only in assessing paranormal claims, but psychological phenomena in general.

REFERENCES

Alcock, J. (1995). The belief engine. *Skeptical Inquirer, 19,* 255–263.
Anderson, C. A., & Lindsay, J. (1998). The development, perseverance, and change of naive theories. *Social Cognition, 16,* 8–30.

Angelo, T. A., & Cross, K. P. (1993). *Classroom assessment techniques: A handbook for college teachers* (2nd ed.). San Francisco: Jossey-Bass.

Ayeroff, F., & Abelson, R. P. (1976). ESP and ESB: Belief in personal success at mental telepathy. *Journal of Personality and Social Psychology, 34,* 240–247.

Bacon, F. (1620). *Novum organum* (B. Montague, Ed. & Trans., 1854). Philadelphia: Parry & MacMillan. Retrieved March 26, 2004, from http://history.hanover.edu/texts/Bacon/novorg.html

Banzinger, G. (1983). Normalizing the paranormal: Short-term and long-term change in belief in the paranormal among older learners during a short course. *Skeptical Inquirer, 10,* 212–214.

Benassi, V. A., Singer, B. F., & Reynolds, C. B. (1980). Occult belief: Seeing is believing. *Journal for the Scientific Study of Religion, 19,* 337–349.

Benassi, V. A., Sweeney, P. D., & Drevno, G. E. (1979). Mind over matter: Perceived success at psychokinesis. *Journal of Personality and Social Psychology, 37,* 1377–1386.

Bloom, B. S. (Ed.). (1956). *Taxonomy of educational objectives: The classification of educational goals: Handbook I, cognitive domain.* New York: Longmans, Green.

Brumby, M. N. (1984). Misconceptions about the concept of natural selection by medical biology students. *Science Education, 68,* 493–503.

Burkan, T. (2004). *A firewalking theory that can benefit everyone.* Firewalking Institute of Research and Education. Retrieved March 20, 2004, from http://www.firewalking.com/theory.html

Clarke, D. (1991). Students' beliefs and academic performance in an empathic course on the paranormal. *Journal of the Society of Psychical Research, 58,* 74–83.

Eylon, B., & Linn, M. C. (1988). Learning and instruction: An examination of four research perspectives in science education. *Review of Educational Research, 58,* 251–301.

Forer, B. (1949). The fallacy of personal validation: A classroom demonstration of gullibility. *Journal of Abnormal & Social Psychology, 44,* 118–123.

Gallup, G. H., & Newport, F. (1991). Belief in paranormal phenomena among American adults. *The Skeptical Inquirer, 15,* 137–146.

Gilovich, T., Griffin, D., & Kahneman, D. (2002). *Heuristics and biases: The psychology of intuitive judgement.* Cambridge, England: Cambridge University Press.

Gray, T. (1985). Changing unsubstantiated belief: Testing the ignorance hypothesis. *Canadian Journal of Behavioral Science, 17,* 263–270.

Guzzetti, B. J. (2000). Learning counter-intuitive science concepts: What have we learned from over a decade of research? *Reading and Writing Quarterly, 16,* 89–98.

Halpern, D. F. (1998). Teaching critical thinking for transfer across domains: Dispositions, skills, structure training, and metacognitive monitoring. *American Psychologist, 53,* 449–455.

Irwin, H. J. (1990). Parapsychology courses and students' belief in the paranormal. *Journal of the Society of Psychical Research, 56,* 266–272.

Jansen, K. L. R. (1990). Neuroscience and the near-death experience: Roles for the NMDA-PCP receptor, the sigma receptor and the endopsychosins. *Medical Hypotheses, 31,* 25–29.

Jones, W. H., & Zusne, L. (1981). Teaching anomalistic psychology. *Teaching of Psychology, 8,* 78–82.

King, P. M., & Kitchener, K. S. (1994). *Developing reflective judgment: Understanding and promoting intellectual growth and critical thinking in adolescents and adults.* San Francisco: Jossey-Bass.

Kloss, R. J. (1994). A nudge is best. *College Teaching, 42*(4), 151–159.

Knefelkamp, L. L. (2003). The influence of a classic. *Liberal Education, 89,* 10–15.

Kuhn, T. S. (1970). *The structure of scientific revolutions* (2nd ed., enlarged). Chicago: University of Chicago Press.

Langer, E. J. (1975). The illusion of control. *Journal of Personality and Social Psychology, 32*, 311–328.

Larsen, C. (2002, October). *Spoon-bending: How Uri Geller really does it.* Retrieved April 16, 2004, from http://www.skepticreport.com/print/urispoon-p.htm

Lehman, H. C., & Fenton, N. (1929). The prevalence of certain misconceptions and superstitions among college students before and after a course in psychology. *Education, 50*, 485–494.

Leikind, B. J., & McCarthy, W. J. (1985). An investigation of firewalking. *Skeptical Inquirer, 10*, 23–34.

McClenon, J., Roig, M., Smith, M. D., & Ferrier, G. (2003). The coverage of parapsychology in introductory psychology textbooks: 1990–2003. *Journal of Parapsychology, 67*, 167–179.

McCloskey, M., Caramazza, A., & Green, B. (1980). Curvilinear motion in the absence of external forcers: Naive beliefs about the motion of objects. *Science, 210*, 1139–1141.

Messer, W. S., & Griggs, R. A. (1989). Student belief and involvement in the paranormal and performance in introductory psychology. *Teaching of Psychology, 16*, 187–191.

Mitroff, I. I. (1974). Norms and counter-norms in a select group of the Apollo moon scientists: A case study of the ambivalence of scientists. *American Sociological Review, 39*, 579–595.

Munro, G., & Munro, J. (2000). Using daily horoscopes to demonstrate expectancy confirmation. *Teaching of Psychology, 27*, 114–117.

National Science Foundation. (2002). *Science and engineering indicators—2002.* Arlington, VA: National Science Foundation (NSB-02-1). Retrieved April 2, 2004, from http://www.nsf.gov/sbe/srs/seind02/start.htm

Newport, F., & Strausberg, M. (2001). *Americans' belief in psychic and paranormal phenomena is up over last decade: Belief in psychic healing and extrasensory perception top the list.* (Copyright © 2004, The Gallup Organization, Princeton, NJ.)

Nickerson, R. S. (1998). Confirmation bias: A ubiquitous phenomenon in many guises. *Review of General Psychology, 2*, 175–220.

Perry, W. G. (1970). *Forms of intellectual and ethical development in the college years: A scheme.* New York: Holt, Rinehart & Winston.

Resnick, L. B. (1983). Mathematics and science learning: A new conception. *Science, 220*, 477–478.

Russell, D., & Jones, W. H. (1980). When superstition fails: Reactions to disconfirmation of paranormal beliefs. *Personality & Social Psychology Bulletin, 6*, 83–88.

Seckel, A. (1989). Rather than just debunking, encourage people to think. *Skeptical Inquirer, 13*, 300–304.

Singer, B. F., & Benassi, V. A. (1981). Occult beliefs. *American Scientist, 69*, 49–55.

Skinner, B. F. (1987). What religion means to me. *Free Inquiry, 7*, 12–13.

Tobacyk, J. J. (1983). Reduction in paranormal belief among participants in a college course. *Skeptical Inquirer, 8*, 57–61.

Trocco, F. (1998). How to study weird things. *Skeptical Inquirer, 22*, 37–41.

Ward, R. A., & Grasha, A. F. (1986). Using astrology to teach research methods to introductory psychology students. *Teaching of Psychology, 13*, 143–145.

Woods, P. J. (1984). Evidence for the effectiveness of a reading program in changing beliefs in the paranormal. *Skeptical Inquirer, 9*, 67–70.

Zusne, L., & Jones, W. H. (1989). *Anomalistic psychology: A study of magical thinking* (2nd ed.). Hillsdale, NJ: Lawrence Erlbaum Associates.

CHAPTER 17

Motivating Students Through Personal Connections: Storytelling as Pedagogy in Introductory Psychology

Craig E. Abrahamson
James Madison University

My first impression of a professor at the beginning of class during my freshman year was that he was a "boring" professor, but, before the end of the first two weeks of that semester, I realized that he was the most engaging instructor that I had ever had because he seemed to be talking just to me.

This chapter explores the following topics: methods of creating interpersonal connection in teaching introductory psychology, creating a mutual relationship the first day of class, utilizing storytelling as a method for teaching concepts, the history of storytelling in education, narratology in context, using the learning story, and a special case of using hypnotic trance in storytelling. Examples throughout the discussion demonstrate how storytelling can be an effective mechanism for motivating students not only to learn course content but also to utilize the principles of introductory psychology as potential tools for self-discovery.

CREATING INTERPERSONAL CONNECTION
IN INTRODUCTORY PSYCHOLOGY

Interaction between instructors and students is the interconnected spheres of both thought and emotion (Biber, 1967), and within this process the instructors reflect a sense of themselves, students, and the content in an integrated fashion. Within the classroom, sensory activity is continually taking place, and the assimilation of new information fits into the students' past experiences by producing a reflective and reflexive response as the assimilation draws from memory and produces emotion (Gold, 2002).

The active learning process often causes an emotional response, so it is essential for the instructor to encourage the students from the beginning of a course by showing faith in each student's ability to learn about human behavior in this introductory context. The instructor should recognize and appreciate each student's real effort during classroom tasks, such as class participation, thus facilitating the student's desire to learn (Carlson & Thorpe, 1984) and generating interpersonal connectedness among students and the instructor.

Instructors of introductory psychology need to continually utilize positive reinforcement when students participate in the learning process, not all of which comes from verbal communication. Much can be communicated through body language. The instructors also need to be continually aware of what types of messages body language is communicating. Students are able to read their professors quite readily. Thus, when students appear to be actively engaging in the learning process in the classroom through their own verbal and nonverbal expressions, instructors need to be aware also that they are expressing their appreciation of the class through body posturing or verbal expressions.

For example, during a class discussion regarding the possibility of inherited physiological tendencies in personality types, a student began describing her beliefs. Another student interrupted to comment that he could tell that I didn't agree with her because of my facial expressions. I concurred with his assessment immediately and stated that I would share my thoughts once the student finished talking. If I had not openly admitted my own feelings, I would have lost the class's trust and our rapport would have been compromised.

When interpersonal connectedness is truly a part of the classroom dynamic, it is possible to motivate students to interact with the course content and to apply it to their own lives, which is one of the powerful realities of teaching an introductory psychology course. With a foundation of trust and mutual respect, students and instructors can work and share together in an atmosphere that is nonthreatening (R. W. Johnson & D. W. Johnson, 1982), and the story continues to be enhanced.

CREATING A MUTUAL RELATIONSHIP
ON THE FIRST DAY OF CLASS

For an atmosphere of motivational learning to exist in the classroom, there must be a relationship between students and the instructor that is founded on mutual sharing of personal experiences, values, beliefs, and course content. A good relationship is the foundation for all learning (McEwan & Egan, 1995), change takes place in the context of a relationship (D. W. Johnson & F. P. Johnson, 2003), and it must begin with the instructor's getting to know each student, even in large classes with more than 100 students. Through this personal connection, the content can become personally meaningful for the students. The content in introductory psychology courses is ideal for this motivational learning to be actualized.

For the past 25 years, I have set two primary objectives for the first day of class of each semester. One is to obtain some primary educational and personal information from each student. After identifying myself, I tell them that for me to be effective in the learning process on which we are about to embark, I need information about each student before I can share any aspects of the course with them. I ask the class to record the following information on a sheet of paper that will be handed in: name, e-mail address, phone number, year in school, and major, and nickname, if preferred.

Next, I inform them that their answers to a series of questions will not affect their grade and will be treated with complete confidentiality. The primary purpose for this writing exercise is to begin the students' storytelling process, whereby I can learn about them through their own stories (e.g., their names and faces, along with the personal information that they have shared). Their evaluations consistently indicate that students feel empowered when they write about themselves in this nongraded assignment.

I then ask them what specifically they want to learn in this introductory psychology course, what they expect from me, and what they expect from themselves. I compare myself to a waiter in a restaurant that wants to know what they would like to eat before they see the menu, an unexpected analogy that always generates laughter, letting me know that the students are engaged. I tell them that I want to be aware of their learning desires as they relate to this class before I might change their perceptions by discussing the course syllabus.

Their next task is to answer, in a minimum of two sentences, the following question: "From a personal perspective, why are you taking this course?" As they respond to my questions, I talk about how I will be spending the late afternoon, sitting comfortably in my office reading their papers and getting to know them; how I am looking forward to this activity, particularly because I won't grade this batch of papers; and how their responses will give me insight into their personalities.

When the students have answered these questions, I instruct them to pass to me their student photo-ID cards. Then they asked to write a minimum of six paragraphs describing themselves from a "personal perspective," including experiences with family, friends, and school. I encourage them to share aspects of themselves that will help me get to know them. I set aside 20 minutes for this part of the exercise, giving them more time if needed. While they write, I leave the room to photocopy their cards so that later I can begin the process of connecting their writing with their faces. My being out of the room while they pen this section creates fewer restrictions in their personal sharing.

I normally have no more than 60 students in my introductory classes, so the previous orientation is workable. A colleague who had an introductory psychology class of 300 students attempted a similar process. He found the student writings useful but less effective due to the class enrollment. If instructors can assimilate the students' personal stories into their memory, they can select stories and examples for that class that will relate more directly to individual students. The professor should make a concerted effort to learn each student's first name, thus facilitate the relationship-building process.

In order for educators to utilize fully the powerful impact that the process of student sharing can have on students' mastering course content, the educators have to change their thinking about the goal of teaching. When I first started having students complete this initial exercise, I thought I was wasting class time because there is so much course content to cover in an introductory psychology course. Instructors must resist the temptation of seeing teaching as a process of primarily transmitting content, for it gets in the way of student understanding and applying new knowledge (Wood, 1998).

Through the years, I have talked with colleagues who teach introductory psychology courses about using the first day of class to begin creating a positive and mutual relationship with students and have received mixed responses. It appears that about two thirds of my colleagues feel that this "important" relationship will develop naturally over the course of the semester without using specific mechanisms to initiate it. The other one third endorsed the use of "ice-breakers" on the first day of class so that students get to know each other and pointed out that, as instructors of introductory psychology, we need to make certain that the main focus is on course content and expectations.

The second objective for the first class of each semester is to explain in detail the syllabus and my expectations of each student. In addition to the usual personal data, I give out my home phone number for emergency use. One semester, a student called me at home at 6:00 a.m. to tell me he would not be in class because his grandfather had a stroke and he had to leave campus immediately to be with his family. I normally receive only about 5 to 10 such phone calls at home per semester, although I teach four courses per semester with 20 to 60 students in each. These calls, without exception, have all had a sense of legitimate urgency.

In regard to my expectations of the class, I talk specifically about the course requirement of "class participation" that enhances the course as the instructor and students all feel free to share their own perspectives on the topics of the course. The instructor and students don't need to agree with each other but must show tolerance for another's perspective to enhance "critical thinking." After identifying myself as a storyteller, I explain that I will relate personal accounts and those of people who have shared their stories with me—all stories relevant to concepts they will master in the introductory psychology class. I will encourage them to share their own stories at appropriate times during the course. The goal for the first class period is for students to experience a sense of initial ownership to the class as a group and regarding the course content. Thus, an instructor begins the process of building a positive relationship with students.

STORYTELLING: A METHOD FOR TEACHING CONCEPTS

Storytelling is an important technique in the process of learning and understanding (Langer, 1997), whether it occurs in or out of the classroom. People gain a better understanding of one another using concrete examples rather than abstractions and generalizations that have little relation to one's experiences, because the sharing of experiences through the device of storytelling enables individuals to build the bridge of understanding between one another (Maguire, 1998). This technique facilitates commonality and the shared resonance of experiences within the content of introductory psychology.

It should be emphasized that not all instructors feel comfortable discussing their own personal stories initially. To become a storyteller, an instructor teaching introductory psychology courses should first listen to people telling stories on the radio, on a tape recording, or at live presentations. Ballads or other forms of music in which the lyrics are a narrative are also useful. Initially, instructors can rely on stories from these sources until they are comfortable integrating some personal ones.

The student evaluation for the course should include a section where students assess specific aspects of storytelling. Their feedback can assist the professor in refining the different approaches to storytelling. The instructor could also utilize a midterm assessment on which students indicate how effective specific stories (ones identified in the assessment document) have been as aids to their understanding of course content. Students may submit these writings anonymously so that they may write candidly without fear of reprisal.

Through interacting with colleagues on campus and at conferences where I have given a significant number of presentations on the pedagogy of storytelling, I have received a number of different perspectives on various methodologies of storytelling. One significant approach is to relate in story form different professional and nonprofessional readings to which one has been exposed. Another helpful idea is to read published stories to students that pertain to specific content in the introductory psychology course. One advantage to teaching introductory psychology courses is that the focus is on understanding human behavior. Thus, there are many opportunities in locating human stories to illumine the course content. For example, an instructor can invite specialists in particular areas of psychology to give presentations to the class. Another technique employing computer technology utilizes short "clips" of individuals telling their own "stories," which emphasize specific course content. Also, several introductory psychology textbooks have accompanying discs on which there is information in story format to emphasize important concepts and terms. Instructors can also utilize storytelling in this format in their classes.

The story provides a context for individuals to better understand others by providing a key to their own vast experiences. Thus, the student is able to relate in a meaningful way to the instructor's point of view by working through personal experiences that result in a more profound and lasting understanding than would have been possible through generalizations (Rorty, 1991). The instructor and the students come together on cognitive and emotional levels that allow students to relate to the instructor from their own personal framework and to grasp the instructor's presentation of various concepts at the same time. This engagement represents a remarkable, and yet common, interpersonal experience.

I told an introductory psychology class the following story to explain the concept of cognitive dissonance. While employed as a social worker for the Salvation Army in Phoenix, Arizona, I was asked to deliver (for a sick coworker) the prepared hot lunch to a center approximately 15 miles from the main facility. When I arrived at the center located in a high crime urban neighborhood, I locked the car before taking one of three large containers of food inside. When I returned to the car to get the next container, I realized that I had locked my keys inside the car. At that moment, a "low-riding" pink Cadillac stopped in front of me. A hulking man exited the car and said, "Got a problem?" Needless to say, I was scared, especially when he took a long knife out of his pocket. However, he quickly used the potential weapon to unlock the door. When he smiled and said, "Be careful around here," I experienced two inconsistent perceptions of that individual (i.e., cognitive dissonance).

About 10 years after I told this story to a class, a former psychology student approached me on a golf course and asked, "Hey, was that story about the pink Cadillac true?" I replied that I would answer his question if he could tell me to what concept the story related. Although the man badly mispronounced the concept, he still knew the answer. This encounter affected me in two ways: It reinforced my conviction about the power of storytelling and proved that through storytelling an instructor can attach emotional meaning to a contextual concept in such a way that facilitates its transfer into a student's long-term memory.

One important value of storytelling from a cognitive perspective is that it becomes a mutual creation involving interaction and understanding between instructor and student (Peck, 1989). The story can create a mutual bond, as students are able to personally identify with the story and the instructor if the story comes from a life experience to which a student can personally relate.

One of the advantages of knowing specific aspects of a student's background gleaned from the first class period's writing activity is that the stories will have a relational context and an emotional impact as well as meaning. Thus, the student is better able to comprehend the course content while developing a shared bond with classmates and the instructor. Also, as professors age, they need to receive from students accounts of their own life experiences to bridge the generation gap and maintain rapport with an increasingly younger student body.

HISTORY OF STORYTELLING IN EDUCATION

Prior to the advent of writing, storytelling was the primary tool with which individuals within their communities preserved and shared their heritage. It is found in all learning institutions (Kirkwood & Gold, 1983) and has ensured continuity of experiences from one generation to the next. Storytelling is also the foundation of the teaching profession. Great teachers, from Homer and Plato, through Jesus, Li Po, and Gandhi have used stories, myths, parables, and personal history to instruct, to illustrate, and to guide the thinking of students (Zabel, 1991). Stories are natural formalisms for storing and describing memories and experiential knowledge. Learning throughout the ages has relied on narrative (storytelling) for the communication of ideas and culture (Land & Hannafin, 1996). Oral tales are used by many cultures to shape minds, providing each listener with a concept of self, of knowledge, of relationship to community, and of individual motivation (Fried, 1995).

Learning stories is at the heart of human imagination and human needs. The utilization of story lies near the center of the language universe, imbuing communication with powers beyond the symbolic meaning of words (Berger, 1997). Fisher (1985, 1987) emphasized that humans are essentially storytellers and proposed that all forms of communication are most usefully interpreted from a narrational perspective, because people inherently pursue a "narrative" logic. More (1987) argued that the use of metaphors, images, and symbols have always existed as primary learning tools throughout human history because humans effectively "code with imagery" to remember and understand words and concepts often covered in introductory psychology. Therefore, stories provide mental images for the student to remember and understand concepts.

My American history professor illustrated this concept as he lectured on President Calvin Coolidge while lying on a bed to emphasize that President Coolidge slept more than any other president. At the end of the lecture, the professor jumped out of the bed and proceeded to shake every student's hand as we left the lecture hall. Before he made his leap, he stated that "Silent Cal" could shake more hands per minute that any president in U.S. history. Decades later, the image I have is still very clear because of his use of the "story" and "imagery."

NARRATOLOGY IN CONTEXT

The primary concept of narratology is that human beings love to tell and listen to stories. There appears to be an innate need in humans for chronological and causal connections, and these processes help make us who we are (Scholes, 1981). Narrative can be described as a primary and irreducible form of human comprehension, which is a defining characteristic of human intelligence and of the human species (Mink, 1978). Related to human comprehension is the idea that as humans we have basic stories, or deep structures, for organizing our experiences (Herrnstein-Smith, 1978). These come in many versions of reality that are shaped by the basic stories to which we have been exposed, directly or indirectly. Thus, the interplay of storytelling in the classroom appears to be helpful in the comprehension and application of new knowledge (Mink, 1978).

Researchers have identified an internal cognitive structure for simple stories that has been referred to as story grammar (Stein & Glenn, 1979). Researchers generally agree that story grammars reflect the story structures that are used to understand narratives (Olson & Gee, 1988), and empirical data indicates that the utilization of the story form exerts a powerful influence on memory for simple stories (Yussen, Huang, Mathews, & Evans, 1988). It is clear that storytelling can assist students in learning introductory psychology course content, a statement supported also by my students' comments on course evaluations and midterm assessments for over 25 years.

There are, nevertheless, some potential pitfalls in using storytelling in introductory psychology classes. One fear is that students can develop an assumption that psychology is primarily based on storytelling and not on empirical research. It is necessary to reiterate that storytelling should be used for illustrating examples of specific course content. Another concern is that students, conditioned to hearing stories that provide a break from the covering of content, may begin to regard them merely as entertainment. To curb this tendency, the instructor should ask the students follow-up questions that will result in a discussion about the specific content that the story illustrated. By using this technique and making it personal, the instructor also risks having the students think that they are forming a personal relationship with their professor. To reduce that risk factor, instructors should narrate stories that are not personal, as well as sprinkle anecdotes about their flaws to indicate that they too often make mistakes and have weaknesses. Lastly, another major concern is that the use of storytelling may seduce students into becoming overly intrigued with certain specific aspects of the discipline of psychology. This concern can be tempered by balancing storytelling so that the discipline is showed realistically as a science.

USING THE LEARNING STORY

Many cultures use learning stories to stimulate questions, raise issues, promote debate, and offer listeners a point of view that may challenge their own perspective (Underwood, 1991). Cultures have utilized "traditional stories" passed down through generations that have kept certain cultural traditions intact and been viewed as sacred aspects of society (Kaufmann, 1996). Kirkwood (1983) defined "learning stories" as brief, oral narratives told primarily to instruct, guide, or influence listeners, rather than to entertain. Stories have survived throughout civilization as they give order to human experience (Fisher, 1987).

As humans, our experiences (stories) are organized in time, and this organization gives our life a sense of structure. The other day while reading about past polio epidemics, I immediately remembered myself as a first grader standing in line for my vaccination with my mother at my elementary school. As our life stories are organized in content and in time, the learning story also needs similar structure for the student to absorb many different kinds of information. It should consist of a setting, human or humanlike characters, and a sequence of elements that creates mounting tension and gives rise to reaction (McAdams, 1997). The learning story can provide a sense of order to the teaching and interaction process within the classroom experience. The instructor should begin each class period with a brief overview of what was covered in the previous class period and then present an outline of the content to be covered during the current class session. After proceeding with factual content for about 10 minutes, the professor then tells a learning story, which often creates active student participation, before going to the next topic of discussion. This ongoing sequential pattern of covering content, storytelling, and student participation has its own rhythm during each class period. Students have indicated that they do not find the pattern boring.

As indicated, the traditional learning story comes from traditional contexts and is not entertainment. Student evaluations continue to confirm that my methodology of storytelling is personal, relates to content, and definitely has its entertaining characteristics. This combination is essential, because learning stories appear to enhance student learning. The following is a story to illustrate abnormal behavior as deviating from a norm. While stopped at a traffic light, a young woman driver picked her nose. Asked if they thought her behavior was abnormal, the students laughed but gave no further response immediately. However, when asked if they themselves had ever done such a thing, and the instructor admitted to doing the same act, most students agreed that the behavior was normal.

Each story shared in the classroom must be factual, especially those from the instructor's own experiences. Honesty allows students to know the background of the instructor as a person and also facilitates interpersonal connections. Authentic stories should reflect the ethical standards of the profession of psychology. Although instructors may share many aspects of their personal and professional life, an essential rule to follow is not to share any experiences that have not been resolved. Instructors should hesitate to share experiences that can be viewed as reflecting above average accomplishments, so as not to be seen in an overly positive way. Personal accolades can create even more imbalance in the student–instructor relationship. However, stories about negative life experiences can heighten mutual understanding as well as promote animated discussion.

For example, in a class where the topic was the current findings of alcohol use among college students and the effects of binge drinking, students showed a reluctance to discuss this topic. No one responded when asked if they thought binge drinking was a problem on our campus. The instructor then gave a detailed account of one of his own drinking episodes as a college student, an experience in which he took no pride. Initially, the students looked shocked at the professor's confession. However, by the time he finished, they were relaxed and eager to share their own feelings about this issue and how it can affect various aspects of behavior. If the professor had not shared a personal story, then the opportunity for dialogue with the class on this topic may have been lost.

A SPECIAL CASE: UTILIZING HYPNOTIC TRANCE IN STORYTELLING

A hypnotic trance is a state that most people experience everyday, yet many people have feelings of caution regarding how it could negatively affect them. This trance can be defined as a temporary suspension from ordinary consciousness and cognitive processing (Erickson, 1958). For example, a driver daydreams while stopped at a red light. When the light does turn green, he doesn't know to move forward until the driver of the car behind him blows the horn. According to trance theory, when a person is in a trance, that individual is open to suggestiveness, and the unconscious aspect of the mind will automatically store content to which the person is exposed if it has personal meaning (Erickson, 1959).

Erickson (Erickson & Rossi, 1976a) defined hypnotic trance as the evocation and utilization of unconscious learning. He believed that individuals are most open to learning in this state due to the fact that their usual frames of reference and beliefs are temporarily altered so they can be receptive to concepts and information that may be somewhat different from what already has been assimilated into their cognitive and emotional frames of reference.

Often, when individuals are engaged in listening to a story, they experience an altered state of cognitive processing, which is referred to as a hypnotic trance state (Tinterow, 1970). When students are listening to an instructor tell a story, they can become absorbed in the story. If the story directly relates to specific course content, then a connection is built between content and the personal experience that the instructor is sharing (Collay, 1998). When the story relates in part to a student's own experiences, this state permits an inner dialogue within the student's own knowledge (Carter, 1993). It is useful after completing a story for the instructor to remind the class of the specific content to which the story referred so that the students can properly connect the content and story for the purpose of storing it in their memory.

Erickson used personal accounts of his life experiences as metaphors that directly related to the points that he was making in such a way that it often appeared to create miraculous learning on the part of students (Sarbin & Coe, 1972). The credibility of Erickson's experiences and his innovative use of storytelling have opened limitless possibilities for the applications of learning through storytelling in educational settings. He empirically showed that individuals learn in remarkably different ways when they are subjected to storytelling that captures their attention and absorbs their thought processes (Barber, Spanos, & Chaves, 1974).

As the instructor deliver the story, the students create their own understanding and assimilate the content into their mental awareness in their own individual way. In other words, each student interprets and assigns meaning to the story in a way that makes sense. While covering the concept of learned helplessness (the debilitating consequences of experiences with uncontrollable events in humans and dogs; Seligman, 1975) in a class, a professor discussed the possibility that the learned helplessness could be a product of both the environment and one's individual make up. The instructor related the story of Mike (not his real name). When Mike was about 10 years old, his father built him a simple tree house. During the summer months, Mike loved to play in it and, as he grew older, he would camp in it overnight. By the time Mike was in his late teens, his father had enclosed the tree house. When Mike was in his early twenties, his dad equipped the tree house with electricity, insulation, and running water. This tree house eventually became Mike's permanent home. Mike's parents were content for him to live in their backyard and provided him with all of his financial needs on a regular basis. When Mike reached middle age, he had never been employed, had very limited social contact outside of his immediate family, and remained in his parent's backyard both day and night. With visitors, Mike limited their conversations to no more than 5 minutes. His behavior would be considered antisocial by conventional standards.

Without exception, students entered a trance state as the instructor told this story. Immediately afterward, the class would erupt in a heated discussion. Some students thought Mike had a good life and had made the most out of his circumstances. Others thought he was a lazy bum. Still others thought that Mike's parents had victimized him to the extent that Mike was unable to live a "normal" life. And, some believed that Mike was not very motivated due to his genetic makeup and had made the best of his circumstances.

By discussing this story, students learned the meaning of learned helplessness and become personally involved in understanding its manifestations. The story of Mike makes a lasting impression on students, an impression that strengthens their ability to apply this particular concept to their life experiences. To understand how students experience a hypnotic trance while listening to a story, the following five-stage paradigm of conversational trance induction is instructive (Erickson & Rossi, 1976b). Most students experience these stages as they listen to such a story.

Fixation of Attention

By telling a story interesting to students, the instructor is able to gain their attention. Students are able to relate to Mike as a child who liked to play outdoors because of their own experiences. As the story unfolds and becomes more intriguing in relation to their own development, they experience a degree of being absorbed by the story (i.e., fixation).

Depotentiating Habitual Frameworks and Belief Systems

Through the absorption process mentioned earlier, students are consciously pulled into the story and patterns of sensory-perception alter their state of consciousness into a trance state. They become so completely focused on the story that they are not aware of external stimuli, such as when the class period is going to end. The students become open to a new means of experiencing and learning.

Unconscious Search

The instructor initiates the unconscious process with direct and indirect forms of suggestion (e.g., "Is Mike lazy?"), which create in the students an unconscious search and mental processing of ideas and concepts that in the past appeared closed (e.g., "Maybe Mike is a victim."). They search their memories to resolve the particular experience or conflict and develop a new frame of reference. The experience allows the students to reorganize information and concepts, as well as to develop new concepts and knowledge.

Unconscious Process

The instructor makes direct and indirect suggestions (e.g., "Mike is trapped in his tree house by his parents."), which initiate in the students an unconscious search and facilitates an openness to mental associations, both of which help students bypass their learned limitations (e.g., "Does Mike have the ability to make up his own mind?"). After listening to the story, students have acquired a series of concepts that are perhaps in conflict with the students' previous perceptions, a series of concepts that open their thought processes beyond normal conscious awareness.

The Hypnotic Response

This temporary suspension from ordinary awareness is the outcome of the unconscious search and processes initiated by the instructor when employing the storytelling technique. The response occurs when a story has truly grasped the students' attention. Their perceptions have been temporarily altered by the trance state. This state ends once the story is completed and the instructor initiates a discussion or begins to lecture.

In summary, the utilization of trance within the storytelling process derives primarily from the students' activities (Erickson & Rossi, 1976b). When telling the story, the instructor stimulates, guides, and exercises judgment in the appropriateness of the story as it relates to the understanding of course content. This educational process is the result of the students' life experiences, understandings, memories, attitudes, the prescribed course content, and the course's goals and objectives.

CONCLUSIONS

One of the primary tasks for an instructor teaching introductory psychology is to help students maintain an interest in and gain ownership of course content. Personal connections between the class and the instructor can aid in this process. As discussed throughout this chapter, the relationship needs to be maintained throughout the semester. It is essential for instructors to attempt to join with their students, to try to understand their current perspective(s) on life and where they feel they are heading. The instructor needs to feel an intellectual and emotional empathy with the class and strive to relate to what the students are experiencing as they seek similarities in their own life experiences.

Having taken introductory psychology courses as students themselves, instructors need to reflect not only on what those experiences were like and the scope of the content of the course, but also on the milieu in which they moved while taking the courses. When I read my students' papers from the first day of class, my primary goal is to feel empathy; I almost disregarded the factual content of the writings during my first reading. The bond between instructor and students needs to begin with feelings. The instructor must mentally join their world. Communication between faculty teaching introductory psychology and students is essential within the classroom because it can create a sense of a learning community. Encouraging students to share their stories within classroom discussions can help the instructor reach this goal. Another technique to consider is to create written assignments (e.g., journal article discussions, student research projects, reaction paper to research articles, and retrospective self-reports) that require students to record their own feelings and perspectives about the content being examined.

Introductory psychology courses create the foundation for scientifically understanding the dimensions of human behavior. The story—by instructors and students alike—becomes the common thread to creating personal connections and a sense of togetherness between the instructor and students, which are essential ingredients to this learning process.

REFERENCES

Barber, T., Spanos, N., & Chaves, J. (1974). *Hypnosis, imagination and human potentialities*. New York: Pergamon.

Berger, A. A. (1997). *Narratives in popular culture, media, and everyday life*. Thousand Oaks, CA: Sage.

Biber, B. (1967). A learning-teaching paradigm integrating intellectual and affective processes. In E. M. Bower & W. G. Hollister (Eds.), *Behavioral science frontiers in education* (pp. 111–155). New York: Wiley.

Carlson, J., & Thorpe, C. (1984). *The growing teacher: How to become the teacher you have always wanted to be*. Englewood Cliffs, NJ: Prentice-Hall.

Carter, K. (1993). The place of story in the study of teaching and teacher education. *Educational Researcher, 22*(1), 5–12.

Collay, M. (1998). Recherche: Teaching our life histories. *Teaching and Teacher Education, 14*(3), 245–256.

Erickson, M. H. (1958). Naturalistic techniques in hypnosis. *American Journal of Clinical Hypnosis, 1*, 3–8.

Erickson, M. H. (1959). Further techniques of hypnosis-utilization techniques. *American Journal of Clinical Hypnosis, 2*, 3–21.

Erickson, M. H., & Rossi, E. I. (1976a). Two-level communication and the microdynamics of trance. *American Journal of Clinical Hypnosis, 18*, 153–171.

Erickson, M. H., & Rossi, E. I. (1976b). *Hypnotic realities*. New York: Irvington.

Fisher, W. R. (1985). The narrative paradigm: In the beginning. *Journal of Communication, 35*(4), 121–134.

Fisher, W. R. (1987). *Human communication as a narration: Toward a philosophy of reason, value, and action*. Columbia, SC: University of South Carolina.

Fried, R. L. (1995). *The passionate teacher: A practical guide*. Boston: Beacon Press.

Gold, J. (2002). *The story species: Our life-connection*. Markham, Ontario: Fitzhenry & Whiteside.

Herrnstein-Smith, B. (1978). Narrative form as a cognitive instrument. In H. Canary & H. Kozicki (Eds.), *The writing of history: Literary form and historical understanding* (pp. 83–97). Madison, WI: University of Wisconsin Press.

Johnson, D. W., & Johnson, F. P. (2003). *Joining together: Group theory and group skills* (8th ed.). New York: Allyn & Bacon.

Johnson, R. W., & Johnson, D. W. (1982). Cooperation in learning: Ignored but powerful. *Lyceum, 5,* 22–26.

Kaufmann, W. O. (1996). *The anthropology of wisdom literature.* Westport, CT: Bergin & Garvey.

Kirkwood, W. G. (1983). Storytelling and self-confrontation: Parables as communication strategies. *Quarterly Journal of Speech, 69,* 58–74.

Kirkwood, W. G., & Gold, J. B. (1983). Using teaching stories to explore philosophical themes in the classroom. *Metaphilosophy, 14,* 341–352.

Land, S. M., & Hannafin, M. J. (1996). A conceptual framework for the development of theories-in-action with open-ended learning environments. *Educational Technology Research & Development, 44*(3), 37–53.

Langer, E. J. (1997). *The power of mindful learning.* Reading, MA: Perseus Books.

Maguire, J. (1998). *The power of personal story telling: Spinning tales to connect with others.* New York: Jeremy P. Tarcher/Putnam.

McAdams, D. P. (1997). *The stories we live by: Personal myths and the making of the self.* New York: Guilford.

McEwan, H., & Egan, K. (1995). *Narrative in teaching, learning, and research.* New York: Teacher's College Press.

Mink, L. (1978). Narrative form as a cognitive instrument. In H. Canary & H. Kozicki (Eds.), *The writing of history: Literary form and historical understanding* (pp. 129–149). Madison, WI: University of Wisconsin Press.

More, A. J. (1987). Native Indian learning styles: A review for researchers and teachers. *Journal of American Indian Education, 27,* 17–29.

Olson, M. W., & Gee, T. C. (1988). Understanding narratives: A review of story grammar research. *Childhood Education, 64*(5), 302–306.

Peck, J. (1989). Using storytelling to promote language and literacy development. *The Reading Teacher, 18,* 138–141.

Rorty, R. (1991). *Objectivity, relativism and truth: Philosophical papers.* New York: Cambridge University Press.

Sarbin, T., & Coe, W. (1972). *Hypnosis: A social-psychological analysis of influence communication.* New York: Holt.

Scholes, R. (1981). Language, narrative, and anti-narrative. In W. J. T. Mitchell (Ed.), *On narrative* (pp. 200–208). Chicago: University of Chicago Press.

Seligman, M. E. P. (1975). *Helplessness: On depression, development, and death.* New York: Scribners.

Stein, N. L., & Glenn, C. G. (1979). An analysis of story comprehension in elementary school children. In R. O. Freedle (Ed.), *Advances in discourse processes: New directions in discourse processing,* (Vol. 2, pp. 53–120). Norwood, NJ: Ablex.

Tinterow, M. M. (1970). *Foundations of hypnosis.* Springfield, IL: Thomas Press.

Underwood, P. (1991). *Three strands in the braid: A guide for enablers of learning.* San Anselmo, CA: A Tribe of Two Press.

Wood, D. (1998). *How children think and learn.* Oxford, England: Blackwell.

Yussen, S., Huang, S., Mathews, S., & Evans, R. (1988). The robustness and temporal course of the story schema's influence on recall. *Journal of Experimental Psychology: Learning, Memory, & Cognition, 14*(1), 173–179.

Zabel, M. K. (1991). Storytelling, myths, and folk tales: Strategies for multicultural inclusion. *Preventing School Failure, 32,* 28–41.

V

Last Words

Teaching Tips From Experienced Teachers: Advice for Introductory Psychology

David G. Myers
Hope College

Teachers wanting to take their game to a new level are hungry for what this book offers: tips for effective teaching, that is, teaching that informs, stimulates, energizes, and even entertains. Nowhere are best practice tips more needed than in that most important of psychology courses—introductory psychology. This course provides the introductory gateway to other psychology courses. More importantly, it is the course taken annually, in North America alone, by some 1.5 million non-majors, most of whom will never take another psychology course.

My favorite teaching tips, presented here, have been gleaned from the collected advice of master teachers and seasoned with my own experience. Some years ago, my collection began to extend beyond McKeachie's classic *Teaching Tips* (1995). During an extended discussion of teaching tips for new teachers, experienced teachers participating in Bill Southerly's Teaching in the Psychological Sciences listserv (faculty.frostburg.edu/psyc/southerly/tips) offered their secrets of success. Here, drawn from the discussion, are my 10 favorites, in italics, with my own reflections:

- *Be positive.* Correcting mistakes is important, but so is catching students doing something right and reinforcing them. Poet Jack Ridl, a revered professor on my campus and Michigan's Carnegie Professor of the Year, harnesses this principle in his teaching of writing (as I can vouch from Jack's mentoring me with his feedback on several thousand pages of my writing). Jack offers not only specific wisdom—"Your point will have most impact if not buried mid sentence"—but also his delight when catching peak moments: "Dave, can you feel your rhythm here? The cadence is lovely."

- *Give frequent and fast feedback.* It takes no more time to read papers and exams immediately—and to return them the next class period. Students welcome the immediate feedback and instructors are glad to have the chore behind them.

- *Be enthusiastic.* As Ambady and Rosenthal (1992, 1993) found, it takes but a few seconds for observers to "read" a teacher's warmth and enthusiasm, and thus to predict their course evaluations. Some people are naturally expressive (and therefore talented at pantomime and charades); others are less expressive (and therefore better poker players). DePaulo, Blank, Swaim, and Hairfield (1992) showed that even inexpressive people, when feigning expressiveness, are less expressive than expressive people acting naturally. Bill Clinton and Dick Cheney could not, for more than a few moments, imitate each other's styles. The moral: If you're a low key person who needs to express more enthusiasm, then don't worry about overdoing it. What's more, fake it and you may make it.

- *Don't expect them to be as enthusiastic.* Chronically sleep-deprived and sometimes self-conscious collegians may not visibly reciprocate our energy, warmth, and enthusiasm. Nevertheless, energy, warmth, and enthusiasm help awaken minds. And as alumni memories of a class sometimes indicate, the mind behind the blank face may register more than we're aware.

- *Give lots of practical examples.* My first textbook editor, in response to my first submitted draft chapter, offered this advice: "Remember, Dave, for every abstract point you must have a concrete example." This principle of good writing is also a principle of good teaching. When we teach the different reinforcement schedules, a concrete example of each—for example, checking e-mail gets rewarded at variable intervals and sustained at high rates—helps drive the point home.

- *Make questions concrete.* After showing a video I used to ask, "Comments anyone?" and suffer the silence. But then a colleague modeled a more effective strategy for me: "How did you react to the argument that ...?" An easily engaged, specific question can unleash a discussion.

- *Have patience awaiting answers.* Don't answer your own question. Allow a few moments of calm silence, and a hand, or perhaps an expressive face, may signal someone's willingness to answer. As a further step, inviting students first to *write* an answer virtually ensures that they will then have something to say (see the discussion of freewriting in Dunn, Schmidt, and Zaremba, chap. 3, this volume).

- *Do say, "I don't know" and entertain ideas about how to answer a question.* We show our humanity and humility when acknowledging our ignorance. And we can use such times to engage students in thinking like scientist-detectives by brainstorming how to go about answering the question.
- *Assume your introductory students will never take another course in your field.* Focus on the big questions. What from this course should an educated person know? What are the big lessons you hope they will never forget?
- *Realize that in teaching, as in life, two things are certain: You're going to make a fool of yourself at some point, and you're going to have your heart broken.* Although teaching for me has been rewarding, even the best of semesters has offered at least one student evaluation that has seized my attention like a bee sting, as in these answers from one of my students: "What did you find beneficial about this course?" "Nothing!" "What could be improved?" "End the course." "What advice would you give a friend who is planning to take this course?" "Don't."

In hopes of harvesting the teaching tips of our master psychology teachers, William Buskist (2002) interviewed award-winning psychology professors, asking them for secrets of their success. Buskist and his colleagues confirmed some of the highlights (see Table 18.1) in a follow-up study that asked community college faculty and students what they perceived as the qualities or behaviors of effective teachers (Schaeffer, Epting, Zinn, & Buskist, 2003). Both groups agreed that these qualities were among the top 10: approachable, creative and interesting, encouraging and caring, enthusiastic, flexible and open-minded, knowledgeable, realistic expectations and fair, and respectful.

From his dozen years on university teaching award committees, Dean Simonton (2003) also observed the qualities of great teachers. And he observed the qualities of scandalously bad teaching—the sort of bad teaching that brings faculty to the attention of personnel committees or leads to their being denied promotion and tenure. Behaviors related to the Big Five personality traits are the key to success, he observed (Table 18.2). Great teaching is marked by behaviors associated with high extraversion, agreeableness, conscientiousness, and openness, *and* by behaviors associated with low neuroticism.

LEARN STUDENTS' NAMES IMMEDIATELY

"Remember that a [person's] name is to [that person] the sweetest and most important," advised Dale Carnegie (1936/1990) in *How to Win Friends and Influence People* (as one of his six "ways to make people like you"[1]). At various times, I have used three strategies for mastering students' names.

---

[1]The other five also are applicable to teaching: Become genuinely interested in other people. Smile. Be a good listener; encourage others to talk about themselves. Talk in terms of the other person's interests. Make the other person feel important—and do it sincerely.

TABLE 18.1

Advice for Teachers From APA Division 2 Award-Winning Teachers

- First, know the content.
- Study the science and art of teaching.
- Observe great teaching and reflect on what might work for you.
- Meet with people who value teaching.
- Be willing to experiment.
- View tests as learning, not just testing opportunities.
- You won't always be effective, but strive to daily give your best.
- Be enthusiastic!

- Demand the best, with patience.
- Genuinely care about students.
- Talk with students outside class.
- Get to know your students.
- Remember being a student.
- Focus on student learning by people with varying needs and skills.
- Always ask for feedback; be grateful for criticism.
- When the passion ends, quit; if your humor is gone, become an administrator.

Note: Data gathered by William Buskist.

TABLE 18.2

Big Five Personality/Behavior Differences Between Best and Worst Teachers

The best teachers exhibit	The worst teachers exhibit
• High extraversion	• Low extraversion
– Before-class chats/enthusiasm/ interactive (e.g., shows of hands)	– Arrive late/leave early/avoid eye contact/inaudible/
• High agreeableness	• Low agreeableness
– Learn names/liberal office hours	– Dislike Q's/minimal office hours
• High conscientiousness	• Low conscientiousness
– Read text/complete syllabi	– Unprepared/bad syllabi/dated
• Low neuroticism	• High neuroticism
– Relaxed/easy-going/flexible	– Anxious/defensive/inflexible
• High openness to experience	• Low openness to experience
– Show connections/use cartoons, newspapers, TV shows, movies	– Narrow perspective/Imposes own views/disdains application

Note: Observed by Dean Keith Simonton.

To these teaching tips and marks of master teachers, I add six more, drawn from my own experience of what has worked best while teaching dozens of sections of introductory and social psychology.

Rehearsal Exercise

In classes of 35, I have simply invited the first person to say his or her first and last name, the second person to repeat that name and to add their own, the third person to repeat the first two names and add their own, concluding with my repeating all 35 names, followed by my own. I would tell students that "we're here to help each other when names are forgotten—someone's forgetting provides our opportunity to learn and remember." Still, forgetting happened less often than I expected. Moreover, memory lapses—often for the name immediately before one's own, for which there had been no rehearsal—provided opportunities for a preview of memory principles. Likewise, my noting the contrasting relaxed and tense body postures of students who'd completed or were awaiting the task provided both humorous relief and a preview of stress and physiological arousal. Even so, the exercise, which also breaks ice by engaging every student in saying something takes but half an hour (for a related view, see Abrahamson, chap. 17, this volume). (Obviously, however, Jim Maas, who has taught 65,000 introductory psychology students at Cornell University, could not have done this in one of his student sections of 1700.)

Photo Lineups

Needing more help as the years went by, I next turned to photographing each class. To create a panoramic sweep, three or four pictures can be stapled to a sheet on which students have written their names according to that day's seating. With a half hour of study at home, plus occasional retrieval practice—often just before class—their names become accessible during class discussion.

Flash Visits

Perhaps I have more capacity for anxiety than most faculty. Starting a new class has always provoked excitement but (while facing new students whose friendship and enthusiasm has not yet been won) also feelings of threat. To jump-start the friendship formation (as well as the name learning), I have dedicated one day within the first week to scheduling students for 5-minute get-acquainted conversations in my office. Meeting, say, 10 students an hour, I could talk with the 70 students in two sections of introductory psychology (well, the 60 that remember to show up) during 7 intense but enjoyable hours. After some easy questions—Where are you from? What drew you to Hope College? What interests do you have? Have you any questions I could answer?—I thank them for coming by and invite them to come back anytime. When next meeting the class, I have found myself noticeably more comfortable, as if surrounded by friends.

MINIMIZE EXAM-RELATED DISAGREEMENTS

I suspect we all dislike handing back exams, and what we dislike even more is taking class time to be publicly challenged regarding the interpretation of multiple-choice questions or points awarded on essay questions. To preclude such hassle, I have asked students to speak to me about their exam-related questions after class. This also, I have explained, spares the rest of the class having to sit through my dealing with individuals' problems.

I have additionally given students an option when they confront a seemingly ambiguous question. The option is to not answer the multiple-choice question, and instead to write a short essay that answers the question. If they can display an accurate understanding, then they receive full credit. If not, they don't (and they will have passed up their chance to guess the right answer). Out of 35 students, a half dozen typically have elected this option in responding to one or two questions. Their doing so virtually eliminates complaints about unfair questions. Sometimes it also alerts me to a question that does have a valid alternative interpretation. (Other faculty achieve the same ends by allowing students to skip a question or to complete a form on which they can challenge a teacher's answer.)

CREATE THE SPACE

Theater directors and sports fans appreciate that a "good house" is a full house. As social facilitation research reminds us, the presence of others is arousing. It intensifies reactions. Some years ago, Freedman and Perlick (1979) had an accomplice listen to a humorous tape or watch a movie with others. The accomplice could more readily induce fellow audience members to laugh or clap when they all sat close together. Likewise, a class of 35 students feels more warm and lively in a room that seats just 35 than when scattered around a room that seats 100. With heightened arousal and more awareness of one another's responses, jokes become funnier and discussion more animated.

To create a "good house" for our classes, we can create an optimal classroom ecology. If possible, schedule the class for a room barely big enough to contain it. Arrange chairs in an arc so people can see one another's faces, while still orienting toward the instructor. Arrive early, stack extra chairs in a back corner, and group the others close together (or rope off the back rows).

BEWARE THE CURSE OF KNOWLEDGE

Technology developers, authors, and teachers often find it irresistibly tempting to assume that what's clear to them will be clear to others. We realize that others lack our expertise, yet, after teaching a class 25 times, we underestimate how confusing an explanation can be. I may feel certain that I have clearly explained "negative reinforcement," and so am astonished when nearly half the class persists in thinking it is punishment (see Chew, chap. 15, this volume).

"The curse of knowledge" describes our egocentric inability to see the world as it looks to those without our knowledge. Ask someone, "How long do you think it takes the average person to solve this anagram—to see that *grabe* can be unscrambled into *barge*?" Knowing the answer, it seems easy, perhaps a 10-second task. But, as Kelley and Jacoby (1996) showed, if given similar anagrams without knowing the answer (*wreat*), the task proves surprisingly difficult.

Likewise, Keysar and Henly (2002) pointed out that speakers readily overestimate their effectiveness in communicating meaning. They asked speakers to read an ambiguous sentence (e.g., "Angela shot the man with the gun") in a way that communicated one of its two possible meanings. The speakers routinely overestimated their listeners' accuracy in perceiving the intended message. They presumed that what was obvious to them would be similarly obvious to their audience. This curse of knowledge is surely a source of much miscommunication not only among friends and lovers, but also between teachers and students, and authors and readers. Whatever can be misunderstood will be. Once we know something it becomes difficult to appreciate what it's like not to know. But we can, by restraining our assumptions, better enable students to cross the bridge from ignorance to knowledge.

LECTURE LESS

After authoring my own text, which stole my best lecture material, I was motivated to subdue my talking head and to offer students briefer synopses of key or difficult concepts interwoven with experiences that more actively engaged them (see later). The resulting student evaluations proved gratifying, and without any performance decline on exams that covered all text chapters.

In hindsight, this makes sense. Given that even average readers can absorb words at double the speed of a teacher's speaking—and can pause to reread difficult material—lecture is an inefficient means of transferring words from one head to another. I believe I speak for fellow text authors in suggesting that, compared to lecture-based teaching, learning from textbooks can offer broader, less idiosyncratic, more representative, and more carefully checked coverage of a discipline. And I am confident I speak for the community of text authors in saying that all introductory texts are superior to their authors' pre-text lectures. Thanks to the magnitude of effort and the extensive quality controls, the resulting teaching package is more comprehensive, tightly organized, carefully reviewed, painstakingly edited, efficiently presented, and attractively packaged than any instructor could home brew (see Griggs, chap. 2, and Gurung & Daniel, chap. 4, this volume). In the spirit of Winston Churchill's remark about democracy, textbooks are the worst way to present information, except for all the others.

ACTIVATE STUDENTS

Writing for the *APS Observer* a decade ago on "The Merits of Classroom Demonstrations," Bernstein (1994, p. 25) observed that "my 27 years of teaching have left me convinced that the best use of class time is not so much to teach things as to do things—tell stories, give examples, present new concepts, and of course offer demonstrations—in ways that motivate the students to read the book, ask important questions, and learn for themselves.... Classroom demonstrations, like other breaks from the straight lecture mode, can provide highlights that make teaching more enjoyable for you as well as the students."

I concur, and have devised or gleaned from others a series of demonstrations that are mostly quick (less than 10 minutes), utterly reliable, dramatic (it doesn't take a statistical caliper to see the effect), pedagogically effective, and just plain fun. Thus, at different times of the semester my students have, for example, been found to be:

- groaning, grinning, and laughing—after virtually 100% have labeled "unsurprising" a seemingly commonsense finding that is actually opposite to what the people on either side of them also claim, in hindsight, to have known all along
- squeezing each others' shoulders and ankles in a human chain—demonstrating psychological measurement principles while measuring the speed of neural transmission
- befuddled by pseudoparanormal ESP tricks
- experiencing perceptual adaptation with special glasses that displace the visual field
- displaying dramatically greater memory for visually than acoustically encoded sentences
- exhibiting common illusory thinking tendencies
- illustrating group polarization after discussion in small groups

All such demonstrations are fun and games, but with a purpose that links to, and makes memorable, a basic principle.

Nearly 20 years ago, Colorado State psychologist Frank Vattano and I sat down with a Corporation for Public Broadcasting executive, hoping to persuade her to allow highlights of the PBS series, "The Brain," to be made available to psychology teachers as affordable brief clips (rather than expensive 60-minute programs). To our delight, she did commission Frank to repackage the series in teaching-friendly modules, and then invited him to do the same with "The Mind" series. Thanks to these and subsequent resources, in nearly every class period we can now offer one or more brief video clips that enliven lecture and stimulate discussion. If we have been considering split-brain research, we can display a split-brain patient being tested. If we have been demonstrating illusory thinking principles, we can meet Daniel Kahneman and Amos Tversky on screen. Judging by the response of my students, this simple innovation—replacing long films and videos with vivid 3- to 10-minute clips that are directly pertinent to the topic at hand—has been a boon to the teaching of psychology.

Finally, I have engaged my students in active processing through out-of-class computer simulations. The best of today's interactive programs can engage students as experimenters (as when training a rat), as subjects (as when being tested on a memory or perceptual illusion task), and as learners in a dynamic tutorial (as when harnessing dynamic computer graphics to teach concepts such as neurotransmission).

So, learn names and make friends, minimize exam hassles, create the space, beware the curse of knowledge, lecture less, and activate students—those are my echoes to the accumulated wisdom of master teachers of psychology, including the best practice wisdom of the master teachers in this volume.

Their wisdom is worth attending to, for those 1.5 million introductory psychology students will form a large part of tomorrow's educated public. For most of them, introductory psychology is our one chance to cultivate an appreciation of the wonder of important phenomena in their lives, to convey the inquisitive spirit in which psychologists *do* psychology, to restrain intuition with critical thinking, to season judgmentalism with compassion, and to replace misconception with understanding. There is so much fascinating and useful information to be gleaned about nature and nurture, sleep and dreams, intuition and illusion. And there is so much mythical pop psychology to be remedied. Educated people should be prepared to question assertions that sleepwalkers are acting out their dreams, that hypnosis uncovers long-buried memories, that our two cerebral hemispheres are functionally equivalent, that newborns are dumb to the world, that repressed traumatic experiences tend to be massively repressed but recoverable much later, or that money and the unsustainable lifestyles of the rich and famous make for happiness.

There is so much to teach and so important to do it well. I tip my hat to Dana Dunn, Stephen Chew, and this volume's other contributors for being our guides in taking our game to the next level as we bring best practices into our own classrooms.

ACKNOWLEDGMENT

This chapter is adapted from an essay that appeared as a guest "Teaching Tips" article in the *APS Observer,* 2005.

REFERENCES

Ambady, N., & Rosenthal, R. (1992). Thin slices of expressive behavior as predictors of interpersonal consequences: A meta-analysis. *Psychological Bulletin, 111,* 256–274.

Ambady, N., & Rosenthal, R. (1993). Half a minute: Predicting teacher evaluations from thin slices of nonverbal behavior and physical attractiveness. *Journal of Personality and Social Psychology, 64,* 431–441.

Bernstein, D. (1994, July/August). Tell and show: The merits of classroom demonstrations. *APS Observer*, pp. 24–25, 27.

Buskist, W. (2002). Effective teaching: Perspectives and insights from Division Two's 2- and 4-year awardees. *Teaching of Psychology, 29,* 188–193.

Carnegie, D. (1990). *How to win friends and influence people.* New York: Pocket Books. (Original work published 1936)

DePaulo, B. M., Blank, A. L., Swaim, G. W., & Hairfield, J. G. (1992). Expressiveness and expressive control. *Personality and Social Psychology Bulletin, 18,* 276–285.

Freedman, J. L., & Perlick, D. (1979). Crowding, contagion, and laughter. *Journal of Experimental Social Psychology, 15,* 295–303.

Kelley, C. M., & Jacoby, L. L. (1996). Adult egocentrism: Subjective experience versus analytic bases for judgment. *Journal of Memory and Language, 35,* 157–175.

Keysar, B., & Henly, A. S. (2002). Speakers' overestimation of their effectiveness. *Psychological Science, 13,* 207–212.

McKeachie, W. J. (1999). *Teaching tips: Strategies, research, and theory for college and university teachers* (10th ed.). Boston: Houghton Mifflin.

Schaeffer, G., Epting, K., Zinn, T., & Buskist, W. (2003). Student and faculty perceptions of effective teaching: A successful replication. *Teaching of Psychology, 30,* 133–136.

Simonton, D. K. (2003, February). *Teaching and the big five: Or what I've learned from a dozen years on teaching award committees.* Paper presented at the Society of Personality and Social Psychology teaching workshop, Los Angeles.

About the Editors

Dana S. Dunn, a social psychologist, is professor of psychology and chair of the Learning in Common Curriculum Committee at Moravian College, Bethlehem, PA. He received his PhD from the University of Virginia in 1987. A fellow of the American Psychological Association, Dunn is active in the *Society for the Teaching of Psychology* and a participant in the 1999 APA-sponsored Psychology Partnerships Project (P3). His research and writing interests include the teaching of psychology, social psychology, and rehabilitation psychology. The author of three previous books—*The Practical Researcher, Statistics and Data Analysis for the Behavioral Sciences,* and *A Short Guide to Writing about Psychology*—Dunn is also co-editor (with Chandra Mehrotra and Jane Halonen) of *Measuring Up: Educational Assessment Challenges and Practices for Psychology.*

Stephen L. Chew is professor and chair of psychology at Samford University in Birmingham, Alabama. He received his PhD in experimental psychology from the University of Minnesota in 1984. He taught for nine years at Gustavus Adolphus College before becoming chair of psychology at Samford in 1993. In 1998, Chew was chosen as a Carnegie Scholar as part of the Carnegie Academy for the Scholarship of Teaching and Learning (CASTL). He received the Buchanan Award for Classroom Teaching Excellence from Samford University in 1999 and in 2001 was named Professor of the Year for Alabama by the Carnegie Foundation for the Advancement of Teaching. He has been a keynote speaker, presenter, and workshop leader at numerous conferences on teaching in general and teaching of psychology specifically. His research interests focus on memory, and on cognition and instruction.

Author Index

Note. Page numbers in *italic* denote pages on which full bibliographical references appear.

A

Abelson, R. P., 232, *242*
Abrahamson, C., 7, *245*
Adams, J. Q., 95, 97, *107*
Akert, R. M., 113, *126*
Alcock, J., 232, *241*
Al-Hilawani, Y. A., 42, *53*
Allain, V. A., 198, 200, *207, 208*
Allen, B. P., 95, 97, *107*
Allen, M., 3, *8*, 167, 168, *173*, 189, *193*
Allport, G. W., 97, *107*
Ambady, N., 262, *269*
American Anthropological Association, 95, 98, *107*
American Association of University Professors, 154, *155*
American Council on Education, 84, 92
American Psychological Association (APA), 95, *107*, 151, *155*, 161, 168, 169, 170, 171, *172*
American Psychological Association Board of Educational Affairs, 75, *78*
Anderson, C. A., 214, *222*, 239, *241*
Anderson, E., 163, *173*
Anderson, J. R., 85, *92*
Angelo, T. A., 76, *78*, 238, *242*

Anonymous, 118, *126*
Apple, K. J., 198, *208*
Appleby, D. C., 57, 59, *69*, 160, 191
Arguello, A., 168, *173*
Aronson, E., 34, *37*, 90, *92*, 113, *126*
Aronson, J., 34, *37*
Association of American Colleges, 200, *207*
Association of American Universities, 154, *155*
Astin, A. W., 195, 196, *207*
Astleitner, H., 145, *155*
Atkinson, C., 144, 146, *155*
Atkinson, R. H., 58, *69*
Ayeroff, F., 232, *242*

B

Bacon, F., 230, 232, *242*
Bagui, S., 145, *156*
Bagwell, C. L., 34, *39*
Baker, D., 104, *107*
Baker, S., 3, *8*
Balasubramanian, P., 151, *156*
Balch, W. R., 44, 47, *53*
Balogh, D. W., 167, *173*
Bamshad, M., 104, *107*
Banaji, M. R., 212, *223*

Subject Index